Zoning and Property Rights

Zoning and Property Rights
An Analysis of the American System
of Land-Use Regulation

Robert H. Nelson

The MIT Press
Cambridge, Massachusetts, and London, England

This book was set in V-I-P Palatino by The MIT Press Media Department Computer Composition Group and printed and bound by Halli-
day Lithograph Corporation in the United States of America

Library of Congress Cataloging in Publication Data

Nelson, Robert Henry, 1944–
  Zoning and property rights.

  Includes bibliographical references and index.
  1. Zoning—United States. 2. Land use—Planning—United States.
3. Right of property—United States.
I. Title.
HD260.N44   333.7'0973   77–22784
ISBN 0–262–14028–4

For my grandmothers, Hildur Nelson and Martha Palonen

Contents

3 Zoning and Public Land-Use Planning 52

4 The Unhappy Consequences of Prohibiting Sale of Zoning Rights 84

5 Zoning Evolution in Historical Perspective 112

Preface

The idea for this book developed gradually. I had originally intended a much shorter, more descriptive work, but as I studied the literature on zoning and other land-use controls more closely, I became increasingly dissatisfied. Most of the discussions available struck me as unenlightening. Not even the few good scholarly studies could meet a critical need: a convincing explanation of the basic objectives of, and need for, zoning. Zoning law was confusing, and local legislative and court decisions concerning zoning often appeared arbitrary. Other observers had noted similar problems, as indicated by the frequency with which terms such as "myth" and "fiction" can be found in recent discussions of zoning theory.

The lack of a clear understanding of the basic objectives of zoning and other land-use controls is cause for concern. Very few areas of government activity are more important than zoning. Zoning policies have major implications for the quality of the physical environment, the distribution of income, transportation, housing, local taxation, and racial and class segregation. Yet, when new land-use controls have been introduced, they have often lacked clear justification or reasonable assurance that they were actually in the general public interest, and frequently their consequences have departed significantly from the original intentions. The weaknesses of zoning theories have contributed to the lack of influence intellectual and expert discussions have had on the development of a system of land-use controls in the United States. The most recent example of the dominant role popular pressure has played is the rapid spread of local ordinances controlling growth in the 1970s. These controls have been almost entirely citizen initiated and represent a trend almost diametrically opposite to the most widely made expert recommendations.

As I became aware of this situation, it seemed to me that a broad analysis was needed to determine what the objectives of zoning in fact were and whether those objectives were justifiable. Not finding a great deal of help in the zoning literature, I gradually turned my efforts toward making such a study myself. This book is the result; it analyzes the development of zoning, its objectives, its accompanying myths and fictions, and its greatest successes and failures. It also examines some new kinds of land-use regulations that have been developed in the past few years, their purposes and probable consequences, and their future prospects for the regulatory system more generally.

My professional background is in economics, but for the study of zoning a strictly economic approach is clearly too narrow. The book does focus on the changes that zoning has made in property rights and their social and economic consequences, and to this extent it makes an economic analysis. But it also deals with zoning history, the role of planning in zoning development, and the political aspects of zoning administration and zoning legal theories. Only by bringing together all these elements can one achieve a clear and convincing picture of what the zoning problems are and what corrective actions are needed.

The basic conclusion of the book is that existing zoning institutions should undergo major revision. Certain practical functions of zoning are valuable, but they can be better accomplished privately under new land-tenure instruments designed along the lines proposed in this book. Other functions of zoning are socially undesirable and should not be maintained. I am equally skeptical of recent environmental land-use regulations and local restrictions on growth.

The book also concludes that formal public-planning institutions—and government generally—should play as small a role as possible in determining the specific uses of land. Their primary role should be to establish the necessary institutions and to provide a proper legal framework within which private decision making can operate. The extensive direct involvement of public agencies in current land-use determination is largely a result of the inadequacies of the legal framework that supports existing institutions.

Part I of the book analyzes the very circuitous evolution of the new collective property rights represented by zoning. Part II describes some recent environmental land-use regulations and growth controls and shows how current tenure trends have taken on a feudal cast. Part III proposes a new system of metropolitan land tenure to replace zoning.

This book is intended not only for economists but for all professionals in land-use fields. I hope that general readers, who for one reason or another have a particular interest in problems of land use, will find it of value as well—there should, at least, be no technical obstacles to their understanding.

I began the book in 1974 while a member of the research staff of the Twentieth Century Fund, which supported my work by releasing me from most of my duties for much of that year. Along the way, a number of people have read versions of the book and have provided helpful comments. I would like to thank Gene Bardach, Don Bieniewicz, John Booth, Bill Fischel, Jim Mann, my sister Valerie Nelson, and Lou Pugliaresi for their comments. Robert Lerman read a previous draft, and his comments and much appreciated encouragement helped to make possible the improvements necessary for reaching a final version.

My wife Jill has edited all the manuscript in its several versions and has provided strong support for my efforts, including financial support during her four months as our sole breadwinner.

Beverly Bergman did her usual excellent job of typing the manuscript and its revisions.

Zoning and Property Rights

Introduction

The development of zoning has represented a major change in property-right institutions in the United States. The essence of a property right is the authority it creates to control the use of property. The areas of control within this authority can be divided up and held by different parties—for example, mineral rights are often held separately from other property rights for the same site. Under condominium ownership, some property rights are personal and others are collective. Similarly, zoning divides control of the use of land, and thus the property rights to that land, between the personal owner and the local government. As a consequence, even though it is not usually realized, zoning in effect creates collective property rights that are held by local government.

Few subjects have generated so much controversy as questions of property rights. They play an essential role in economic organization because they provide the principal incentives for productive activity. They also have a great influence on the distribution of the benefits of a social and economic system and thus on the degree of social equality the system provides. The basic purpose of the collective property rights created by zoning is to provide an incentive for establishing and maintaining high-quality neighborhoods and communities. Without protection from undesirable uses, high-quality neighborhoods or communities might not be formed because the potential residents would have no protection for their investment against uses threatening the environment. Zoning thus performs a role on a collective level essentially the same as that performed on an individual level by personal-property rights. Personal-property rights, of course, provide the incentive to acquire and maintain individual property. The impact of zoning on social equality is also comparable on a collective level to the impact of personal-property rights on an individual level. Individuals who are well-off are able to protect their possessions from use by others, especially the poor, through the exercise of property rights. Zoning similarly enables residents of desirable neighborhood and community environments to restrict entry, and thus use by others, in this case on a collective level.

Some of the fundamental issues raised by zoning are also identical to those raised by personal-property rights. Are the social incentives supported by zoning worth the social inequality that zoning promotes? What ways are available to diminish the inequalities without at the same time eliminating the desirable incentives?

This book does not provide answers to these very difficult questions. On other grounds, however, it strongly indicts zoning and recommends its abolition in its existing form. In an economic system based on market exchange, property rights are normally transferred by sale. In the land market, the owner has always had the right to sell his personal-property rights. As we have seen, however, zoning establishes a division of property rights at any given site into their personal and collective aspects, and zoning institutions have not provided any effective mechanism for transferring those collective zoning rights. Unlike most other property rights, they have never been legally salable.

In a rapidly changing society, major modifications in the basic types of land use in neighborhoods and communities are sure to be needed and to occur from time to time. In order for such changes to take place under zoning, both the personal and collective rights at sites for new development have to be assembled. The collective rights are legally exercised by local governments. Developers have therefore had to go to local governments to obtain a transfer of these rights, that is, to obtain a zoning change. Since no provision has been made to pay for this transfer legally, they frequently pay for it illegally, often in the form of bribes to local officials. On many occasions, developers have acquired very valuable property rights at little or no cost to themselves simply by purchasing restrictively zoned land at a low price and then pressuring local government for a change in zoning that transfers to them the right to develop the land for much more profitable uses.

These and some other unsavory aspects of zoning are the consequences of government's failure to provide satisfactory mechanisms for the transfer of those collective property rights that are created by zoning. In a market system, the results of removing these essential rights from the system of exchange could hardly have been different. In the final part of this book, a new system of metropolitan land tenure is proposed. Its most important features are the provisions made for the sale of zoning rights through normal market procedures.

These basic issues and problems of zoning have been largely obscured during the development of this institution, a situation not unusual in land-tenure matters. The evolution of the land-tenure system in the United States—in fact, throughout most of the world—has long been one of many small incremental changes made in response to immediate practical needs. In the nineteenth century, the settlement of the western United States and the tenure pattern established there were major national concerns, but there was very little understanding at the time of the basic policies involved. Benjamin Hibbard, a leading historian of nineteenth-century policies governing the public domain, described them as "a series of expedient actions put into practice from time to time which must perforce be gathered together, classified as best they may be, and called the public policies."[1]

In the twentieth century, the evolution of zoning has not changed very much. It was inaugurated in New York City as the result of efforts by Fifth Avenue merchants to obtain protection from the expanding garment industry. It then spread throughout the United States in response primarily to demands for desirable residential neighborhoods and protection from the encroachment of lower-quality housing. Subsequent changes in zoning have generally come about through the gradual evolution of local practices and have typically not been widely recognized until after the fact.

In the nineteenth-century settlement of the western United States, the actual consequences of policies governing the public domain were very often obscured by the strong ideological justifications—such as the importance of protecting the small farmer—given for them. Much the same can be said about zoning. Its evolution has been characterized by misunderstanding, confusion, myth, and a general failure to achieve what could reasonably be called rational policymaking. While it is always much more difficult to assess developments as they occur, it appears likely that the same will be true of changes in land tenure that are now taking place largely under the influence of the environmental movement.

I The Evolution of New Collective Property Rights

Introduction to Part I

In *The Zoning Game* (1966), probably the most influential book of the decade on land-use regulation, Richard Babcock asked, "Why do we have zoning anyway?" and then replied, "It is indicative of the chaotic nature of the subject that there is no generally accepted answer to this question."[1] Although zoning has existed in the United States for sixty years, its purposes and objectives have never been well understood. To discover them, it is first necessary to investigate historically the development of land-use controls, the changes that have evolved in zoning practices and in the actual utilization of zoning, and to view—with some skepticism—the intellectual justifications most frequently given for zoning. It will be especially important not to allow zoning's misleading appearance to prevent the discovery of its actual significance.

1 Zoning Protection for Neighborhood Quality

Zoning was introduced in the United States as a reform of the nuisance law that had been made necessary by the rapidly increasing complexity of modern urban life. The Supreme Court, after considerable hesitation, had in 1926 approved the constitutionality of zoning protection for neighborhoods from uses which, while not "nuisances" in the old legal definition, had very similar effects on neighborhood quality.

The Nuisance-Law Origins of Zoning

Rights to personal property have traditionally been highly valued in the United States, but limits have always been placed on their use when they could seriously interfere with the rights of other individuals. In the American legal system, the laws governing these limits are authorized as being appropriate police powers of the state; to fall into this category they must involve the protection of health, safety, morals, or other fundamental social interests. Some land uses can in fact harm or endanger neighbors. A dumping ground might breed disease, attract rodents, threaten fire, or represent any number of other dangers to nearby properties. Less seriously—and here to some degree harm becomes dependent upon prevailing standards—any land use that produces stench or noise or ugliness, that seriously offends long-standing moral values, or in some other way causes affront to neighboring property owners, can be said to harm those neighbors. Two classically cited examples are a smoking factory and a stockyard.

A clear authority exists under the police power for government to control land uses that are either physically harmful or offensive to commonly accepted community values. Such controls have traditionally been called "nuisance laws." All societies have probably had some kind of nuisance control, whether legally codified or enforced through social sanctions. They were part of the law in Elizabethan England and existed in the United States from the earliest colonial times. One 1692 Massachusetts law confined certain nuisance uses to special districts within urban areas. By the nineteenth century, a wide variety of regulations on property had been employed, including, among others, controls on the flammability of housing materials, provision of drainage facilities, erecting of fences, and the locating of slaughterhouses, of cemeteries, and of dams that could cause flooding.[1]

Of course what is regarded as harmful often changes with time. By the early part of the twentieth century, governments in the United States were increasingly willing to restrict use in order to protect nearby properties from consequences that were then coming to be seen as harmful: Boston, Indianapolis, Milwaukee, and Washington, D.C., had laws creating districts where building height could be regulated, with one main reason—to ensure that ample sunlight would reach every property. The law was upheld for Boston by the Supreme Court in 1909.[2] In 1915, the Court also upheld a local nuisance ordinance that was being used to prohibit the operation of a brickyard and cited as reasons the yard's excessive smoke and bad smell.[3] That an existing facility was forced to shut down, with heavy financial losses to its owner, indicated the strength of the support being given by the Court to the government's power to regulate nuisance.

Controls on nuisance still play their role in land-use regulation. Together with zoning ordinances, they can keep junkyards, billboards, sex shops, and other uses regarded as offensive by the community out of areas where they are not wanted and where the population is sufficiently powerful to invoke such sanctions. Nuisance ordinances can also be used to regulate conflicts among neighbors over noises, smells, and activities of one neighbor that might be considered harmful or dangerous to the others.

The Introduction of Modern Zoning

Modern zoning originated in Germany in the late nineteenth century. In the United States, it is usually said to have begun in 1916 with the New York City zoning ordinance, although by that time, Los Angeles had already had a regulatory system for seven years that divided the city into residential- and industrial-use districts. But the New York ordinance was the most comprehensive up to that time, and it represented a landmark in the history of land-use regulation in the United States. After 1916, zoning ordinances using the New York model were rapidly introduced throughout the country. By 1926, at least 425 municipalities representing more than half the urban population of the United States had enacted them. Under the original New York ordinance, the city was divided into residential, commercial, and unrestricted-use districts. Districts were also mapped out in which building height was regulated, following earlier precedents for height regulation in other cities. (New York had studied the Boston height regulations closely before designing its own ordinance.) A third type of districting imposed "area" (court and yard) controls on buildings.

Zoning was originally widely regarded as constituting a reform of nuisance law, and as having similar purposes. As such, like the nuisance law, it was viewed as a legitimate exercise of the police powers of the state. Zoning had to have its legal basis in the police power because it placed substantial new restrictions on the use of personal property without offering public compensation. In his famous brief to the Supreme Court defending zoning, Alfred Bettman argued: "The need of zoning has arisen to a considerable degree from the inadequacy of the technical law of nuisance to cope with the problems of contemporary municipal growth."[4]

Bettman criticized nuisance law for being uncertain and vague. A landowner could not know whether a prospective use would be allowed at a location without a separate legal determination in each case. Court decisions were unpredictable, depending on the judge and on other circumstances. Because there was no requirement for prior public approval, a location might already have been put to some use before any action was considered against it. Given the large numbers of potential nuisance conflicts and the growing problems arising from failure to deal with them in cities becoming ever larger and more complex, Bettman concluded that a justification for zoning and its concomitant exercise of police powers lay in its ability to deal with the inadequacies of nuisance law.

Considerable doubt was expressed at the time about the actual purposes of zoning, and whether they were in fact appropriate to the strong, financially uncompensated restrictions (in contrast to eminent-domain proceedings) on use of personal property allowed under the police power. It was generally agreed, for example, that exercise of police powers would not be appropriate for enforcing purely aesthetic standards. Edward Bassett, one of the leading architects of zoning, believed that "as a general rule . . . zoning regulations may not be based on esthetic considerations. A zoning regulation controlling the color or the architectural style of buildings would not be upheld today by the courts."[5] Originally, many aspects of zoning controls were brought into question, including the critical feature of restrictions on the location of multifamily housing:

When Greater New York was zoned there was no segregation of residence districts according to the number of families in a dwelling. It was feared that courts would not uphold districting on that basis because of the difficulty of showing that the number of families, apart from space requirements per family, was substantially related to the health and safety of the community. . . . [6]

The necessity for justifying zoning regulations as having the police-power functions of protecting health, safety, and morals led both to frequent confusion about zoning's actual purposes and to many contrived arguments relating zoning to legitimate police-power functions. Bassett provides an illustration of the nature of some of the arguments that were made:

Quiet and the presence of natural surroundings and even vegetation, on account of its production of oxygen, may be important elements in preserving health. . . . It has been said that beautiful architecture is in the same way conducive to health, or at least to comfort and well-being. If all people were alike, this might be true. . . . [7]

The Supreme Court finally ruled on the constitutionality of zoning in 1926. The Court had previously shown a very great respect for the sanctity of private-property rights, and there was much uncertainty as to how it would decide. Despite its previous record, the Supreme Court upheld zoning by a six-to-three vote. While acknowledging that the resemblance could not be pushed too far, the Court based its approval in part on the close similarities it found between zoning and the nuisance law. In dealing with the key question of a high-density land use in a low-density neighbohood, the Court stated: "Under these circumstances, apartment houses, which in a different environment would be not only entirely unobjectionable but highly desirable, come very near to being nuisances."[8] Considering the significance of the case, the Court's opinion was brief and uninformative on many other important zoning issues. There was almost no examination of the possible far-ranging social and economic consequences of zoning, even though some had been brought up in material available to the Court, resulting in a great deal of speculation about the considerations that motivated its Justices.

Reflecting its early history, zoning today is still frequently justified as accomplishing standard police-power purposes. For example, while discussing zoning minimum-lot-size requirements, law professor Robert Anderson observed in 1968:

Minimum lot area restrictions tend to serve the standard purposes of the police power by insuring adequate light and air and by reducing the danger of the spread of fire. At least these are the objectives commonly listed by the courts when they approve area restrictions. . . . [9]

The Basic Need for Protection of Neighborhood Quality

Nuisance law and early zoning ordinances had the common aim of protecting the neighborhood. Under zoning, however, neighborhoods were not generally protected from a use that would actually harm or endanger other neighborhood uses or that could reasonably be said seriously to offend accepted moral values. For example, in a residential district, zoning automatically prohibited all commercial uses, even though most would probably not have had any of the harmful consequences traditionally regarded as a nuisance. The minimum-lot-size requirement has been one of the most important zoning controls. In a neighborhood zoned for one-acre lots, a three-quarter-acre lot was automatically prohibited, no matter how attractive the house and landscaping planned for it might have been.

In practice, if not in early statements of zoning theory, one of the purposes of zoning has been to protect neighborhoods from uses that threatened in some way to reduce the quality of the neighborhood environment. In many cases, this understanding of the purpose of zoning has been described as intending to prevent the reduction of the overall property value of a neighborhood by excluding a particular use. As the National Commission on Urban Problems (the Douglas commission) phrased it in 1968: "The purpose of zoning becomes, in effect, to keep anyone from doing something on his lot that would make the neighborhood a less enjoyable place to live or make a buyer less willing to buy."[10]

It has often been assumed that zoning protects neighborhoods from entrants attracted by factors other than the neighborhood environment. A particular store owner might decide that a neighborhood location would be convenient to potential customers in the community, or that the neighborhood might be an attractive location for an apartment building because of its proximity to a nearby highway interchange or commuter station. But, in fact, much more systematic factors are generally at work.

The need for protection of neighborhood quality arises from the nature of the incentives that lead an individual to select a particular neighborhood to live in. The quality of a person's housing is determined not only by the attractiveness of his own property but also by the attractiveness of those surrounding it. Partly because he does not have to pay to establish or maintain the quality of the surrounding properties, he will have a strong incentive to locate where neighboring properties are attractive. As a result, the location preferred by most people—including many of only average means—will be an upper-class neighborhood.[11]

In areas less intensively developed than those in inner cities, the most important single indicator of housing quality is density. Because neighborhoods with low density generally have a high environmental quality, developers of high-density housing will have a strong incentive to locate it in low-density neighborhoods. Moreover, high-density housing economizes greatly on land costs, so that prices of land in even the most desirable neighborhoods are usually affordable. As a result, if neighborhood entry were not controlled, there would be a strong tendency for high-quality, low-density neighborhoods to decline. If accessibility to the center of a city and other locational features were not factors, the result in a housing market without controls on neighborhood entry would be a mix of housing densities and consequently similar environmental quality in almost every neighborhood. Given individual property-owner incentives,

neighborhoods of noticeably higher quality, whether the judgment is based on density or other factors, would always tend
to attract new entrants until their quality was reduced to the
average.

The means of dealing with this critical problem is, of course,
land-use regulation. Zoning ordinances establish minimum lot
size, floor space, road frontage, setback distance, side and
rear yard size, and other similar minimum quality standards for
each neighborhood, while building codes and subdivision regulations establish other types of quality standards for the structures themselves.

The opportunities for preserving a neighborhood by enforcing
regulations that protect it against lower-quality uses accrue
most of all to the better-off members of society. They are the
ones who can afford to live in low-density neighborhoods and
whose high-quality environments are threatened by the prospect of high-density housing occupied by the poor. One state-
ment clearly showing this understanding of zoning appeared in
a 1940 study by the well-known planner, Hugh Pomeroy:

The important thing is to provide protection for the character of
the neighborhood. . . . Low density neighborhoods occupied by
higher income families should not be faced with the danger of
intrusion or encroachment by small lot developers which would
destroy their character. The danger is always that the less intensive occupancy will be impaired by encroachment by more intensive occupancy. . . . [12]

Or, as one zoning-law expert stated more recently, "It is feared
that less expensive homes than those erected by the first settlers
of an area will diminish property values and destroy the atmo-
sphere established by the construction of expensive homes on
spacious grounds. . . ."[13]

Because high-income suburban neighborhoods have very low
densities, the problem there is especially acute. In large cities,
on the other hand, land in better-quality neighborhoods is often
sufficiently expensive (because these areas are already developed at higher densities) that only additional housing for higher-income families can be built to begin with (assuming any
new housing is feasible). The particular timing of the rapid
spread and acceptance of zoning in the 1920s can be explained
as being a response to the increasing threat to the new subur-

ban neighborhoods that accompanied the mass introduction of the automobile and the consequent spread of low-density suburban living.

The essential protection that zoning provided for the newly emerging suburban neighborhoods of the prosperous is a possible explanation for the surprising approval granted to it by the conservative Supreme Court of the 1920s. The Court in fact indicated that it was clearly aware of this purpose behind neighborhood zoning. It emphasized that an apartment house in a low-density neighborhood was "a mere parasite, constructed in order to take advantage of the open spaces and attractive surroundings created by the residential character of the district."[14] Apartment houses seek out low-density neighborhoods precisely because the surroundings are desirable, and, in doing so, they damage that desirability, while not contributing anything to neighborhood quality—hence their "parasitic" behavior.

In recent years, the essential role of zoning in protecting neighborhood quality, especially in middle- and upper-income residential neighborhoods, has been widely recognized. One of the most perceptive analyses of the American zoning system was made by the English city planner, John Delafons, who demonstrates the benefits of an outsider's perspective. In 1962, he remarked:

The main reason for the popularity of zoning was that it maintained the character of the best residential districts, or, in the case of smaller towns and villages, of the whole community, by severely restricting the scope for new development or changes in the intensity and type of use of existing property. . . . [15]

In 1968, the Douglas commission observed:

Regulations still do their best job when they deal with the type of situation for which many of them were first intended; when the objective is to protect established character and when that established character is uniformly residential. It is in the "nice" neighborhoods, where the regulatory job is easiest, that regulations do their best job.[16]

In 1974, in the *Belle Terre* case, the Supreme Court, in the first zoning case it had heard in more than forty years, strongly reasserted its earlier approval of zoning protections of neighborhood quality. The village of Belle Terre, New York, with only

two hundred and twenty homes and seven hundred people,
effectively constituted one neighborhood. Justice William Douglas wrote in the majority opinion:

A quiet place where yards are wide, people few, and motor
vehicles restricted are legitimate guidelines in a land use project
addressed to family needs. This goal is a permissible one. . . .
The police power is not confined to elimination of filth, stench,
and unhealthy places. It is ample to lay out zones where family
values, youth values, and the blessings of quiet seclusion and
clean air make the area a sanctuary for people.[17]

Neighborhood zoning generally protects well-off people from
the entry of the less well-off. But one might note that zoning
has also on occasion been employed to protect poorer people
against better-off people, when they in turn become, in the
words of the 1926 Supreme Court, the "parasites." Consider
SoHo, a New York neighborhood with old manufacturing lofts,
that has attracted many artists. Because a sizable number of
well-to-do New Yorkers like to live in neighborhoods with artists, the artists of SoHo were threatened by an influx of nonart-
ists, with possible eviction from the neighborhood because of
increased rent levels, a situation that had already occurred
in nearby Greenwich Village. Following the example of many
suburban neighborhoods, the SoHo artists decided to meet the
threat by establishing restrictions on entry. In 1971, they persuaded the New York City government to establish an Artists
Certification Committee that would certify applicants as professional artists and then to make such certification a zoning requirement for SoHo residency.

Zoning as a Collective Property Right to the Neighborhood Environment

Because zoning has generally been administered to suit the
wishes of the most directly affected property owners, its purpose has often been seen as the protection of private property. Delafons was particularly explicit: "It was as a means of
strengthening the institution of private property in the face of
rapid and unsettling changes in the urban scene that zoning
won such remarkable acceptance in American communities."[18]
His assessment of zoning controls was that "American land use

controls, in effect, were designed to promote private property interests." He quotes approvingly from a 1953 New Jersey Superior Court opinion that is unusually blunt in its favorable attitude toward zoning: "The real object . . . of promoting the general welfare by zoning ordinances is to protect the private use and enjoyment of property and to promote the welfare of the individual property owner. In other words, promoting the general welfare is a means of protecting private property."[19]

An ordinary personal-property right—as applied, for example, to an automobile or a piece of furniture—gives the owner the authority to control its use. Zoning creates authority to control potential uses and other major changes in property in a neighborhood, and it thus, in effect, creates a new property right —that of regulating certain matters significantly affecting the neighborhood environment. One New Jersey judge put it this way in a local bar-association speech defending the virtues of zoning: "A valid zoning ordinance . . . gives to a property owner a right which did not exist before the ordinance was adopted, that is, the right to prevent a use which is forbidden by the ordinance. . . . In other words, valid zoning ordinances create valuable property rights. . . ."[20]

Although zoning rights are held by local government, in all except a very few instances, local legislatures can be counted on to follow the residents' wishes in administering the zoning of a neighborhood. Thus, despite the standard police-power justifications given for zoning over many years, the fundamental significance of neighborhood zoning is that it creates a collective property right to the neighborhood environment that is effectively held and exercised by its residents. The same collective right to control neighborhood uses and quality can be obtained privately through collective property rights established under condominium ownership. In some cases, zoning is superfluous because ordinary personal-property rights can provide the same protection; if a neighborhood is entirely owned by a single private developer, he can exclude any use he sees fit simply by exercising his personal-property right. Private covenants can accomplish zoning purposes as well; changes in use in a neighborhood may be restricted by covenants designed to maintain the quality of the existing environment.

In order to obtain protection of neighborhood quality by these strictly private devices, however, it is necessary to assemble an entire neighborhood under single ownership prior to its development. In an existing neighborhood, with a variety of property owners, it would be very difficult—if not impossible—to obtain unanimous voluntary agreement to a set of covenants or other binding restrictions on neighborhood property uses. Because most neighborhoods have either been developed piecemeal or their properties sold to many successive owners after development, zoning institutions have had to be created to allow property owners in such neighborhoods to acquire collective control over their environment. Unwilling property owners can be required under zoning to accept new collective rights to the neighborhood environment, a form of coercion that would not be possible using private methods.

Zoning has thus represented a basic change in property-right institutions. Well before the similar developments of condominium ownership, it imposed a division of neighborhood property rights into their personal and collective aspects. The individual property owner retained certain exclusive personal rights, such as control over the use of the interior of his property, while others were held and exercised collectively by neighborhood residents. Under zoning, collective rights are administered by local legislatures acting virtually as trustees for neighborhood residents; under condominium ownership, they are administered by a privately elected condominium association.

The collective property rights created by zoning have had social and economic consequences similar to those of other property rights. They have provided important incentives to establish and maintain neighborhoods of high quality. Creators of such neighborhoods need not fear that their efforts will be wasted because people with new, unwanted uses in mind will decide to share their advantages. Because of neighborhood zoning, a wide choice in neighborhood types and qualities is available to suit many individual preferences and means.

Like other property rights, zoning rights have important consequences for the distribution of income and wealth. They make it possible for residents of desirable neighborhood environments to avoid sharing their environment with the poor. In creating a new collective property right, neighborhood zoning produces a distribution of benefits and costs of neighborhood environmental amenities that matches the distribution of ordinary private goods and services—to each according to his personal means. Segregation of neighborhoods by income as a result of zoning rights is widespread, but comparable segregations characterize most private consumption. The rich travel in airplanes instead of buses, eat in better restaurants, visit more elegant resorts, and send their children to more prestigious colleges. Because of zoning rights, they also obtain better housing in higher-quality neighborhoods.

In sum, although zoning represented a major infringement on personal-property rights by collective authority, it was not, though it has often been seen as, a threat to the concept of private property. Properly understood, zoning was a new and well disguised extension on the collective level of private property concepts. More than anything else, zoning's consistency with the traditional respect for private property in the United States accounts for its wide acceptance and constant use.

Recent Evolution Toward Greater Neighborhood Control and Discretion

Since the rapid spread of zoning in the 1920s, its method of neighborhood protection has changed little. Undesired-use classifications are excluded from a neighborhood, and many changes in existing structures are also controlled. However, neighborhood zoning does not provide the degree of control and discretion of a full property right to the neighborhood environment that, for example, condominium ownership provides. The rigidity of zoning-use classifications has made it impossible to admit particular desired uses if they belong to the wrong classification: a small convenience store, a place to eat, greater mixtures of lot sizes, or some multifamily housing might all be significant assets to a neighborhood, if attractively designed. Nor does zoning provide control over architectural characteristics or minor alterations in neighborhood properties: for example, there is no way of preventing one neighborhood property owner from painting his house some disagreeable color, from erecting an intrusive fence, or from planting a tree where it blocks the neighbors' view. Within the last few years, pressures have begun to develop for greater collective neighborhood control and discretion in dealing with such matters.

Until recently, two factors inhibited movement toward greater neighborhood control and discretion. First, so long as aesthetic sensibilities favored highly homogeneous neighborhoods at low densities in rural settings, not much was lost through the rigidity of zoning-use classifications. Second, had this not been the case, neighborhoods would probably still have preferred the rigidity of zoning to the exercise of greater discretion. Because residents have had to rely on the wider community to administer neighborhood zoning protections, they have never been completely confident that neighborhood wishes would be followed in all instances. Supported by the courts, zoning rigidity has provided neighborhood residents with a highly valued assurance that the community would not at some future date allow undesired uses into the neighborhood against their wishes.

In the last decade and a half, a new aesthetics judgment on neighborhood quality has begun to make its presence felt. Neighborhoods with only one kind of use are now often seen as boring, bland, and, consequently, less desirable. Diverse mixtures of uses, including stores, restaurants, small manufacturers, and different types of residences are now regarded as desirable. Jane Jacobs made one of the first and best-known formulations of this view; here she describes her own neighborhood:

The continuity of this movement (which gives the street its safety) depends on an economic foundation of basic mixed uses. The workers from the laboratories, meat-packing plants, warehouses, plus those from a bewildering variety of small manufacturers, printers and other little industries and offices, give all the eating places and much of the other commerces support at midday. . . . We possess more convenience, liveliness, variety and choice than we "deserve" in our own right. . . . If the neighborhood were to lose the industries, it would be a disaster for us residents. . . . Or if the industries were to lose us residents, enterprises unable to exist on the working people by themselves would disappear.[21]

A second important factor creating pressure for greater control and discretion in neighborhood zoning has been the higher density of more recent suburban development and the growing trend toward rehabilitation of well-located, high-density neighborhoods in older central-city areas. At higher levels of density, the exact lot layout, housing design, landscaping, house color, and other minor details become much more important to neighborhood quality. The resulting interdependence has created a need for a finer degree of neighborhood control than that afforded by traditional zoning. Responding to this need, many large-scale developers, for example, have required home purchasers to agree to comprehensive land-use controls in their neighborhoods. The recent spread of condominium ownership can be attributed in part to a growing desire for more comprehensive control over neighborhood quality than is obtainable under traditional zoning.

Despite legal, intellectual, and other objections, property-right institutions have exhibited a remarkable ability in the past to respond to new popular demands. The beginnings of a response to demands for greater collective control and discretion over neighborhood quality can be seen in a rapidly spreading use of historic-district regulation. The courts have determined that the status "historic" legally justifies public imposition of a comprehensive set of regulations clearly directed at aesthetic concerns and involving so much discretion that they would not be permitted in any ordinary neighborhood. In such districts, permission is generally required for all significant changes in the exterior of properties. For example, under the provisions for historic districts contained in the new Model Land Development Code of the American Law Institute, district approval can be required for any modification of the "height, shape, size, placement, use, color, style, and texture of structures and landscaping and relationships to surroundings."[22] Transplanting a shrub on the front lawn from one spot to another, for example, will usually require historic-district approval.

Thus far, historic-district regulation has had a minor impact on the overall control of neighborhood quality throughout the United States. But, given strong popular pressures, considerably greater use of this instrument—and perhaps some new legal inventions with the same objective—can be predicted. For example, the residents of one block in New York City recently filed suit to compel the city to designate their block for historic-district status. A *New York Times* article described quite candidly the motives behind much historic-district regulation: "Historical district status generally increases real-estate values and, as a result, many neighborhoods of no real architectural quality have been demanding it as a social stabilizer."[23] A recent Urban Institute study of the Model Land Development Code commented on its provisions for special districts and suggested the far-reaching implications of these provisions for control of neighborhood quality:

Two points are of special note. First, the variety of things that can be afforded protection as special preservation districts and landmarks is very broad. Almost no restriction whatever is placed on the sort of property whose use can be limited. . . . Second, the local government or agency may invoke a broad set of criteria to prohibit development within the designated area. This includes offering practically any reason justified under the broad purposes of the Code, and permits the regulation of any sort of activity. In sum, this would permit regulating all types of activity (in these areas), for any "socially and economically desirable" end.[24]

The creation of tight public controls of a highly discretionary nature over neighborhood quality would virtually eliminate any substantive differences between such controls and those obtained under collective private-property rights. But numerous subterfuges would no doubt have to be employed and formal differences maintained, such as the assertion of "historic" value and other grounds for special treatment, to justify legally public controls. Rather than go through such contortions, it might be preferable to acknowledge the real purpose and openly to create new collective private-property rights where the majority of neighborhood residents want them.

2 The Extension of Zoning Protection to the Community

The reason why societies have to control land uses is that these uses are highly interdependent. Interdependencies among uses within neighborhoods differ in important ways from uses within communities. (As used here, the term "community" is political and refers to a unit of local government.) Unlike neighborhood residents, community residents may not necessarily be greatly concerned about the physical appearance of properties, so long as they are outside the immediate neighborhood. Social interchange among community residents is less frequent and more formal than it is among neighborhood residents and it is most likely to occur in public schools, social clubs, public parks, shopping areas, and other public places. The most important common bond among residents of a community is probably their shared fiscal circumstances, and this bond has no counterpart among neighborhood residents.

Although the differences between neighborhood and community regulatory purposes have not traditionally been emphasized, they are nevertheless very important. Protection of the community became an accepted zoning purpose long after the same protection for neighborhoods had already been established. Different legal rationales were required to gain this acceptance, and different social and economic issues were raised.

Community Zoning Purposes

The most controversial role of zoning has been that of protecting the character of communities. With zoning, communities with advantages in physical and social environments and public services are able to exclude uses that would diminish these advantages. The fiscal incentives such communities face are particularly strong. Communities with high tax bases very often bar new uses that would create a drain on their fiscal resources and thus cause the quality of public services to decline. The consequence of many communities following such incentives has been extensive segregation of communities according to wealth and income ("economic segregation").

In the preceding chapter, it was observed that high-quality neighborhoods face a continually high demand for entry from residents of less desirable neighborhoods. In the same way, advantaged communities face a steady and high demand for entry from residents of less desirable communities. By occupying high-density housing and thereby economizing on land costs, less well-off people could generally afford entry into even the wealthiest communities (so long as some land is vacant or otherwise available). In fact, if locational characteristics such as central-city accessibility were not a consideration, and if there were no land-use regulation (or other controls on entry), communities would tend eventually to equal one another in desirability. If one community should then become much more attractive than others, it would encourage new uses and residents to move in from less desirable communities until the attractiveness was reduced. This principle is illustrated among regions in the United States by emigrations from the traditionally poor South to more prosperous parts of the country, and from the East to the open West. Internationally, equalizing tendencies are checked by the barriers to immigration maintained by wealthy countries. On an individual level, people protect their possessions from use by others by exercising their personal-property rights. In a metropolitan area, zoning gives communiies the authority to control use of their land, thereby making it possible for wealthier communities to preserve their high-quality environments and public services.

Zoning, of course, does not give communities direct power to control individual mobility. But the community can limit any new residents to those likely to occupy the development that is permitted. Because occupancy of high-density housing would be the means whereby the less well-off could gain entry into wealthy communities, land-use regulations put particular emphasis on such density controls as minimum-lot-size requirements. Minimum floor space and other zoning requirements also fix lower limits on the cost of any permissible dwelling unit and thus on the incomes of its likely residents. Zoning ordinances sometimes limit the number of bedrooms permitted in apartment units to discourage families with children. Limitations or prohibitions on multifamily housing serve to exclude the poor, the elderly, childless couples, and single people. By these widely practiced devices, communities are actually able to maintain a substantial degree of control over the uses and residents they will accept.

The Evolution of Zoning to Protect Community Character

Zoning was not originally intended to be a device for protecting community character. When it took root in the United States following its introduction in New York City in 1916, zoning was almost solely concerned with neighborhoods. In the early days, it was generally assumed that each community would create sufficient use districts to accommodate almost any need. Legal experts generally held the view that communities had an obligation to accommodate most uses seeking to enter, so long·as prospective entrants were willing to settle in their assigned district (neighborhood).

Zoning was first commonly employed in big cities where areas of widely varying development already existed. Because of their large size, cities accepted as necessary the finding of suitable locations for the many different uses that were important to the city as a whole. Protection of a given community's character did not become an objective of zoning until it had first come into wide use for that purpose in much smaller suburban communities.

One of the first signs that zoning was being used to protect community rather than neighborhood character was the introduction of zoning of large vacant land areas in undeveloped parts of communities. The original architects of zoning gave little thought to the question of how to zone large tracts of undeveloped land, where there was no existing neighborhood requiring protection. Many early proponents of zoning doubted whether zoning of undeveloped land was either proper or desirable. Edward Bassett commented: "The early arguments for zoning were all related to the needs of centers of population, like cities and villages. It was assumed that country districts and farming localities could not be zoned."[1]

It was not long, however, before signs appeared that zoning would be used to protect the general character of the communi-

ty. In 1924, a Judge Westenhaver observed in a zoning case
before him:

> [The objective of the ordinance is] to place all the property in an
> undeveloped area of 16 miles in a straight-jacket. The purpose
> to be accomplished is really to regulate the mode of living of
> persons who may hereafter inhabit it. In the last analysis the
> result to be accomplished is to classify the population and seg-
> regate them according to their income or situation in life. . . .[2]

In large part because he did not see a sufficient public purpose in economic and social segregation of communities, Judge
Westenhaver declared unconstitutional the entire zoning ordinance in the town of Euclid, Ohio. On appeal, however, the
U.S. Supreme Court overturned his ruling, establishing the legal
precedent on which zoning was to be based for the next fifty
years. In its decision, the Court made little distinction between
protection of the neighborhood and the community and did not
deal with the issue of economic and social segregation. Its ne-
glect of these important issues was surprising, because at the
time many observers had noted that Euclid's zoning ordinance
seemed to have a different and less legally defensible purpose
than many of the better-known big-city ordinances. In fact,
some proponents of zoning suspected that Euclid's ordinance
had been especially chosen for challenge as being the most likely to produce a decision against zoning's constitutionality.

Partly because the Supreme Court had not addressed the matter directly, the issue of the legality of using zoning practices to
protect community character was not fully resolved until the
mid-1950s. By then, a solid legal foundation had been built,
and, based on precedent, the courts in most states could routinely be counted upon to give their approval to large minimum
lot sizes, minimum floor spaces, and other now familiar community zoning practices.

The problem was that protection of community character
could not be adequately justified under the legally necessary
explanation that zoning was basically a reform of nuisance law.
Nuisance regulation dealt with threats by one property to the
health, safety, or morals of residents of nearby properties. While
neighborhood zoning greatly expanded the nuisance concept, it
was at least consistent with the principle of regulating adverse

impacts on nearby properties. But community zoning was not so much concerned with the impact of any one property as it was with the cumulative impact of many properties in the development of new residential neighborhoods. To have asserted that the effect of a new residential neighborhood on the rest of the community was comparable to the effect of a nuisance on a neighborhood might well have been rejected by the courts.

In a number of cases in the history of zoning, when a new need did not fit old legal theories, new legal rationales were devised. Community zoning followed this pattern. In the 1926 *Euclid* case, the Supreme Court had indicated that, as legislative acts, entire zoning ordinances should not be overturned unless clearly shown to be arbitrary or unreasonable. In the late 1930s, partly because of adverse reaction to Supreme Court interventions to overturn New Deal legislation, legal opinion in the United States was shifting to the view that the judiciary should be much more circumspect about interfering with legislative enactments. The courts applied this principle to zoning and concluded that, as legislative acts, community zoning ordinances should generally be presumed valid unless very clear abuse of local legislative authority could be proved. The result was that the courts declined in all but the most extreme cases of abuse to consider the merits of challenges to community zoning ordinances. A 1951 decision by the New York Court of Appeals illustrated the general attitude taken:

[The] decision as to how a community shall be zoned or rezoned, as to how various properties shall be classified or reclassified, rests with the local legislative body, its judgment and determination will be conclusive, beyond interference from the courts, unless shown to be arbitrary, and the burden of arbitrariness is imposed upon him who asserts it. . . . [3]

Commenting on the effect of such attitudes, law professor Robert Anderson wrote: "Notwithstanding the differences in language used to describe the kind and degree of proof needed to upset a zoning ordinance, it seems clear that in nearly all of the states the burden of proof can properly be described as an 'extraordinary' one."[4]

The second and equally important defense of community zoning was the planning theory of zoning. While careful planning had always been considered a step preparatory to enacting or making major changes in zoning ordinances, it was not until the 1930s that city planning commissions responsible for preparing comprehensive land-use plans were widely established in the United States. At the same time, it was also argued in the courts with increasing emphasis that the fundamental purpose of zoning was to provide an instrument—together with installation of public facilities—for implementing formal public plans. By the end of the 1930s, this planning theory of zoning was winning wide acceptance as the basic reason for zoning.

As explained above, nuisance-law rationales for neighborhood zoning could not offer a good justification for community zoning, but the planning theory of zoning was able to fill the gap. The objective of comprehensive public planning went much beyond coordinating small-scale interactions among individual properties in neighborhoods. Rather, the foremost planning aims were to create attractive whole communities, cities, and especially regions. This much broader objective clearly required control of general patterns of development and, in particular, of the development of new neighborhoods. In this way, community control over development of new neighborhoods could easily be justified.

An especially critical element in the planning theory of zoning was the conviction widely held at the time that planning was a scientific and technical skill. Much as a court would today accept expert testimony on a medical, engineering, or other scientific subject, the courts agreed that land-use matters could also be decided by expert opinion. Moreover, because planning was believed to be scientific in nature, land-use planning was asserted to involve determinations that were nonpolitical, thereby making possible judgments among competing social interests on the basis of a wide public welfare. Naive as it may seem to many people today, for years it has been an assumption on which the legitimacy of zoning has rested that land use could be decided by community planners who possessed a technical knowledge and professional commitment that assured that the plans they prepared for a given community would reflect a broader interest. As a result, so long as zoning actions were "in accordance with a comprehensive plan," the courts accepted them as advancing the broadest welfare and did not pursue the matter further.

The necessity of comprehensive community planning, the reflection of technical expertise that comprehensive planning was presumed to represent, and the assurance thereby provided that planning and zoning consistent with plans would serve a broad public interest have been the basic ingredients in legal reasoning on zoning since the rapid growth of community zoning in the suburbs after World War II. A 1968 decision of the New York Court of Appeals provides an excellent illustration of those still widely accepted basic themes:

Underlying the entire concept of zoning is the assumption that zoning can be a vital tool for maintaining a civilized form of existence only if we employ the insights and the learning of the philosopher, the city planner, the economist, the sociologist, the public health expert and all the other professions concerned with urban problems.

This fundamental conception of zoning has been present from its inception. The almost universal statutory requirement that zoning conform to a "well-considered plan" or a "comprehensive plan" is a reflection of that view. . . . Without [a comprehensive plan], there can be no rational allocation of land use. It is the assurance that the public welfare is being served and that zoning does not become nothing more than just a Gallup poll. . . . [5]

In sum, on the grounds that they were legislative acts and based on a comprehensive plan, the courts declined to consider the social implications and consequences of community zoning protections. Given the obstacle that community zoning posed for those strongly committed to a more egalitarian and homogeneous society in the post–World War II period, this court attitude may have been the only means by which community zoning could legally have been sustained.

Once given judicial approval, communities made frequent use of zoning powers to control entry, especially in the years after World War II when suburban growth was extremely rapid. Statistics describing land-use patterns and regulatory practices are generally poor. Thus, there are no good national figures available to describe community zoning practices. One 1960 study for the New York metropolitan region provides some indications of what the situation was among the more than five hundred zoning jurisdictions in the region:[6] outside New York City, a tiny 0.4 percent of residentially zoned land permitted multifamily use; on the average, the median minimum permissible lot size in a zoning jurisdiction was one-third of an acre (just short of 15,000 square feet); minimum lot sizes of one acre or more were required on 48 percent of all residentially zoned vacant land in the region; in wealthy Westchester County, one acre, or larger, minimum-lot-size requirements covered 78 percent of vacant land.

By the late 1960s, zoning exclusion of high-density uses and their potential low- and moderate-income occupants from large parts of the suburbs was receiving widespread national attention. Several national commissions and study groups investigated zoning practices. The Douglas commission stated:

Zoning . . . very effectively keeps the poor and those with low incomes out of suburban areas by stipulating lot sizes way beyond their economic reach. Many suburbs prohibit or severely limit the construction of apartments, townhouses, or planned unit developments which could accommodate more people in less space at potential savings in housing costs. . . . [7]

The Advisory Commission on Intergovernmental Relations reported: "To a significant extent [the crisis of the cities] is a problem caused by long-standing economic and social discrimination by well-to-do suburban communities and the fact that the low income people have been virtually imprisoned within the boundaries of the central city. . . . "[8]

Dimensions of Fiscal Inequality

One of the most significant consequences of community zoning policies has been the creation of large disparities among communities in tax base per resident. While relative physical and social environmental qualities of communities are generally difficult or impossible to measure, some figures on relative fiscal circumstances can be obtained. These figures provide a useful indication of the degree of overall inequality that results from community zoning.

Following their economic incentive, communities usually do not admit uses that would significantly reduce their property-tax base per resident, forcing uses that would to locate in communities with a lower tax base and with less incentive to exclude them. Combined with an uneven distribution of commercial and industrial property, wide differences among communities in tax base per resident result.

A high community tax base allows several options. A well-off community might provide unusually good public services, which it could afford without especially high tax rates, or it might provide average public services and low rates. More typically, there is a compromise.

One of the best and most comprehensive studies of local property taxation was made in New Jersey in the early 1960s.[9] New Jersey provides a particularly strong incentive for communities to engage in fiscally motivated zoning practices because it contributes one of the lowest proportions of state to local expenditures of any state in the United States. Table 1 shows the consequences of this in 1960 in Hudson County. As is the case among many communities, the higher the average income in the community and the higher the tax base per resident, the lower the tax rate tends to be. In brief, in cases such as this the local property tax on homeowners is highly regressive.

While the property tax tends to be regressive because of fiscally motivated zoning, it also tends to be regressive because the average percentage of income spent on housing declines as income rises.[10] To the extent that property-tax payments are closely correlated with housing expenditures, which they must be to a substantial degree, the property tax will be regressive even among those residing in the same taxing jurisdiction who pay at the same rate. In this respect, a property tax is similar to a sales tax.

Table 2 shows the percentages of income paid directly in property taxes by homeowners in various income classes nationally (renters, of course, do not pay property taxes directly). It is evident that, by this measure, homeowner property-tax payments are highly regressive. No one has calculated exactly how much of this regressiveness results from the sales-tax element of the property tax and how much from differences in tax rates among communities.

Property taxation is most regressive in cases where public-

Table 1 Property Taxation in Hudson County, New Jersey, 1960

Municipality	Effective Property Tax Rate (%)	Rank	Real Property per Resident	Rank	Median Family Income	Rank
Hoboken (city)	7.34	1	$1,966	12	$5,435	12
Union City (city)	6.88	2	2,277	10	5,815	11
Jersey City (city)	5.85	3	2,232	11	5,950	9
West New York (town)	5.45	4	2,492	8	6,199	8
Guttenberg (town)	4.50	5	2,383	9	5,913	10
Bayonne (city)	4.43	6	3,700	6	6,423	7
North Bergen (township)	4.08	7	4,067	4	6,910	4
East Newark	3.65	8	2,929	7	6,480	5
Weehawken (township)	3.34	9	3,749	5	7,011	3
Harrison (town)	2.70	10	4,729	2	6,449	6
Kearny (town)	2.27	11	4,315	3	7,015	2
Secaucus (town)	1.66	12	5,973	1	7,161	1

Source: Morris Beck, *Property Taxation and Urban Land Use in Northeastern New Jersey* (Washington, D.C.: Urban Land Institute, 1963), p. 62.

Table 2 Real Estate Taxes as a Percentage of Family Income for Elderly and Nonelderly Single-Family Homeowners, by Income Class, 1970

Family Income	Real Estate Tax as a Percentage of Family Income	
	Elderly (age 65 and over)	Nonelderly (under 65)
Less than $2,000	15.8	18.9
$2,000–$2,999	9.5	10.1
$3,000–$3,999	8.0	7.2
$4,000–$4,999	7.3	5.5
$5,000–$5,999	6.2	5.1
$6,000–$6,999	5.8	4.3
$7,000–$9,999	4.8	4.1
$10,000–$14,999	3.9	3.7
$15,000–$24,999	3.3	3.3
$25,000 or more	2.7	2.9
All incomes	8.1	4.1

Source: *Federal-State-Local Finances: Significant Features of Fiscal Federalism,* Advisory Commission on Intergovernmental Relations (Washington, D.C., February 1974), p. 201.

service expenditures do not vary much among communities with different tax bases. Expenditures for fire protection, highway maintenance, government administration, and some other basic responsibilities are likely to be insensitive to the tax base. But expenditures for such public services as education are frequently very responsive to it.

School property taxes constitute more than 50 percent of all local property-tax collections. Community incentives are basically the same for educational finance as for financing public services as a whole. But school property taxes are not as regressive as local property taxes generally. For example, in 1969 two of the highest school property-tax rates in California were found in Palo Alto and Berkeley, not because of low tax bases but because those communities place an unusually high emphasis on education through the influence of their many residents who are Stanford or University of California employees. Wide variations in tax bases result, therefore, in large disparities among communities in expenditure levels for education.

The great differences in resources available for education became the concern of the California Supreme Court in the much publicized *Serrano* case. [11] The court cited the extreme examples of Beverly Hills and Baldwin Park—both located in the Los Angeles metropolitan area. During the 1968–69 school year in Beverly Hills, the school system had available a tax base of $200,000 per student and spent $1,244 per student; the effective school property-tax rate was 0.52 percent. [12] By contrast, in Baldwin Park, the system had available a tax base of $16,000 per student and spent $595 per student; the school property-tax rate was 1.07 percent, double that for Beverly Hills.

The Fleischman Report on financing education in New York State cited Great Neck and Levittown on Long Island as other examples of the inequality of educational finance. [13] In the 1968–69 school year, the two towns taxed themselves at identical rates, but Great Neck received revenues of $2,077 per pupil— almost twice the $1,189 Levittown could spend.

Over the years, the large differences in community tax bases per resident and the associated problems of property-tax regressiveness and large disparities in public service expenditures have been the subjects of wide criticism. Recently, however, a number of economists have issued some caveats concerning the meaning of numbers such as those shown in Table 2. It has long been recognized that, because of capitalization of property taxes, the final incidence of property taxes may differ substantially from the direct incidence of tax payments. [14] Another concern is that the taxpayers with low incomes shown in Table 2 may include a substantial number of considerable wealth whose low incomes are either temporary or are the incomes of well-off but retired elderly. A number of studies have concluded that, even though housing expenditures increase less than proportionally with current income, they increase roughly proportionally with long-run income prospects ("permanent income"). [15] Another important consideration is that property taxes are collected on commercial as well as residential property. Some students have asserted that partly because a major portion of the property tax is paid on commercial property, and thereby indirectly taxes heavily the investments and wealth of well-off people, the property tax is progressive in its overall incidence.[16] In 1975, challenging longtime conventional views, economist Henry Aaron of the Brookings Institution concluded with respect to recent reassessments of property tax incidence:

The importance of this revision in analysis of tax incidence for evaluating the property tax can hardly be exaggerated. Indeed, the tax becomes one of the more progressive elements in the national tax system rather than one of the most regressive . . . . Advocates of greater progressivity in the system should recognize that the property tax advances rather than obstructs achievement of egalitarian objectives.[17]

Despite this new view of the property tax, there still seems little question that the effect of zoning on the system of local finance is to promote greater inequality. Analyses such as Aaron's do suggest, however, that this effect may have little to do with the property tax and much more to do with the fact that local governments have responsibility for paying for public services. Local reliance on income taxes, for example, would involve the same incentives for zoning exclusion of low-income residents. Finally, if the property tax is actually now progressive in its final incidence, zoning inequality may then show up in that the property tax would be even more progressive in the absence of zoning or other similar controls on community entry.

The Increased Awareness of Community Zoning Inequality

Although the discriminatory consequences of community zoning have received broad public attention only in recent years, they have had a long history and have occasionally provoked comment. In the *Euclid* case, which established the constitutionality of zoning, the federal district judge who first heard the case accurately perceived the purpose of Euclid's zoning and found it unacceptable. Newton Baker, the unsuccessful attorney for the opposing Ambler Realty Company, argued without success in his 1926 Supreme Court brief: "Nor can police regulations be used to effect the arbitrary desire to have a municipality resist the operation of economic laws and remain rural, exclusive and aesthetic, when its land is needed to be otherwise developed by that larger public good and welfare. . . . "[18]

From the 1940s on, zoning was not given much attention for more than two decades. Although there was little comment about it generally, a few observers perceived in the 1950s that community zoning practices could be damaging to the interests of the poor. In 1953, Harvard law professor Charles Haar commented on a New Jersey Supreme Court decision upholding minimum floor-space requirements in Wayne Township, New Jersey:

The preservation of expensive homes (whose assessed evaluations can be maintained at a high level and which cost little for the community to service) apparently becomes a proper function if suitably dressed up as a zoning ordinance. . . .

The New Jersey court substituted shibboleths for reasoning and used liberal shibboleths to attain an illiberal result—a decision which can only still further distort the problem arising from the complex relationship of city and county.[19]

In the early 1960s, a few judicial opinions indicated a growing court concern about community zoning policies. In a much noted 1962 New Jersey Supreme Court dissent to the approval of a total exclusion of trailer parks from a zoning jurisdiction, Justice Frederick Hall was critical:

[Legitimate zoning purposes] are perverted from their intended application when used to justify Chinese walls on the borders of roomy and developing municipalities for the actual purpose of keeping out all but the "right kind" of people or those who will live in a certain kind and cost of dwelling. What restrictions like minimum house size requirements, overly large lot area regulations and complete limitation of dwellings to single family units really do is bring about community-wide economic segregation. . . . [20]

By the mid-1960s, urban racial and poverty problems had become matters of intense national concern, and suburban restrictions on the availability of low- and moderate-income housing constituted a major and conspicuous obstacle to their solution. Several national commissions strongly recommended zoning reform. The Kaiser committee on urban housing recommended granting the federal Department of Housing and Urban Development powers to override local zoning in cases where it prevented construction of federally subsidized low- and moderate-income housing projects. This recommendation was based on the belief that "when zoning standards applicable to a substantial area are framed or administered so as to screen out the poor from the right to occupy dwellings to meet their needs, serious questions of unconstitutional discrimination arise—particularly when the area is adjacent to a large city and the majority of the poor are nonwhite."[21]

The Douglas commission in 1968 similarly condemned highly restrictive zoning policies: "Practices of this kind are socially deplorable. Economically, they are especially harmful where they have the effect of separating lower income persons from job opportunities. This regulatory conspiracy against low-income housing must be broken."[22] The commission recommended reforms including denial of land-use regulations to municipalities with less than 25,000 population or of less than four square miles in area; denial of regulatory powers to local governments without plans ("development guidance programs"); greater state planning and supervision of land-use regulation, particularly the availability of low- and moderate income housing; and establishment of special federal and state policies to promote greater availability of housing in proximity to employment locations, again especially for low- and moderate-income groups.

The Small Success of Zoning Reform

Despite strong recommendations by prestigious national commissions, only a few reform steps have been taken in the intervening years. A few efforts have been made to establish regional institutions to plan low-income housing. In 1970, in the Dayton metropolitan area, a much praised agreement was reached voluntarily among metropolitan communities to follow a formula prepared by the Dayton area regional planning commission to distribute 14,000 units of federally subsidized low- and moderate-income housing. In Washington, D.C., and other metropolitan areas, fair-share formulas—although having no legal force or necessary agreement from communities—have been prepared by metropolitan planning agencies for distribution of low- and moderate-income housing throughout the metropolitan area. Although it is not likely that these formulas would have been followed to any great extent in any case, the cutoff in federal housing subsidy funds by the Nixon administration in 1973 prevented their implementation.

Massachusetts is the only state that has taken direct legislative action to distribute low-income housing among suburban communities. In 1969, it enacted the Massachusetts Zoning Appeals Law (the so-called Anti-Snob Zoning Law) to create a system of state review of proposals submitted by nonprofit sponsors for low- and moderate-income housing. Zoning decisions of local governments can be appealed to a newly established Housing Appeals Committee. In considering whether a project should be permitted in a particular community, the relevant criteria include the amount of low- and moderate-income housing already built in the community and the compatibility of the proposed housing design with the existing community environment. Under the law, the overall low- and moderate-income housing supply cannot be required to exceed 10 percent of total community housing and the overall amount of land used for low- and moderate-income housing to exceed 1.5 percent of total community land. Until 1973, the law's implementation was held up by a court challenge.

In 1968, at the height of the turmoil following the assassination of Martin Luther King, Jr., Governor Nelson Rockefeller persuaded the New York State legislature to establish the Urban Development Corporation (UDC), aimed partly at increasing provision of low- and moderate-income housing. One important and controversial feature of the legislation was the provision of authority for UDC to override zoning and other community land-use regulations. Although UDC treated this authority with great circumspection, using it in only a few instances against the wishes of local government, the legislature subsequently voted to rescind the authority. Finally, in 1973, rather than veto it, as he had done before, Governor Rockefeller faced what appeared to be the unavoidable and signed the rescinding legislation. In 1974, the U.S. Commission on Civil Rights reported that "the UDC has built relatively few low-income units and it has not been active in suburban communities."[23]

Court challenges to community zoning have met with minimal success. Legal challenges must deal with a troublesome practical problem. While it is easier to win court cases on an individual-project basis, given the heavy legal costs involved, only a few can be litigated at a time, and such cases therefore do not have much effect on overall zoning practices. It would be much more effective to obtain a court-ordered rewriting of entire community zoning ordinances. But to single out one community to rewrite its ordinance discriminates against that community if other communities are engaging in the identical zoning practices. Moreover, to open up one community to low- and moderate-income housing projects while others exclude them might subject that community to a flood of new housing projects.

The better solution would be to require a regionally coordinated set of adjustments in all community zoning ordinances to increase the regional availability of low- and moderate-income housing. But in most areas there are no regional institutions with the responsibility or capacity to calculate the proper adjustments. Aware of the far-reaching social and economic consequences of zoning decisions and the broad knowledge of social and economic facts and conditions needed to make these decisions responsibly, the courts have felt themselves poorly equipped to become virtual regional planning bodies for low- and moderate-income housing. This difficulty has been an inhibiting factor preventing them from taking stronger action against zoning practices.

A major victory in legal challenges to community zoning was finally won in the New Jersey Supreme Court in 1975. The court ruled that the New Jersey communities in rapidly developing areas that contain plentiful supplies of vacant land must zone to accommodate a wide variety of housing types and qualities:

The universal and constant need for such housing is so important and of such broad public interest that the general welfare which developing municipalities like Mount Laurel must consider extends beyond their boundaries and cannot be parochially confined to the claimed good of the particular municipality. It has to follow that, broadly speaking, the presumptive obligation arises for each such municipality affirmatively to plan and provide, by its land use regulations, the reasonable opportunity for an appropriate variety and choice of housing, including, of course, low and moderate cost housing, to meet the needs, desires and resources of all categories of people who may desire to live within its boundaries. . . . [24]

The New Jersey Supreme Court did not address the major practical problem noted above, namely, who is to determine what a reasonable range of housing types and qualities is for Mt. Laurel. It remains to be seen how this difficulty will eventually be handled.

Despite the Mt. Laurel decision, the full implications of which are still a long way from being worked out, community zoning reform has had little overall success. Princeton professor Michael Danielson assessed the situation in 1976:

The retreat of Congress and the federal executive from any substantial commitment to opening the suburbs, the failure of almost all of the states to restrict local land-use powers, and the reluctance of the most metropolitan councils to press for dispersed housing, all reflect sensitivity to suburban interests which severely limits the prospects of effective unilateral action from above. . . .
Few state courts have imposed significant restrictions on suburban land-use controls. Only New Jersey's supreme court has directly confronted suburban exclusion. . . . [25]

Practical problems have not been the only explanation for strong resistance to reform. There is obviously wide popular support for community zoning policies, and it seems to have increased considerably in recent years. Community zoning in fact meets important needs that have not been sufficiently appreciated.

Justifications for Zoning Protection of Community Character

The intensity of recent criticisms directed toward community zoning policies has led many people to assume that such policies have no legitimate justification. But there are many social and economic benefits from having communities with homogeneous populations. The community political process may function more successfully, expending less time and effort (and emotion) in trying to reach political compromises. A well-defined set of community objectives and a feasible plan for achieving them are much more likely to emerge when the community population is homogeneous. By contrast, in big cities, where decisions generally result from compromises among numerous factions, the political process often seems incapable of decisive action.

There are also important economic advantages deriving from a homogeneous population. Specialized shopping and other facilities can be made available to meet its particular needs. Social and other private clubs will be able to orient their programs toward meeting common local needs. Most important, the provision of public services can be designed to meet specific demands of a population that has similar requirements.

Whenever individual demands for local public services differ widely, as they do for education, major problems result when a diverse community must provide them on a uniform level. For example, in a community where many levels of wealth and income are represented, wealthier residents will usually want high levels of public service but will be unable to persuade the majority, which will be unwilling to pay for them. On the other hand, the poor might prefer low levels of some services, particularly luxury services, and low taxes, but they will also probably be outvoted. Elements of the community that depart greatly from the norm will usually be unable to obtain satisfaction for their particular public-service requirements.

Julius Margolis, economist and past director of the Fels Center of Government at the University of Pennsylvania, has described the advantages of a homogeneous community. After commenting on some of the inequalities and other problems resulting from zoning policies, he observes:

Against these losses should be placed the virtues of a more homogeneous community. If neighbors share preferences about public services, it is easier to get consensus about the quantity and quality of those services. There will be less controversy about the issues of a playing field or a science lab, a park versus a library. Not only will the decision making costs be less but there is a greater probability that the outputs would be more satisfactory for most of the residents. A set of public services which matches the preferences of the residents is no mean accomplishment. . . . On the contrary, a whole new school of thought has developed which elevates these gains to the level of dominant objectives. . . . [26]

The school to which Margolis refers has regarded the small-to-medium-size suburban community as serving an economic function very similar to that of a private club.[27] Both the private club and the exclusive suburban community make it possible for groups of similar individuals to obtain goods and services that require collective provision and in the quantities and qualities suited to their closely shared means and preferences. The close resemblance is illustrated by the relatively insignificant differences between a municipal golf course in a small, wealthy community of golfers, where use is limited to community residents, and a private golf club in, and with a membership from, the same community. Community zoning requirements can then be understood as the public equivalent of entrance fees and other requirements for admission to private clubs.

The private-club analogy points to some of the complexities in the issues raised by community zoning policies. Few people contest the right of better-off individuals to form exclusive private clubs. There would probably be little social benefit in prohibiting club membership fees and club exclusiveness. Rather than increasing social equality through broadening club memberships, such prohibitions would in many cases result in the dissolution of the club. Similar problems are encountered in prohibiting zoning restrictions in wealthy communities.

If local communities were required to be integrated economically, many individuals with high incomes who favored high public-service levels would be likely to turn to private provision of what has heretofore been a public service. That is what high-income people residing in big cities who send their children to private schools, for example, are already doing. One might even find that wealthy individuals would join together to create communities with very low tax rates and offering very little in the way of public education and other public services, thereby eliminating much of the incentive for the less well-off to enter the communities. In those communities, by common understanding, all the wealthy citizens would simply obtain privately such services as education, recreation facilities, and garbage collection. Police protection might even be provided privately to some extent as the wealthy congregated in large privately managed developments with guards, entry gates, and other protections paid for by the residents—as is already the practice, for example, in large communities of the elderly that demand especially high protection.

One way to prevent the community from withdrawing public provision of education (and other normally public services) would be to finance those services through state (and federal) revenues. But it would then be necessary to allocate those revenues approximately equally among communities according, for example, in the case of schools, to their student population. Once again, in many communities there would be a large gap between the public-service demands of many citizens and public-expenditure levels on their behalf. Rich communities might have less qualified teachers, larger class sizes, and fewer specialized courses than they are willing to pay for; and poor communities might receive more audiovisual gadgetry, swimming pools, and gym equipment than they regard as worth being taxed for.

Because of the political influence of the wealthy, state financing of education would probably result in a large increase in statewide expenditures, bringing all community educational expenditures into the range of current levels for wealthy communities. This result might well involve an undesirably large commitment of national resources to education. A number of doubts have, of course, been publicly expressed concerning the educational benefits of increased expenditures beyond a certain point. Frequently, the high educational expenditures of wealthy school districts include luxuries with little educational content for the benefit of children whose parents can easily afford them.

Besides allowing flexibility in public-service provision, there may be still other fundamental reasons in favor of homogeneous communities. Recent indications suggest that the strong advocacy of social homogeneity of the late 1960s is more a last gasp than an indication of things to come. The trend of recent years has been toward an increasing segregation of economic classes and other groups. Large numbers of better-off persons clearly prefer economically segregated living patterns and, in a significant departure from the past, are becoming less reluctant to say so. In fact, there are strong trends toward greater social segregation of living patterns generally, although combined with greater racial integration.[28] Some examples are "singles" apartment complexes, retirement communities, university towns for youth, and rural communes.

Although often not sufficiently emphasized, the intense commitment to social integration of the last few decades has rested on a belief that a common social ideal exists—essentially that of the educated, scientific, rational, liberal man. While it may be unfortunate, the trend of recent years has been antiscientific, antirational, and antiliberal. A result of this is the growing notion of a society in which people with a wide diversity of views and behaviors may coexist in separate communities.

Robert Nisbet, Albert Schweitzer Professor in the Humanities at Columbia University, has pointed to major shifts now occurring:

Strange specters hover over the landscape. In place of the accustomed ideals (especially in the minds of intellectuals) of political nationalism, of ideological uniformity, of integration of groups, classes, and sections of the country, and of homogeneity of mind and culture to match homogeneity of law and political practice, we find ourselves in the presence of unwonted ideals of ethnic particularism, localism, regionalism, and . . . pluralism. . . . [29]

As an example of this trend, a recent much-commented-upon work by Harvard philosophy professor Robert Nozick argues that, given the virtual certainty of many different philosophies and values, the only ethically justifiable society is one of a broad range of choices among diverse communities in which people holding similar philosophies and values congregate. In any other society, coercion by the state to impose one particular group's philosophy and values on others would be necessary: "Nozick, finding incredible the supposition that there is one best society for everyone, proposes instead a "meta-utopia"—a framework for many diverse utopian experiments, all formed of voluntary communities, so that no one can impose his version of utopia on others. . . . "[30]

Such an approach has long been reflected in local-option laws controlling the sale of alcoholic beverages. An important recent example is provided by the 1973 *Miller* decision of the U.S. Supreme Court allowing much greater state and local discretion in controlling sale of pornography.[31] Current proposals for the segregation of public beaches into sections for clothed and for nude bathing provide an unusually clear illustration of the principle of social segregation as a practical solution to the problem of divergent moral and philosophical views. Such approaches all assume considerable separation of community and other living patterns.

The growing emergence in the United States of localism and regionalism, distrust of national authority, loss of faith in the possibilities of scientific—and almost inevitably, therefore, centrally directed—progress, and resistance to social change seems in fact to be part of a worldwide phenomenon. In a 1975 *New York Times* report on European trends, Flora Lewis examined some similar contemporary European attitudes:

What is happening is that tradition and ethnic separateness are being increasingly asserted not only among nations but among their supposedly assimilated regions. Being up to date no longer means rejecting the past and its patterns but emphasizing them with vigor, even violence.

Corsicans, Bretons, Welshmen, Scotsmen, even the 80,000 French-speaking Swiss of the Jura Mountains who want to be detached from the German speaking canton of Berne and form one of their own—all are demanding narrower, not broader, social structures, less incorporation, not more.[32]

Consistent with trends in the 1970s, the U.S. Supreme Court has refused to disapprove the practice of economic discrimination to establish and maintain homogeneous communities. In its 1971 *Valtierra* decision, the Supreme Court upheld a provision of the California Constitution requiring prior local approval by voter referendum before low-income housing could be constructed in a community. Justice Hugo Black showed little hesitation in his opinion for the majority upholding the right of community residents to vote to exclude low-income housing, even explicitly approving of their taking fiscal factors into account. (The same right would without question have been denied if the referendum had concerned "black" rather than "low-income" housing.)

The people of California have also decided by their own vote to require referendum approval of low-rent public housing projects. This procedure ensures that all the people of a community will have a voice in a decision which may lead to large expenditures of local governmental funds for increased public services and to lower tax revenues. It gives them a voice in decisions that will affect the future development of their own community. This procedure for democratic decision making does not violate the constitutional command that no state shall deny to any person the "equal protection of the laws."[33]

A 1974 report by the National Committee Against Discrimination in Housing concluded:

The weight of judicial opinion in the relative handful of decisions that have interpreted Valtierra appears to read that decision to mean that wealth [as opposed to race] is not a suspect classification, and that economic discrimination does not rise to an equal protection violation. . . . [34]

As previously noted, Justice William Douglas gave a strong endorsement to neighborhood zoning in his opinion in the 1974 *Belle Terre* case. It may surprise many people that the two principal Supreme Court opinions upholding forms of neighborhood and community economic segregation were authored by Justices William Douglas and Hugo Black, two of the fiercest Court opponents of racial segregation. Their opinions in fact seem to reflect a deeply rooted American view that a person should be able to join with others of similar means and preferences to establish and maintain an environment to their liking. Unlike other areas of private consumption, satisfaction of personal preferences for an immediate neighborhood and community environment can be accomplished only through employment of public—or at least collective—regulatory powers. In essence, this view holds that the immediate environment is a private good, subject to standards of private consumption rather than to the requirements that normally must be met by public actions.

Zoning as a Collective Property Right

Zoning gives community residents the authority to control use of their environment and public services. While community zoning powers are not as total or as discretionary as are the ordinary rights of private-property ownership, they constitute in essence—as neighborhood zoning does also—a collective property right to the community environment and to its public services. Partly because of this right, as we have seen, the small-to-medium-size community comes very close to the features of a private club. Private clubs accept only those persons whom the club members want; zoning gives community residents the authority to limit entry to the types of people they want. Private clubs have membership fees; zoning that regulates minimum lot size, floor space, and other quality standards sets a fee (property-tax payment) for use of the community's environment and services.[35]

To the extent that these property-tax payments go directly for public services, they are very similar to a user charge. User charges are widely employed in the United States to finance sewer, water, transportation, and other public services. The fiscal consequences of zoning are very similar to financing local public services through user charges. A few observers have suggested wide adoption of user charges to finance local services.[36] This policy would eliminate much of the existing fiscal incentive for communities to deny entry to less well-off persons, although high user charges in wealthy communities would effectively keep out the poor and thus would share many of the consequences of current zoning practices.

The inequalities that result from community zoning are the natural consequences of creating collective property rights to community environments and public services. As with ordinary personal-property rights, these rights allow the wealthy to avoid sharing their environment with the poor. The distribution of community environmental and public-service benefits is generally the same as the distribution of the benefits of private clubs or of ordinary personal property—to each according to his private means. Society has accepted these distributional consequences—over much opposition, of course—at least partly because incentives are also created for the establishment and maintenance of high-quality community environments and public services. Without zoning protection, greater sharing of high-quality environments and public services might not result; rather, many such environments and public services might never be established and, where already established, might be allowed to decline in quality. The role of private clubs and other unambiguously private social institutions would probably greatly expand. Perhaps partly to avoid that eventuality, society has chosen to treat the small-to-medium-size suburban community, although nominally a public institution, effectively as a private one.

As the community size grows, the analogy between communities and private clubs becomes strained. The jurisdiction of some local governments covers large areas comprising populations of several hundred thousand people—this is the case, for example, in certain areas where counties have major governing roles. In these circumstances, although zoning purposes are essentially unchanged, the community ceases to be comparable to the club. Rather, a more apt analogy is that between the large community and a nation-state, where zoning rights can be compared with national immigration controls. The rights of property ownership to an area and of sovereign control over that area are basically the same.

Community Zoning Evolution Toward a Full Collective Property Right

As it was originally administered, community zoning included only a portion of the rights that private club members possess to their collective property. The community could exclude almost any use classification it wanted, but it had to adhere rigidly to classifications once they were enacted into law. The resulting lack of discretion in zoning law was a serious limitation on the benefits of zoning to community residents. It was quite possible, on the one hand, that a particular use within an excluded use classification might actually have enhanced the community environment or, on the other, that a use in a permitted classification might prove detrimental.

The same problem could—and did—occur in neighborhood zoning. But in most neighborhoods, zoning rigidity was considered an asset because neighborhood residents could not otherwise be fully confident that the wider community might not at some point admit undesired uses against their wishes. Because it had full control over its zoning, the community did not face this uncertainty. The advantages of greater discretion therefore substantially outweighed any disadvantages. With broad discretion in deciding whether to accept individual project applications, the community could examine the particular aesthetic quality of prospective development, consider all its specific fiscal and environmental implications, guide development into specific areas at the times desired, and generally make any fine distinctions it saw fit.

Initially, the problem was that the existence of broad discretion in community zoning was directly contrary to the basic principles of proper zoning practice that had been established in early zoning theory (partially reflecting the original design of zoning to suit neighborhood aims). The original architects of zoning saw its rigid use classifications as an effective and probably constitutionally necessary way of ensuring against possible misuse of strong zoning controls. While acknowledging the unavoidability of some zoning changes, they made it clear that zoning should be altered only occasionally, and they attempted to make zoning change difficult by requiring specific legislative action for each case. Zoning architects regarded any widespread practice of granting zoning changes in response to individual applications from developers or property owners as threatening discriminatory treatment of favored parties and probably as unconstitutional. Alfred Bettman, for example, commented:

That zoning is regulation by zones or districts, as distinguished from regulation by individual lots or small vicinities, is a principle on which both the moral and legal validity of zoning have been based. . . . Were we to continue to treat the single piece of land or small group of lots as the unit of regulation, but transfer the power to regulate to a public legislative or administrative organ, that would not be zoning even though it were to be held constitutional, which is not likely.[37]

Although greater discretion in controlling community entry had many advantages, such past warnings carried sufficient weight to prevent communities for a long time from employing regulatory methods that explicitly left development permission to the discretion of local officials. Rather, as has typically been the case in the history of zoning, changes in practice crept in gradually and informally, with little awareness of the eventual result.

Zoning laws had always allowed for exceptions—"variances" —in cases of unusual hardship or other special circumstances. In some communities, the granting of variances at times had become so liberal as to amount to discretionary zoning administration. In the period after World War II, floating zones and special-permit districts introduced limited forms of discretion. Floating zones were zoning classifications not attached to any specific geographic area, but fixed on the zoning map of the community at the discretion of administrators, normally in response to a proposed project within the classification. Special-permit districts gave zoning administrators the authority to approve certain special categories of projects in those districts at their discretion. The first explicit systems of administrative discretion intended to receive wide application were not introduced until the 1960s, however, under provisions for planned-unit developments. Under these provisions, developers provide detailed specifications for their proposed project (generally of fairly large scale), which are then frequently modified in negotiation with the community. Other than health and building codes, few standards for granting planned-unit-development permission are fixed in advance, although the community may attach many stipulations during negotiation.

Regulatory provisions for planned-unit development in fact simply gave formal recognition to an informal method of project-by-project review that had already been in use for some time and that has continued in wide use in communities. While the form of traditional zoning was preserved, the practice was changed greatly. Communities simply adopted highly restrictive zoning ordinances that prohibited almost all development. Each prospective use then had to receive a specific zoning-change approval, which would be granted only after a community review of project specifications and, in many cases—especially if the project were large—negotiation with the developer.

By the late 1960s, as part of a broad examination of the land-use-control system, it was generally acknowledged that in large numbers of communities—especially in rapidly developing areas—traditional zoning had, in effect, been converted into a system of administrative discretion. The Douglas commission characterized such zoning practices as "wait and see" zoning:

Large lot zoning can effectively prevent economically attractive development until the municipality grants rezoning. When the owner applies for that rezoning, the municipality has an opportunity to look over the proposal and give it the broadest of discretionary review. Such a "wait and see" approach to regulation is now gaining acceptance very rapidly.[38]

The Model Land Development Code described the very wide administrative discretion that resulted:

Since the intent of these holding zones is to assure that any future development will require an amendment to the regulations and thereby receive discretionary review by the municipality, the process of deciding individual applications for rezoning has become the important element of zoning. A person who looks at the text of a zoning ordinance or the zoning map in order to ascertain the community's policies toward land use may be accumulating only meaningless information. . . . [39]

Reflecting their unwillingness to interfere in zoning matters, courts have generally tolerated these practices. But while approving the exercise of broad local discretion, the courts have been concerned to ensure that zoning changes were fairly granted. For example, courts have many times ruled that a zoning change granted for one site had to be granted for nearby properties as well, if their owners requested it.

The introduction of broad administrative discretion eliminated much of the practical, if not the formal, difference between community zoning rights and condominium, private club, and other strictly private collective property rights. Most recently, in 1976, the United States Supreme Court took another step that narrowed the still substantial formal differences. In a case involving the community of Eastlake, Ohio, it declared that communities could require public referenda to approve all zoning changes.[40] To make major decisons concerning collectively owned private property, it is, of course, also a common practice to conduct a vote of all shareholders or members.

But there is still one important aspect in which zoning does not provide the full rights of ownership of a collective property right. Community residents cannot sell their zoning rights. A few communities have attempted to evade court disapproval, however, in effect selling their zoning rights by charging high subdivision, water, sewer, or other entry fees, much above the actual costs of the new development borne by the community. Only developers willing to pay these charges would receive the needed change in zoning.

So far, the various fees, charges, and taxes have probably not produced much revenue for communities above the costs of new development. But a recent complaint by a developer's attorney concerning a case in Livermore, California, under court challenge, suggests the considerable potential:

The city storm drainage fee is $328 a unit. The city water storage fee is $266 a unit. The sewer connection fee is $1050 a unit. The subdivision improvement inspection is $45. The plan inspection is another $45. A fee called a tax on residential construction is $584 a unit. The park development fee is $403 a unit. The tract map processing fee is $25 a unit. . . .

The school district . . . charges $800 per letter per house.

The total of all these fees, in addition to some county water district fees which I have not mentioned because they are not imposed by the city, approach $4000 a house. . . . [41]

While the future is always difficult to predict, it would not be surprising to find high community fees of this kind eventually becoming the practical means by which communities could effectively sell their zoning rights. This could well be in the public interest, as Chapter 4 will examine. Creating collective property rights without also establishing an adequate mechanism for transfer of these rights when needed to allow for changes in land use has had very unhappy consequences for land development. Comprehensive public-land-use planning, which has been the means intended to guide new development, has instead been far more important for its legal and intellectual role in theories of zoning.

3 Zoning and Public Land-Use Planning

The role of public land-use planning in the legal justifications for community zoning was described briefly in the previous chapter. This role is of such importance in the general development of zoning that it requires particular attention. Since the 1930s, zoning has been given its principal intellectual and legal justification through its use as one of several key instruments for implementing comprehensive public land-use plans. The greatest misconceptions concerning zoning in recent years have involved the role of public planning. Before the system of land-use regulation can be improved significantly, a much better public understanding of the planning role in zoning is needed.

Zoning has proved generally effective in protecting the environments of existing neighborhoods and communities. It has had less success in accomplishing another traditional major zoning purpose, that of guiding new land development according to a preestablished plan. The greatest failings of the American system of land-use regulation have involved the manner in which transitions in land use have occurred.

The Need for Public Planning

During the process of land development each step ideally ought to be closely coordinated with other steps. But the piecemeal nature of land development, the very large number of participants involved, the competitive relationship among private (and also to some extent public) participants, the frequently poor understanding of the workings of social and economic forces in land markets, and various other factors have often resulted in a lack of coordination. The desirability of improvement in this regard has long been perceived, and public land-use planning has been widely proposed to provide the coordination needed for land development.

The previous two chapters were concerned with neighborhoods and communities. Patterns of land use can also be examined within regions and the nation and, occasionally, even across nations. A region is similar to a neighborhood in that it is a geographic area identified by certain social and economic ties within its boudaries. By contrast, the boundaries of a community are politically determined, and they often cut arbitrarily across social and economic interrelationships. In examining the overall process of land development, the basic units are the neighborhood and the region (or the various subregions).

Coordination of neighborhood development is obviously desirable. Heavy industry should not be located in areas that are likely to become residential neighborhoods, and residences should not locate in areas about to be turned over to heavy industry. Coordination in the development of properties for the same or similar use is also desirable. For example, within a residential neighborhood, the architecture of one house may clash with the architecture next door. A particularly conspicuous example of poor coordination among nearby uses is the strip development of commercial districts along major highways. Used-car lots, gasoline stations, hamburger stands, drugstores, and other facilities are often jumbled together to the great detriment of the district's appearance. (Compare, for example, the large suburban shopping centers coordinated by a single owner-developer.) The frequent absence of planning in neighborhood (or district) development is a primary cause of what is judged by many to be the low aesthetic quality of the American urban landscape. It is also, although to a lesser degree, probably a cause of more basic economic inefficiency in serving needs for which neighborhoods are intended.

Many planners have long advocated that government comprehensively plan future physical development, with planning of individual neighborhoods necessarily a starting point. In a well-known speech to the American Society of Planning Officials, John Reps, the leading American historian of city planning, lamented the low aesthetic quality of the urban landscape in the United States and recommended public planning for further development:

I start from the premise that the American urban environment is grossly unsatisfactory when compared to what we are capable of achieving. It is inefficient, inconvenient, unattractive, uneconomical, and unloved. The tragedy is that this condition is also unnecessary. . . .
I do maintain that public plans, deficient though they may be in many respects, far exceed in quality in almost every case what actually emerges as the built environment.[1]

A second broad objective of public planning has been to improve the coordination of regional development. Regional planning involves coordination among air- and water-quality programs; installation of major transportation facilities; sewer, water, and other public-facility installation programs; the location and timing of new residential, commercial, and industrial development; and many other regional matters.

The absence of regional coordination can be costly. If public facility installation is not coordinated with new development, public-service demands can exceed capacity in areas where development occurs rapidly and unexpectedly. Highways can become congested, schools overcrowded, and sewage-treatment plants overloaded. As new public facilities have to be installed hurriedly, their costs may be greater than they would have been had development been planned in advance. Unnecessary costs can be incurred if new development skips over vacant areas already equipped with public services. The inefficiencies of such "leapfrogging" development have attracted wide comment:

This process of leapfrogging or scatteration brings only costs. Firm figures are hard to come by, but our calculations indicate that direct public costs (for highways, sewers, water supply, parks, and some other services) may come to $150 per family per year. . . . it seems that the costs of sprawl are significant even in an age of affluence.[2]

Without adequate regional coordination, highway transportation programs might further encourage new low-density development, threatening to defeat the purposes of programs designed to reduce air pollution or to preserve greater open spaces. Preservation of undesirably large open spaces could defeat programs to open up more land for low- and moderate-income housing.

The basic desirability of regional planning and coordination has long been recognized. The Standard City Planning Enabling Act issued by the Department of Commerce in 1928 recommended that each state create regional planning bodies (although with only advisory responsibilities). The authors of the Enabling Act explained:

Every growing town or city with an agricultural or undeveloped belt around it not only needs good highway connection with the country, for example, but desires to forestall the strangling effect of ill-planned or unplanned suburbs. To some suburbs and towns the maintenance of clear roadways and good rapid transit facilities which pass through other jurisdictions is of most vital importance. Inadequate approaches to an important bridge in one municipality may become an intolerable burden to the citizens of others. Objectionable uses of land in one community may adversely affect another, as in the case of slaughter-houses with their offensive odors, or of factories set directly next to a city residence district.

Orderly development from this point of view of the region as a whole must come eventually through comprehensive planning by regional commissions, which define and analyze regional problems, and devise practical measures for carrying them out. . . . [3]

Zoning as an Instrument of Comprehensive Public Planning

It has frequently been remarked that zoning is "negative." By this is meant that zoning has had its greatest successes in excluding development in order to preserve the character of an existing neighborhood or community. If the process of land development resulted in unattractive and inefficient neighborhoods and communities, however, regulations that could only protect existing character would clearly leave a great deal to be desired.

An even more critical concern has been that, even though zoning controls may only be intended to protect individual neighborhood and community environments, they automatically exert substantial control over broad patterns of regional development. The cumulative consequence of many individual neighborhood and community zoning actions will be to direct development away from those areas in the region that exclude it and toward those areas that accept it. Without regional coordination of zoning jurisdictions, their cumulative control over broad development patterns will tend to be haphazard and unpredictable. In such a situation, there is a danger that the overall consequences for regional development might be harmful to the broad public interest.

The desire to prevent this possibility has been a basic reason behind the creation of planning institutions. Most observers have suggested that, without comprehensive planning, the desirability and even constitutionality of zoning would be called into serious question. As a result, there have been many attempts to integrate zoning into public planning. A generally accepted view has been that "the zoning plan is, or should be, aimed at achieving the objectives of the land use plan."[4]

The conviction that zoning must be designed so that it is consistent with a comprehensive land-use plan is an old one. As long ago as 1924, the Standard State Zoning Enabling Act stated:

[Zoning] regulations shall be made in accordance with a comprehensive plan and designed . . . to provide adequate light and air; to prevent the overcrowding of land; to avoid undue concentration of population; to facilitate the adequate provision of transportation, water, sewerage, schools, parks and other public requirements. . . . [5]

When zoning ordinances were first widely introduced, many communities had no formal planning capacity and could not follow the recommendation of the Zoning Enabling Act. The Standard City Planning Enabling Act of 1928 was partly aimed at remedying that situation. After its publication, comprehensive planning was introduced in many communities throughout the United States. The number of city planning commissions grew from 390 in 1927 to around 1200 in 1937.[6] Between 1933 and 1936, the number of metropolitan and regional planning agencies grew from 85 to 506. Accompanying the rapid spread of formal planning institutions, the view was increasingly accepted that the purpose of zoning should be to provide a key tool for implementing public land-use plans. Acceptance of the planning theory of zoning had progressed by 1942 to the point where Alfred Bettman could observe:

The old idea was that zoning was chiefly for the protection of nice residential neighborhoods. . . . The early forms of zoning were inactive, for they sought only to keep existing conditions. The proper concept of zoning, which is being generally accepted, is that it is an instrument for the constructive guidance of land for private uses. Zoning should be thought of not as a negative device for keeping something out, but as a positive tool for causing the city to grow according to a logical plan.[7]

According to traditional planning philosophy, the planning process should follow a well-defined procedure in which zoning would have a particular role. Planning would begin with a careful study of the current situation and trends in a given planning jurisdiction, then it would project residential and other future land-use demands, and then commercial, public-service, and other supporting facilities would be determined. Finally, expected future development would be allocated among geographic areas in the jurisdiction according to various planning considerations. One result would be a detailed land-use map—part of the master plan—showing the precise type of future development intended for each geographic area. As one study put it, "The conventional analogy is that the comprehensive plan is like the blueprint of an architect's design for a building."[8]

Zoning is only one of a number of public controls over land use. Highway, sewer, water, and other public-facility installations have also been regarded as playing key roles in achieving plans. As areas were developed according to plan, the community would coordinate development with the installation of highways, sewer lines, schools, and other needed public facilities. The essential role of zoning and other land-use regulations was to ensure that development would be in accord with the plan for the area as development proceeded within it. As planner Hugh Pomeroy commented in 1940: "The planning process consists of four successive steps: (1) securing adequate basic data; (2) analysis of the data; (3) preparation of guiding plans which constitute a master plan for the community and (4) use of various controls and procedures to make the plans effective. . . ."[9]

The evolution of zoning purposes is seen in the changes in zoning practice. As zoning came increasingly to be regarded as an aid in implementing public land-use plans, three major changes in practice took place. As already discussed, the first zoning ordinances were not intended to control uses in undeveloped areas—"country districts," in Bassett's phrase. Obviously, if zoning were to be a useful aid in achieving planning objectives, the scope of zoning would have to broaden. This tendency appeared early on, and as the planning theory of zoning received greater acceptance, control of land use in undeveloped areas became a prime zoning function.

Originally, zoning ordinances were hierarchical (or "cumulative"). Uses were classified by the ordinance in order of their offensiveness. Single-family homes on large lots were typically considered least offensive (or most desirable) and heavy industry most offensive. Each type of use was permitted in any district in which uses considered more offensive were allowed to locate. As a consequence, all uses could locate in a heavy industrial district, while only one use could locate in districts allotted to single-family homes on large lots.

The hierarchical character of early zoning appears to have been dictated by the original view that zoning should serve primarily protective purposes. If the main purpose of zoning was to protect certain uses from proximity to much less desirable uses, there was little reason—or possibly even legal justification—to prohibit a more desirable use from locating in a district populated by less desirable uses. But if zoning were to become an effective public tool to be used for planning purposes, it was essential to eliminate its hierarchical character. Residential and other high-quality uses might locate in currently undeveloped areas planned for future industrial and commercial use, and then once they were located there, it might well prove impossible to install the uses planned. Even if it was possible, it would frequently result in an unattractive neighborhood. Despite many strong statements stressing the need for planning, the secondary concern of original zoning architects in implementing plans is clearly shown by the hierarchical character of early zoning. But since World War II, many communities have created districts—especially industrial and commercial—in which only the specified uses have been permitted to locate.

A third change that took place in zoning was an increase in the number and refinement of zoning district classifications. The New York City ordinance of 1916 had had only three types of use districts—residential, commercial, and unrestricted. If planners were to control future development with any precision, many more exact district classifications would be needed. By the 1950s, a reform of the Chicago zoning ordinance resulted in sixteen major district classifications and over seventy subdistrict classifications. Many other communities introduced similar, if not so far-reaching, changes in their zoning ordinances.

The Role of Planning in the Theory of Zoning Law

Since the early twentieth century, there has always been at least a small group of planning advocates who have proclaimed large benefits to be gained from greater public planning of development. But, despite the work of Lewis Mumford and a few others, this group has never enjoyed popular acceptance. Neither has it created a large or sustained body of work of widely acknowledged intellectual distinction. Instead, the legal profession has provided the most effective advocacy of land-use planning in the United States. The original zoning architects were almost all lawyers. Subsequent leadership in the introduction of public land-use planning was also provided by some of these same lawyers—men such as Edward Bassett, Alfred Bettman, and Frank Williams.

From the first introduction of zoning, many legal experts argued that zoning had to be accompanied by public planning, and that, if it were not, it might well be declared unconstitutional. As already noted, the Standard State Zoning Enabling Act stated in 1924 that zoning must be "in accordance with a comprehensive plan." According to one author of the Enabling Act:

A court should not be asked to assume that the particular zoning ordinance before it bears a reasonable or substantial relationship to the promotion of the public health and the other public benefits . . . unless the ordinance really has that relationship; . . . the justification of a zone plan . . . comes from the fact that those who made the plan made it purposely, and more or less scientifically and organically. . . . [10]

By planning, Bettman, Bassett, and other early zoning architects meant primarily the exercise of careful deliberation, the marshaling of all needed facts, and the drawing upon all available technical expertise to ensure that zoning was in the public interest. With time, zoning-law experts increasingly asserted the necessity of having exact maps of future land uses and other formal statements of objectives. By the mid-1950s, matters had progressed to the point that Harvard law professor Charles Haar could argue that it was necessary to produce a formal master plan that, although malleable to some degree, would constitute an "impermanent constitution" for the zoning system.[11] In his well-known article, "In Accordance with a Comprehensive Plan," he stated that "a fundamental and necessary interrelationship exists" between the zoning ordinance and the public plan: "For to the extent that zoning is properly conceived of as the partial implementation of a plan of broader scope, zoning without planning lacks coherence and discipline in the pursuit of goals of public welfare which the whole municipal regulatory process is supposed to serve."[12]

Legal theorists still justify zoning as a means of implementing public plans. Law professor Robert Anderson stated in 1968 that "zoning continues to be regarded as a legal device for the implementation of a plan for community development."[13] By the title of his massive study of zoning law published in 1975, *American Planning Law*, Norman Williams equates zoning law with planning law.[14]

The new Model Land Development Code of the American Law Institute maintains traditional legal rationales for land-use regulation. With regard to a major new regulatory role proposed for state governments, the code's authors explain that "an ongoing planning process is clearly a prerequisite to satisfactory performance of the regulatory functions authorized."[15] A local plan must be prepared in a sufficiently detailed and specific fashion that its guidance of future development can "withstand a test in court in regard to its reasonableness or its appropriateness and completeness in relation to any particular government action which may later be taken."[16] While the Model Code would not absolutely require planning, it strongly advocates creating state and local plans and reducing the regulatory authority of governments without them.

One concern of the legal profession has been that public planning is needed to ensure that many uncoordinated zoning controls do not cumulatively exert a tight control over regional development that is purposeless, haphazard, and contrary to the larger public interest. The insistence of the legal profession on the necessity of planning has also resulted, perhaps in even greater part, from a fear of deliberate misuse of zoning powers by local public officials. Zoning is particularly open to misuse for the benefit of favored private parties. Permission to develop land for a high-value use is worth large sums of money to private developers, and large financial losses can result from failures to obtain it. Zoning regulations are administered by local governments that often are subject to little journalistic scrutiny or other outside examination. For these reasons, there has been an ever-present concern to avoid their misuse.

This concern has been justified by events. Almost from the beginning, there has been a steady stream of reports of political wheeling and dealing by developers to obtain favorable zoning changes from local governments. Instances of outright bribery and corruption have periodically come to light. One result has been a constant effort to circumscribe the opportunities for discretionary actions by local officials in zoning administration. The Englishman, Delafons, was particularly struck by the determined effort to keep discretion out of the American system:

Since the values conferred or denied by land use controls are great, their administration affords exceptional opportunities for graft and by the same token exposes them to exceptionally strong pressures. The result, in America, has been a determination to eliminate the scope for discretion in land use controls by formalizing them in a set of standard regulations and by laying down in advance the conditions under which, if at all, change may be allowed.[17]

One of the distinctive features of the American system of land-use regulation, when it is compared with other countries, is its direct incorporation of zoning requirements into statutory law. The assignment of direct responsibility for drawing zone boundaries to the local legislature was intended to limit discretion and thereby to reduce the danger of zoning misuse. Incorporated directly into statute, zoning left little discretion (nominally administration consisted only of enforcing the existing laws), and each subsequent zoning-district change had to be specifically enacted by the local legislative body. The courts also received direct responsibility for the review of all zoning matters. Court review has played an especially critical role in the operation of zoning. Probably because they have shared the general concern about possible zoning misuse, courts have seldom hesitated to overrule particular zoning decisions of local officials when they believed them unfair, arbitrary, discriminatory among property owners, or simply without sufficient rational justification.

Americans are so accustomed to direct incorporation of zoning regulations into statutory law that many probably have not considered that there are other possibilities. Yet, in Britain and other countries government agencies have the main responsibility for establishing and administering land-use regulations, somewhat as American regulatory agencies, such as the Interstate Commerce Commission or the Civil Aeronautics Board, establish and administer regulations over private industries.

If the purposes of zoning were limited to protecting the character of already built-up neighborhoods and communities, little discretion in administration would be needed. When public control over the process of land development becomes a zoning purpose, however, a certain amount of discretion is clearly unavoidable. In zoning administration, the most important discretion takes the form of local legislative changes in the zoning ordinance, so-called zoning amendments or rezonings. Such changes are normally of two types: occasional comprehensive revisions of the entire ordinance, and specific actions on applications of individual landowners (the latter are often received in large numbers).

Most legal experts have traditionally been convinced that, as Charles Haar explained, "exercise of the legislative power to zone should be governed by rules and standards as clearly defined as possible, so that it cannot operate in an arbitrary and discriminatory fashion, and will actually be directed to the health, safety, welfare and morals of the community. . . ."[18]

In the traditional legal view, planning has been an effective means of protecting against misuse of the considerable discretion that is unavoidable in administration of zoning. The planner has been given the responsibility for determining whether proposed zoning changes would serve legitimate public interests. First, in the creation of a zoning ordinance and later in comprehensive revisions, legislative actions could be based on detailed land-use planning maps. In considering applications for rezoning of individual parcels, the local legislature could also refer to the land-use planning map and receive advice from the planning commission. Moreover, the planning map and planner recommendations were to be more than simply advisory, because they were to be a basic resource of the courts, providing a standard for judicial review of zoning administration.

This view of the planner role probably reached its strongest articulation and fullest intellectual acceptance in the 1950s. Commenting on Charles Haar's views on the planning role, University of Chicago law professor Allison Dunham explained:

[Professor Haar] seems to recognize that a plan should be more than advisory so that it may become part of the owner's arsenal of facts on which to exercise choices concerning land use and, more importantly, part of the material which a court may use to determine whether the administrator is acting in accordance with law. . . .

The important thing is that [the master plan] be adopted without knowledge of any particular case of land use; that it be definite enough so that it can be objectively determined whether administrative action conforms to it or not; and that it be adhered to when government action is taken.[19]

The Planner as Protector of the Public Interest

An essential, although often implicit, link in legal reasoning is the assumption that comprehensive public plans will guide development to meet the broader public interest. In zoning and planning theory, acceptance of the planner's ability to identify the public interest has rested first on the planner's independence from local elected officials and, second, on the belief that the planner has the special technical expertise required for understanding and administering public controls over the land-development process.

The Douglas commission commented that "planning functions were originally lodged in independent planning boards as part of a general movement in the 1920s to isolate important activities from the 'corrupting influence' of politicians."[20] Early proponents of planning even optimistically envisioned that independent planning commissions would assume many direct responsibilities for land-use control. The Standard City Planning Enabling Act advised giving community planning commissions broad powers:

City departments submit to [the planning commission] for consideration important questions affecting streets, highways, building setbacks, sewers and water pipes, conduits, bridges, viaducts, tunnels, parks, playgrounds, the water front, public buildings, private buildings on public land, transit lines and public utilities and franchises. These departments are required to comply with the adopted plan, unless the planning commission finds it wise to accept suggestions by amending the plan. Otherwise the department must take the matter before the Council. . . . [21]

According to the enabling act, planning-commission disapproval of city department requests on land-development matters could be overturned only by a two-thirds vote of the local legislative body (usually the city council). Planning commissions were not to be elected, but were to be made up of distinguished local citizens appointed by the mayor. Historically, independent citizen planning commissions were in fact widely created, but in most cases they were primarily given advisory responsibilities.

One reason for proposing to give the planning commission what amounted to governing responsibilities was founded on the belief that successful planning and coordination of land development required independence in order that special technical knowledge about the design and organization of regions and communities might be applied. Planning knowledge was often described as "expert" and, especially, "scientific," and it had to be acquired through training in technical planning concepts.

The strong proponent of planning, Alfred Bettman, describes this view:

There is always present . . . the conflict between political considerations and scientific or expert considerations. By "political" I do not mean "partisan," but the hearkening to the clamor of the moment, decisions made by easy compromise between pressure groups. In order that mistakes in these decisions may be reduced, the factor of expertness of science needs to be injected to a greater degree.[22]

Another well-known planner stated: "Planning is as much a technical subject as engineering or law and its importance may be much more far reaching than some detail of engineering construction or some question of legal interpretation. . . . "[23]

Reflecting the very strong faith of the period in the powers of technology, acceptance of the need for special expertise in land-use matters was widespread from the 1920s through the 1950s. It entered, to a certain extent, into the Supreme Court decision to uphold zoning in 1926. The Court seemed impressed by the weight of expert opinion marshaled in support of zoning and, at one point, noted: "The matter of zoning has received much attention at the hands of commissions and experts, and the [favorable] results of their investigations have been set forth in comprehensive reports."[24]

In more recent years, Alan Altshuler, among others, has shown some skepticism about the assumption that special expertise is needed in the planning role: "The case for efforts at genuinely comprehensive planning has generally rested heavily on the thought that planners can resolve conflicts among goals in expert fashion. If they cannot, if they can only articulate specialist goals, then elected officials would seem required to act as the comprehensive arbiters of conflict. . . . "[25]

The Impact of Planning on Community Development

The reader of legal articles and court decisions about zoning might easily come away with the impression that comprehensive public land-use planning was a highly developed technical skill with a long record of successes in its guiding of development. Only in recent years have some dissenting opinions intruded, and these have not been sufficient to constitute a noticeable inclination in court reasoning toward abandoning the planning theory of zoning. If anything, the necessity of comprehensive planning seems to have been asserted by the courts with more vigor than ever.

The observer of the actual process of community and regional development in the United States will come away with an altogether different impression. The history of comprehensive public land-use planning in this country is in fact one of an almost total lack of influence. As long ago as 1935, the leading planning proponent, Alfred Bettman, had confessed some doubts whether planning would prove to have the influence that had been expected:

Planning has been talked and written about to such an extent as to give the impression that planning has a definite meaning in our minds, and that this meaning and its actual application in practice have become an established tradition. Those who frankly face the facts realize that we are still far from any such stage. The ease with which local planning commissions were mowed down in the early skirmishes of budget reductions, and the rather small extent to which state and national plans have been actually applied in a selection of public works may be evidence that planning, as a concept, is far from having either definiteness or the strength which comes from acceptance and deep roots. . . . [26]

In the forty years that have followed these remarks little has changed. Delafons commented in 1962:

In America, public planning policies as they are understood in Britain have hardly begun to emerge and certainly never pass beyond the confines of individual municipalities. The principal objective of American controls remains the traditional protection of private property interests. Such objectives as the long term programming of private development, reservation of land for future public use, prevention of piecemeal redevelopment in areas which will later be subject to comprehensive redevelopment and protection of undeveloped land for its agricultural, recreational, or landscape value are generally beyond the scope of present controls and are only rarely admitted as proper or necessary objectives of public policy.[27]

By the late 1960s, it was generally agreed that comprehensive planning had either not taken place or, where attempted, had been almost entirely unsuccessful in its efforts better to coordinate new development. The Douglas commission in 1968 was highly critical of formal community planning efforts:

It could hardly be clearer that formal plans are not furnishing a unifying basis for most local regulations and other needed development guidance measures. Many communities regulate without meaningful plans. Some of those that do have plans pay little attention to them in making regulatory decisions. Still others find that plans provide little guidance in answering many regulatory questions. In any event, the failure to formulate guiding policies precludes effective development guidance. . . . [28]

This view has been echoed by many other students of land use in recent years. In their study, *Planning and Urban Growth*, Marion Clawson and Peter Hall state that "the plain fact is that most of the plans developed by U.S. city planning organizations have had limited effect; implementation has not lived up to the promise of the plan. As a result, a great deal of city planning in the United States has been wasted professional effort. . . . "[29]

Partly because the law creates a special legal status for a

professional planning staff, generally lodged in a community planning commission, and partly because it has typically been assumed that planning was a discipline that required special training in technical and scientific skills, it is usually assumed that successful planning can only be done by professional planners. Because most of the products of professional planning efforts have been laid aside and ignored, it is also frequently concluded that "planning has failed." This view is misleading, however, because it is the professional planners and formal comprehensive plans—not necessarily all planning—that have failed to have much influence on community growth.

Most communities do not make decisions concerning their future development that are haphazard or without any reasonable explanation. They have been guided by certain policy principles and have adopted suitable methods of implementation. If a plan, as it is typically defined, consists of a set of policy principles and methods of implementation, communities have often had plans, and, while seldom written down and labeled "community plan," they have frequently been both successful and influential. For example, in many suburban communities, general policy has included several guiding principles: already developed neighborhoods should be zoned for existing uses, and, once their zoning is set, few, if any, later changes should be made; in generally undeveloped areas, research facilities, "clean" industry, and other nonresidential facilities that offer fiscal gains should normally be permitted; low-density, residential housing, similar to, or higher than, existing housing quality is also suitable for undeveloped areas; and to some extent the community should attempt to channel new development into certain areas while holding it off in others. The method of implementing this plan has been through administration of the community zoning ordinance, partly as prescribed by the zoning map and partly through the exercise of discretion in denying or approving requests for zoning changes. As has frequently been noted, these informal plans have often been successful in suburban communities.

Nor do all communities have plans designed mainly to resist new development. Until fairly recently, most Americans have regarded growth as a sign of progress. In many communities, property owners, local businessmen, construction and other union members, and other powerful local interests have stood to gain from growth. As a result, a substantial number of communities in the past have welcomed rapid development. Formal comprehensive plans have also had very little influence in these communities. But the informal plan to accommodate rapid growth has often been successful.

In brief, the almost complete lack of influence of formal comprehensive planning was not a failure of the idea of planning in itself but a failure of a particular concept of planning and of the institutions that were designed to make it work. Its failure in the United States can be explained in a number of ways, but three factors seem most critical: the absence of regional authority for land-use control; the inability to provide public compensation to those property owners who would be adversely affected by implementation of public land-use plans; and the separation of public planning institutions from basic governing responsibilities.

The Failure to Establish Regional Authority for Land-Use Control

As we have seen, planning must deal with problems that differ at neighborhood and regional levels. The problem of coordinating neighborhood development was greatly simplified by the assumption by planners that neighborhoods should be homogeneous. One neighborhood might contain homes on one-acre lots, another on three-quarter-acre lots, and so forth. Problems of developing commercial districts, with many use types, or of aesthetic clashes in residential neighborhoods were often neglected. The idea was to designate an undeveloped district for a low-density, homogeneous residential use, zone it for that use, and then let it be filled in according to plan. Although community boundaries sometimes cut through the middle of neighborhoods, the assignment of planning and zoning responsibility to communities did not pose any fundamental obstacles to the achievement of such public plans for neighborhoods.

By contrast, most important regional land-use objectives require coordination that extends far beyond the boundaries of individual communities. An individual community almost in-

variably finds it difficult to know how its policies fit into
a regional pattern of land development that is the product of
large numbers of actions involving many small communities.
The achievement of important regional objectives is likely to
require steps in certain communities that are not in the best
interests of its residents. Even with the best of intentions,
one community might be unable to take measures to assist in
achieving regional objectives, unless its actions are closely coordinated with those of other communities in the region. As
experience has amply demonstrated, it is not reasonable to hope
for close coordination among many communities through voluntary cooperation. Finally, communities with the same planning
and zoning responsibilities can vary enormously in size and
administrative capacity. For these reasons and others, in the
ideal circumstances for regional land-use planning there would
be little, if any, role assigned to an entity such as the community.

But despite constant urgings of metropolitan-government re-
formers over many years, the fact is that planning and zoning
have remained the responsibility of the local community. It is
the community that must project its future growth, plan its future development among geographic areas, and employ zoning
and other public controls to implement the plan. The decentralization of planning and zoning responsibilities into the hands
of many independent communities has created a virtually insu-
perable obstacle to effective regional planning and coordination.
In the absence of regional authority, little can be done other
than to request that community planning bodies coordinate
plans with regional planning objectives (to the extent that these
are even known).

Other than in a few large cities and counties, communities
have thus had little influence over broader regional development patterns, and community planners have had to concentrate
their efforts on neighborhood development. Given the original
assumption that neighborhoods should be homogeneous, the
basic question to be decided was the type of homogeneous use
planned for each new neighborhood. Despite the traditional assumption, the professional independence of planners has seldom been so great as to be able to ignore the general feelings of

the community. On the question of new neighborhood uses, the community has most often sought to protect its character, and most planners have planned accordingly. One of the most important roles of community comprehensive planning has always been to provide a legal and intellectual justification for protecting the community character by zoning. So long as a use was "planned," the courts and others have generally been unwilling to interfere. In recent years, a growing awareness of this professional planning role has produced sarcastic remarks, such as "a city does not hire a planner until it decides it does not want anyone else in the city."[30]

Besides the lack of regional authority, another explanation for the general failure of planning to have much influence has been the inability to pay out of public funds those who would be adversely affected by the implementation of public land-use plans.

The Inability to Pay Public Compensation

The successful implementation of comprehensive public plans would generally require discriminatory treatment of property owners in at least three respects. First, unless the neighborhoods were meant to be entirely homogeneous, lots would be planned for various uses. Second, unless the whole community were to be homogeneous, neighborhoods would be planned in various ways. Third, unless the plan were to be implemented throughout the entire community at once, savings in public-facility installation would require the development of one or a few neighborhoods at a time. As a result, implementation of public plans would typically create a wide divergence of property values in a community. The fortunate owners of properties at sites planned for high-value-use development at an early date would benefit handsomely; less fortunate owners of property at sites planned for low-value-use development in the more distant future could suffer severe financial setbacks.

Understandably both the courts and the American public have been reluctant to support a system that in an essentially arbitrary manner generates large gains for certain lucky property owners and imposes losses on other unlucky ones. Whenever this would be the result, the courts have frequently overturned community actions. The constitutional basis for court intervention has been the fundamental requirement that law not treat citizens arbitrarily or capriciously.

One solution to the problem of discriminatory treatment of property owners might have been to compensate financially those who would suffer setbacks from implementation of community comprehensive plans. The measures necessary to provide such compensation, however, have never been introduced.

For development on a neighborhood scale, the inability to pay compensation has dictated minimum lot size and other zoning requirements that treat every small lot in the same way. It might have been preferable to plan and zone for higher-density housing on one neighborhood lot, lower-density housing on another, and an elementary school, variety store, or park at other locations. But these uses would generate widely different land values, and to zone specific lots in this way, without paying public compensation to the losers, would be legally (as well as morally) unacceptable.

Much the same problem of discrimination is involved at the community level, except that on that level it concerns whole neighborhoods instead of individual lot owners. If a community zones one undeveloped neighborhood for two-acre minimum lot sizes and a second for one-half-acre minimum lot sizes, the value of land in the second neighborhood will typically be considerably higher than that in the first. The courts have usually tolerated this kind of discrimination, saying, in effect, that undesirable elements of discrimination must be balanced against greater public benefits from land-use planning. The question of fair treatment of property owners has nevertheless remained a major source of unease. Especially in light of the general ineffectiveness of comprehensive planning efforts, the court justifications for discriminatory treatment of property owners have not persuaded a number of observers. Donald Hagman has emphasized both the discrimination between property owners resulting from land-use regulations—in his graphic terms, causing "windfalls" and "wipeouts"—and the frequent weakness of the justifications made for it:

Persons suffering wipeouts especially cannot be expected to be sanguine in the face of a neighbor's windfall. The myth that some brooding omni-planning in the sky justifies some persons getting the goodies while others are deprived cannot explain away the harsh and fiscally substantial reality that who gets the goodies is essentially arbitrary and capricious. When windfalls and wipeouts were small, a planner's explanation of why A got permission to develop while B did not was likely to be accepted. When the stakes are higher, the explanations are examined more carefully and largely found wanting.[31]

Somewhat inconsistently, while tolerating different treatment of property owners in different neighborhoods, the courts have not allowed communities to treat property owners differently with respect to the time that development of their property is permitted. Although there have been only a few cases in which the issue has been dealt with directly, courts have generally given clear indications that they were not likely to permit a community to zone in a way that allows a certain type of use, but allows it only after some specified future date (which could vary among locations). Thus, while agreeing that some flexibility is needed, concern over discriminatory treatment of property owners has caused the courts to stop short of giving the community authority to control the timing of its development. As a result, much of the flexibility needed for effective implementation of public plans is not available.

The problems of discriminatory treatment led the Douglas commission to conclude that the ability to pay public compensation was a necessary regulatory tool in rapidly developing transitional areas:

Effective development guidance, both in controlling the timing and location of explosive development pressures, and in stimulating such pressure in built-up areas where none exists, requires the use of tools that go beyond noncompensative regulation. Governments should provide for the payment of compensation in certain instances in which regulation substantially reduces property values or in which regulation proves impractical because large value reductions would result.[32]

While the essentially arbitrary financial setbacks that implementation of plans would impose on some unlucky individuals have been of greatest concern, little more justification can be found for creating large property-value increases for the lucky winners. A system of public compensation for the losers should almost certainly be accompanied by a system of taxation or some other method for public capture of large value gains to the winners. But to insulate an owner from future property-value losses and to capture for the public future value gains is to acquire a major part of the normal risks and profits of property ownership. To separate the gains and losses that would have occurred in any case from those that are clearly caused by public plan implementation would also be very difficult. Because of such considerations, a number of land-use students have concluded that the only practical way to implement public land-use plans is for the public to purchase land for the express purpose of implementing public plans. In the last decade, a number of planning proponents have reached this conclusion and have become strong advocates of land-assembly or land-banking programs for public land acquisition in advance of development.[33]

Although the effects of implementation of public land-use plans would be highly discriminatory among property owners, in most cases even the losers would retain at least some reasonable portion of their original property value. But for sites planned as parks, open woods, greenbelts, farmland, and other particularly low-value uses, the planned use might well allow the property owner to retain only a very small portion of the potential value of his site. In those cases, the constitutional basis for a court to overrule community actions is not discriminatory treatment, but the confiscatory effect. Although much less limiting a factor than the far wider problem of discrimination, the inability to pay public compensation in cases where implementation of plans would amount to confiscation of property has also significantly retarded the progress of comprehensive public planning. (Compensation relating to confiscation is a much bigger problem in conservation efforts outside urban areas, where the objective is frequently to prohibit most types of development.)

Public confiscation of property is unconstitutional under the so-called takings clause of the Fifth Amendment, which reads: "Nor shall private property be taken for public use without just compensation." Land-use regulations, of course, do not literally confiscate property, but as a result of legal precedents, especially the 1922 case, *Pennsylvania Coal Co.* v. *Mahon*,[34] zoning and other land-use regulations are subject to legal challenge on "takings" grounds.

In the early twentieth century, underground coal mining in the coal country of eastern Pennsylvania frequently caused the surface to cave in, a phenomenon called surface or mining subsidence. In response to the problem, the Pennsylvania legislature in 1921 enacted a regulation prohibiting mining below public and private facilities, wherever subsidence threatened. Coal companies had long owned underground mining rights throughout eastern Pennsylvania. They claimed that to prohibit coal mining would be—in effect, if not literally—to take their coal without public compensation. In *Pennsylvania Coal*, the United States Supreme Court agreed, with Justice Oliver Wendell Holmes saying for the Court:

It is our opinion that the Act cannot be sustained as an exercise of the police power. . . . What makes the right to mine coal valuable is that it can be exercised with profit. To make it commercially impractical to mine certain coal has very nearly the same effect for constitutional purposes as appropriating or destroying it. . . . [35]

Justice Holmes then stated: "The general rule . . . is, that while property may be regulated to a certain extent, if regulation goes too far it will be recognized as a taking."[36]

In sum, the inability to provide public compensation has greatly limited the options open to planning and the means available to implement any plans made. Without provisions for paying compensation, plans could not specify different uses of sites within neighborhoods; plans could not provide for timing of development; plans could not specify very low-value uses, and plans could not designate different neighborhoods for uses too far apart in value.

The Separation of Public Planning from Governing Responsibility

In addition to the failure to establish regional land-use authority and the inability to pay public compensation, a third critical reason for the general lack of influence of formal comprehensive planning has been the separation of planning institutions from basic governing responsibilities.[37] In most communities, the planning commission has been an independent board of prominent local citizens appointed by the mayor or some other chief executive. While organizational structure has varied to some degree, the professional planning staff has typically been placed under the planning commission. As explained above, this organization reflected a view of the planner as a technical expert endowed with specialized knowledge. The independence of the planning commission was intended to ensure that planners would be free to apply their professional skills in a disinterested manner, insulated from the pressures of direct involvement in politics. At critical junctures, the local executive and legislative branches, the courts, and the public could call on community professional planners for their expert advice.

While this concept of planner independence from the local governing process had great appeal, especially in the decades immediately prior to and following World War II when faith in scientific and technical expertise was pervasive, the practical consequence has been to make formal comprehensive plans largely superfluous. They were supposed to provide a fixed advance standard representing the public interest against which subsequent zoning administration could be measured by both the courts and the public. These plans usually consisted of land-use maps and a set of general principles to guide development. But the general principles usually proved of little help when specific questions had to be decided. The Model Land Development Code observes:

The planning process is said to proceed from the general to the particular. . . .
A difficulty with the approach is that it is nearly impossible to state significant general objectives in the first instance. . . . Specifically what is meant by "orderly" and by "diversity"? Does "orderly" mean development proceeding from present population centers outward rather than "leapfrogging"? Or does it mean starting new population centers in presently undeveloped areas with greenbelts separating the population cores? . . . [38]

Land-use planning maps are specific, but generally ignored. Except for differences in boundaries of districts, the contents of a planning map are virtually identical to those of a zoning map. Given both maps, one is likely to be superfluous. If the districts of the planning map are more expertly drawn, the zoning map probably ought to be changed. If the zoning map is more appropriate, there is little need for the planning map. It could be argued that the planning map can serve as a guide for future zoning changes that are temporarily to be refused. But the courts have generally rejected the legal right of a community to determine timing of development—at least overtly. Plans have not answered the critical question of when and why the zoning change should be approved, and, in fact, while communities have delayed development in this fashion, they have seldom closely followed planning maps in making later rezoning decisions.

Given a planning map and a zoning map, the choice of which is the legally valid map was eventually made by the courts. Despite the critical importance of planner recommendations in legal reasoning to justify community zoning, the courts have almost always chosen the zoning map. In many cases, this choice has resulted in some circuitous court reasoning in which the zoning ordinance itself is discovered to have been the actual comprehensive plan of the community. As one court critical of such reasoning observed, it relies on a "meaningless interpretation" that "zoning regulations . . . must be in 'accordance' with themselves."[39] The likely explanation for such court behavior is that, when issues became concrete, the courts could not find much indication of special expertise in professional planning maps, in any case not enough to require that new plans must be prepared before zoning ordinances could be revised or that existing plans must supersede particular zoning actions of elected local legislatures. The courts thus often ignored in practice the arguments that provided the basic justification for zoning in legal theory.

A second responsibility of the independent planning commission was to provide guidance on those decisions in zoning administration that were unavoidably highly discretionary. But the final responsibility for these decisions was given to the local legislature, which was likely to formulate its own guidelines with the assistance of personal staff. Lodged in a body independent of the legislature, once again the planner role tended to become superfluous.

One good reason for local legislatures' taking advice provided them by professional planners might be the realization that the special skills of the planners could be used to advantage. On discretionary matters, the courts might have required the adoption of planner recommendations by overruling the contrary actions of local legislatures. Generally speaking, however, neither legislatures nor courts have regularly followed planner advice, probably in considerable part because they did not find sufficient justification for preferring planner judgments over legislative judgments.

The frequent superfluousness of, and consequent lack of influence in, the planner role has been the leading cause of a crisis of confidence that hit the planning profession in the 1960s. Richard Babcock suggested the nature of the problem when he referred to the "general neurotic state of the planning profession," the members of which are "not certain what manner of animal they are themselves."[40]

With mounting internal criticism and outside pressure, the planning profession undertook to redefine its mission. Among other things, it was proposed that the distance between planners and the holders of governing authority be diminished. If it were to be eliminated altogether, planners would function as direct subordinates of public officials, with the task of providing various kinds of technical and administrative advice and assistance. The importance of formal plans was much deemphasized. Planner education was made more comprehensive, covering a wider range of economic and other social science methods of analysis and devoting less time to map construction. The subject matter for planning was modified to cover general urban governmental, economic, and other administrative problems.

Two Practical Purposes of Comprehensive Plans

The general failure of formal community planning to influence development should have been apparent to anyone examining the issue carefully well before it received broader attention.[41] The need for regional authority for land-use control was clear to the authors of the City Planning Enabling Act in 1928. The committee which originally developed zoning in New York City recognized that public compensation might be necessary even for the limited zoning powers it was considering at that time. It rejected provision of compensation, with deep reservations, because of the complexity of administering it, as well as other problems. The impracticality of many formal comprehensive plans prepared by communities was obvious fairly early, as shown in the refusal of courts to back them up, despite the clear inconsistency with zoning-law theory. In such circumstances, the persistence of communities in preparing formal comprehensive plans suggests that these plans have had some important practical purposes that have not yet been explored. In fact, there seem to have been two.

First of all, the preparation and publication of comprehensive plans often stirs a strong sense of community achievement and progress among its residents. The average citizen has not had much time to contemplate the subtleties of planning and is not usually aware that comprehensive plans are more often than not disregarded. He assumes, because so many other communities have produced them, because professionals following long-established methods construct them, and because the federal government and other institutions provide funding, that comprehensive plans must be valuable instruments. The sheer bulk of formal planning documents and the obvious effort involved also offer assurance that the community is receiving extensive expert assistance. Delafons commented on this aspect of planning: "It is very clear that many city planning departments, particularly those with a lavish budget and the glossiest publications, serve primarily as a public relations service for the city government . . . "[42] William Whyte has also described the popularity and political advantages of producing comprehensive plans:

What all this amounts to is a lot of public-relations activity, and the consensus it produces is illusion. A revealing aspect of these projects is that though the plans call for the most sweeping exercise of government power over commercial and business interests, they are roundly applauded at their unveiling by commercial and business interests. . . . I have attended many of the civic ceremonies staged for the presentation of these plans, and I am always amazed at the euphoria which characterizes them.[43]

Comprehensive plans have had a second, more critical, practical purpose that probably explains why so many communities go to considerable trouble to produce them. For many communities, a formal comprehensive plan has provided important assurance to the judiciary that land-use regulations were being employed for a broad—"planned"—public interest. Since at least the Standard State Zoning Enabling Act, the legal profession has viewed the existence of a comprehensive plan as a basic and necessary means of ensuring that administration of land-use regulations is not serving private or parochial community interests.

The judiciary has reflected general intellectual trends, and until recently most judges have not been very attentive to issues of land-use regulation. (Richard Babcock noted in 1966 that "judges find zoning a monumental bore."[44]) The judiciary has often accepted—usually implicitly—the view that planning involves fundamentally technical matters and therefore is nonpolitical. Many judges have tended to assume that the answers of the planning profession, like the answers of the medical or any other profession, should generally be accepted. The obvious faith in the values of formal planning among planners and among large numbers of local citizens has also impressed judges.

In these circumstances, preparation of a formal comprehensive plan has assisted numerous communities in defending their zoning ordinances in court. Although few courts have approved zoning actions solely because they conformed to a formal community plan, where a decision was uncertain, the existence of a conforming plan could aid the community in legally sustaining its actions. As one zoning law commentator explained: "It is evident in the cases that the more proof there is of consideration by the legislative body of planning factors involved in the ordinance or in its amendment, the easier it will be to sustain zoning as being in accordance with the comprehensive plan, i.e., as being consistent based on a rational underlying policy."[45]

The planning theory of zoning has provided a key element in rationales for the general judicial practice of noninterference with the basic content of community zoning (while continuing to guard actively against excessively discriminatory or arbitrary treatment of individual property owners). As discussed, despite the inconsistency, the courts have nevertheless not usually required that a formal comprehensive plan be prepared and, where one existed, have almost never required that community zoning conform to it in its details. Still, the actual existence of an identifiable formal plan has made it much more plausible for the courts to determine that, as legally required, zoning was "in accordance with a comprehensive plan." In this way, preparation of a formal plan has often helped to forge an essential link in a chain of judicial reasoning to sustain community zoning. A recent important example of this reasoning involved the controls to set the sequence and timing of development which were amended to the zoning ordinance of Ramapo, New York, in 1969. In a widely commented-upon 1972 decision providing one of the first instances of judicial approval for this type of control, the New York State Court of Appeals held: "The preeminent protection against their abuse resides in the mandatory ongoing planning . . . requirement, present here, which attends their implementation and use . . ."[46]

As indicated, the actions of the courts have been contradictory. As long ago as 1953, Charles Haar observed:

There appears to have been a judicial tendency to interpret the statutory directive that zoning ordinances shall be "in accordance with a comprehensive plan" as meaning nothing more than that zoning ordinances shall be comprehensive—that is to say, uniform and broad in scope and coverage. . . .

A court will merely satisfy itself that the local legislative authority has thought to some extent about the ordinance it is enacting; if so, absent other glaring infirmities, the ordinance is a comprehensive plan.[47]

The courts have interpreted legal requirements for planning in such a way as to give them very little practical effect partly because most of the plans actually produced quickly became outdated and hence obviously unsuited as a guide to development. But most state zoning enabling legislation still requires that zoning be based on a comprehensive plan, resulting in a succession of efforts in some communities to construct new formal plans, particularly at times when community zoning policy faces legal challenge. Then local citizens occasionally even advance the argument that past "planning has failed." This argument, of course, refers only to professional planning and its products, the comprehensive land-use map, and other formal statements. In making such an argument, the community effectively distracts attention from its often highly successful informal plans and their frequent absence of provisions for accommodating any substantial new development. Thus, many new comprehensive plans are predestined to fail, because their most essential practical purpose is not to provide the policy principles for community land-use controls but to camouflage those principles. Overly explicit descriptions of community land-use policies might endanger the planning link in the legal reasoning that sustains the policies, and in some instances it might also be considerably at odds with the community self-image.

Under strong pressure not to infringe on the central land-use-policy concerns of the community, professional planners have been almost obligated to produce comprehensive land-use plans that are innocuous, noncontroversial, and with few practical consequences. Comprehensive plans avoid difficult decisions partly by projecting community land uses far into the future:

The plans are so sweeping. They get everybody off the hook. If they had to make a decision on just one element of the plan, the whole edifice of consensus would come tumbling down. But the plans do not confront people with immediate and difficult choices. They vault over the messy present and near future. They take the big view. They make everybody feel bold.[48]

The most important element of a comprehensive plan has usually been a land-use map showing what planners considered the most desirable use twenty or thirty years hence for various areas of the community. But the critical question for local officials has been whether to permit a proposed development at a particular site now. If the development is inconsistent with the plan, yet clearly beneficial to the community, it is almost inevitable that the plan will be disregarded, in part because it is impossible to place much confidence in a map of projected uses for twenty or thirty years in the future. It is often difficult to predict community circumstances even a few years hence, never mind twenty or thirty. After a few years, in most communities so much development has been approved that is inconsistent with the existing comprehensive plan that no one pays it much further attention (until a new plan is prepared).

Comprehensive plans have not given much consideration to the problem of transition. The land-use map has set forth an arrangement of uses for twenty or thirty years hence, but usually has offered little guidance about how that arrangement might be reached. Plans have not considered the question of what might be done with land while it was waiting for its ultimate development, even though the twenty-year interim was often too long simply to assume that the land should be left idle or in a low-value use. Plans also have not considered the economic feasibility of planned development to the private building industry, but neither have they made provision for public assumption of the building role.

The uses ultimately planned for each part of the community have typically been assumed to be final. Little or no provision has been made for the possibility that changing circumstances might alter the most efficient uses for a particular location. If a community had been developed strictly according to plan, after twenty or thirty years no further development would have taken place. While not every plan has been so unrealistic and most planners have been aware of such practical matters, the basic concept of the formal comprehensive plan has nevertheless contained those major inherent deficiencies.

In sum, the history of formal comprehensive planning in the United States shows a well-intentioned but basically mistaken notion: that the planning of future land use is a technical question for experts to decide. Partly because this basic notion was never really accepted by political leaders or the public, the authority and tools necessary to implement public land-use plans were never created. If continued practice of formal comprehensive planning had been determined solely on the basis of its demonstrated accomplishment, it would not have taken long to acknowledge the mistake. But by the time the failure of planning efforts was clearly discernible, the view that zoning should be a key tool for implementing a comprehensive plan had been made an indispensable part of the legal justification for community zoning policies. As a result, much as the nuisance-law justification for neighborhood zoning, the planning theory of community zoning has maintained a life long beyond the point at which it can reasonably be defended, and it has become another zoning legal fiction that is automatically invoked when needed, according to a formula prescribed by legal precedent. To help to maintain the fiction, large numbers of communities have maintained planning commissions and have prepared formal comprehensive plans.

4 The Unhappy Consequences of Prohibiting Sale of Zoning Rights

According to zoning and planning theory, land development was to be guided by comprehensive public land-use plans. In practice, as we have seen, formal comprehensive plans have had almost no influence. Instead, development has been determined by the interaction of private developer pressures and the exercise of neighborhood and community zoning rights. Before development of land can proceed, it is necessary for a developer to acquire both the personal-property rights and the collective zoning rights to the land. Yet, no formal mechanism—such as a market—exists for transfer of collective zoning rights from neighborhood and community residents.

Owing to the circumstances of their adoption, zoning rights have not been considered salable. As an exercise of the police power to protect public health, safety, and morals, it would be unsuitable for the exercise of neighborhood zoning to be determined—as are most property rights—by the wishes of the highest bidder. Similarly, as an instrument for the implementation of public land-use plans, it would be unethical to offer community zoning rulings for sale. As a result, sale of zoning rights has been considered illegal. Yet, that prohibition combined with the fact that zoning creates a collective property right has had very unhappy consequences. Among other problems, it has created a major obstacle to necessary and desirable transitions in the type of basic use of land in neighborhoods and communities and has frequently forced that transition eventually to occur through extralegal means.

The Problem of Neighborhood Transition

Under feudal land tenure, which reflected the static feudal society more generally, there were few provisions for the sale of land. Typically, a man's possession of land was tied to his social position and his land was not regarded as freely transferable. The development of modern property-right concepts from the feudal period was brought about by the needs of an evolving capitalist economic system. This system placed a far greater premium on change and on the achievement of economic efficiency than had the feudal system. If an item of equipment, a mineral resource, a labor skill, or any other economically valuable property can be employed more effectively or efficiently by one user than by another, under capitalist principles it should be transferred to the better—more efficient—user. The mechanism for this transfer is sale of the property. In a system in which the ultimate goal is higher profit, the fact that the property will have a higher value for the more efficient user will generally ensure that such a transfer will take place. The hallmark of this system is thus frequent change in use of property in search of greater efficiency in higher-value uses led by a quest for profits. The application of such ideas to land transformed the nature of property rights to land.

The introduction of neighborhood zoning protections in the United States represented the establishment of a highly static and, in this respect at least, somewhat feudal scheme of ownership. Zoning was originally created to protect established neighborhoods from intrusion by uses that would diminish their quality. The question of what to do when uses became highly uneconomic for the neighborhood location they occupied seems to have concerned zoning architects very little, if at all. Conceivably, when a much more valuable use arose, the zoning of a whole neighborhood could have been changed all at once at the appropriate time to make way for the new use. But because it would require the simultaneous agreement of the great majority of neighborhood residents, this type of wholesale zoning change was bound to be very difficult to accomplish and, in practice, has almost never occurred.

Thus, for lack of attention to the problem, or perhaps for some other reason, there was no adequate formal provision made for transfer of zoning rights to facilitate transitions to a new type of basic use by a neighborhood. But, of course, modern society is rapidly changing, and, realistically, new economic pressures will eventually require changes in the basic use of most neighborhoods. The introduction of a new neighborhood property right that included no adequate mechanisms for transfer of that right would therefore not be workable.

If neighborhood zoning rights had been handled in a way similar to ordinary private collective property rights, a number of formal mechanisms for transfer of neighborhood rights might have been provided. All changes in neighborhood zoning could have been refused until the neighborhood residents voted—by simple majority, or two-thirds, or perhaps even a higher percentage—to change the neighborhood zoning to allow new higher-value uses. Under such provisions, a favorable neighborhood vote would result only when neighborhood residents had offers sufficiently high to make it worthwhile for a majority or more to move to a new neighborhood. In effect, a favorable vote would show that the offers had met the neighborhood price for sale of both the collective zoning rights to the neighborhood environment and the personal rights to individual properties.

A better method of zoning-right transfer would recognize that zoning division of neighborhood property rights into personal and collective parts is highly impractical for purposes of neighborhood transition. Neighborhood zoning institutions could then have included a formal mechanism whereby a private developer or other party would offer a certain sum of money for the entire bundle of personal and collective property rights in the neighborhood. Again, with a sufficient percentage of neighborhood residents voting to approve, sale of this full bundle of rights could be completed in one transaction. In neighborhoods where pressures for transition are intense, new uses typically have values far higher than existing uses; neighborhood residents would therefore eventually have ample incentive to vote to accept an offer for the entire bundle of neighborhood personal and zoning rights. The huge potential financial incentives for zoning changes are illustrated by a case in the 1960s:

The amounts of money riding on rezonings are enormous: In Montgomery County, Maryland, an affluent area just north of Washington, D. C., an estimated $100 million was added to the value of 4,000 acres of land by rezoning in 1963 and 1964, making possible $500 million worth of construction on that land.[1]

A formal mechanism for selling neighborhood zoning rights should treat zoning as a collective property right which, like business-corporation or private-club collective rights, could be sold by its owners when the collectively held property became much more valuable through another use. But lacking any such formal transitional mechanism, a highly informal means of accomplishing neighborhood transition necessarily evolved. Zoning rights have in fact been frequently bought and sold, but not collectively, and thus not for the benefit of the neighborhood residents as a whole. Rather, the profits of zoning sale have often gone to a few neighborhood residents who have succeeded in getting their zoning changed, usually at the expense of the remaining residents. In many cases, sale of zoning rights has benefited not any neighborhood residents but corrupt local zoning administrators, who have succumbed to the enormous financial pressures for transitions in use that zoning inflexibility can provide.

The Informal Mechanism of Neighborhood Transition

The informal way that transition in neighborhood use has been accomplished under zoning can be illustrated by a hypothetical example. Suppose that in 1830, according to the land-market circumstances of the time, the Greenwich Village neighborhood of Manhattan had had only one use, homes on one-acre lots, and that the neighborhood had in fact been fully developed in this use. Let us say that the Greenwich Village residents, in order to protect their neighborhood quality, had formed a Village association, and each property owner had voluntarily transferred all rights to determine future uses to its board of directors. In a later day, of course, this would have been unnecessary, because zoning would have provided control over neighborhood uses and the local legislature would have filled the role of the board of directors.

After a few years, as the New York economy expanded, developers would begin to see the Village location as suitable for higher-density housing to meet the very rapidly growing demand. If the Village residents then behaved like typical neighborhood residents behave today, they would very likely put strong pressure on fellow residents to resist redevelopment and on their Village board of directors to provide solid assurances that no use changes would be allowed. But as land values continued to rise, eventually some neighbor, who might not be so attached to the neighborhood, would propose to redevelop his land in much higher-value, higher-density housing. He would apply to the board of directors to permit it, or more likely, he

would sell to a developer willing to pay a high price for the land
in expectation of obtaining the necessary board approval.

The Village board of directors would then be in a difficult
position. As time passed, single-family homes and one-acre lots
would become less and less economically justifiable at the
Greenwich Village location. It would be evident that, at some
point, the gains in neighborhood property value would eventually be so large that all but a very few neighborhood residents
would prefer to sell and move. Yet, for the moment, introduction of a few high-value facilities would be highly disruptive to
the great majority of remaining residents. Moreover, approving
a use change at this point would create a large capital gain for
the landowner of the site, an undeserved reward for actions
taken at least to some extent at the expense of his neighbors.
The Village board of directors would therefore very probably
deny early applications for new use approvals.

But economic pressures would continue to rise. Eventually,
possibly when the request came from a developer with close
acquaintances on the board, or when development financial
pressures became sufficiently intense, through kickbacks or side
payments to members of the board, a use change in the neighborhood would be approved. Once the neighborhood transition
had begun, changes would be approved more easily because
opposition would diminish. As the Village neighborhood declined (or changed) in quality, more requests for use changes
would be received as more old neighbors moved out. At some
point, all changes requested would receive approval, because
denial would constitute discriminatory treatment. By 1850, or
thereabouts, the neighborhood of single-family homes of 1830
would have become a neighborhood of row-houses, perhaps
with some commercial uses mixed in that were appropriate to
the changed social and economic circumstances.

Basic changes in neighborhood use are an old and continuing
fact of urban life in the United States. Since the introduction of
neighborhood zoning, the process of transition has in many
cases closely resembled the hypothetical Greenwich Village example just described. The process of transition under zoning
has had certain characteristics in common that have been re-
peatedly pointed out by its observers. First, it produces many

misunderstandings and great ill will between neighborhood residents and developers. While a basic change in neighborhood use may be unavoidable, and desirable for all society in the long run, the neighbors often see developer pressures as a profit-motivated attempt to subvert the land at their expense. Moreover, even if residents accept the desirability of eventual neighborhood change, there is usually still a conflict of interest over its exact timing. At least at first, the majority of neighbors generally want to delay, while developers want to proceed more quickly.

The resentment of neighborhood residents is often heightened because they regard themselves as victims of capitulation by the local legislature to developers. High-quality neighborhoods are almost always under development pressure. Their attractiveness is a lure for all kinds of prospective lower-quality development, and a basic purpose of zoning is to protect them from that development. It is often difficult or impossible for neighborhoods to distinguish between the continual development pressure that results from high neighborhood quality and the pressure of an emerging long-term social and economic trend that makes neighborhood transition both virtually unavoidable and eventually desirable. The understandable tendency of most neighborhoods is always to interpret development pressure as a manifestation of the former, and failure to maintain protection as a sign of inept or even corrupt government.

When a neighborhood comes under strong long-term development pressure, the local legislature is caught in a dilemma. It must resolve a conflict of interest between developers and neighborhood residents regarding the timing of the change in basic use. Whichever way they decide, members of the local legislature are likely to be much faulted—by the developer and perhaps others outside the community for holding back progress, or by the neighbors for selling out.

Neighborhood transition also creates severe strains among neighborhood residents who have different preferences about the best time for neighborhood transition to occur. Nonresident owners may well want to sell for the high-value use right away. Neighbors who do not want to move out of the neighborhood at all may face a severe conflict of interest with neighbors who badly need money or who, for other reasons, are willing to sell and move quickly. The conflict is aggravated because continued high neighborhood quality requires a united neighborhood front. As soon as a few neighborhood sites are developed in new uses, the residents who remain behind are faced with a sharp decline in neighborhood quality.

In part because of strong pressure from neighborhood residents (and sometimes from the rest of the community) and in part because they are seldom able to see long-term social and economic trends, local legislatures often resist the initial developer requests for zoning changes. The result is frequently an intensification of economic pressures for zoning changes up to the point where local government or some neighbors can no longer withstand them. Unfortunately, the final instrument of change too often has been a bribe paid to some key local official.

In short, under neighborhood zoning, transition creates severe strains among neighborhood residents and between residents and both local government and developers. Unlike labor negotiations or other circumstances of conflicting interests, neighborhood zoning institutions include few provisions for bargaining, arbitration, or other procedures for resolving inevitable conflicts in as structured, fair, and equitable a manner as possible.

One undesirable consequence has been that neighborhood transition has often been very ill timed. Where developers have strong influence, neighborhood zoning protection can collapse under the first stresses created by new economic pressures. The residents may be totally unprepared for change, and because of insufficient immediate demand, there may be a long, uncomfortable period of transition in which both old and new uses share the same neighborhood. On the other hand, where residents resist the inevitable turmoil of neighborhood change for too long, the transition may come too late. From an overall social and economic point of view, the efficient use of the land may be excessively delayed.

A second undesirable consequence of the process of neighborhood transition under zoning has been that subsequent neighborhood development is almost entirely unplanned. Because of strong local opposition to neighborhood change, neighborhood redevelopment almost always occurs in piecemeal fashion. Development occurs at those sites where a particular neighborhood resident wants to sell out right away, where a property owner has good political connections, where a vacant site is owned by a nonresident, and so forth. The consequence is haphazard and uncoordinated development of the future neighborhood.

Some Recent Examples of Neighborhood Transition

In the post–World War II period, the suburbs have been the area of most rapid growth in the United States, where the largest number of transitions in basic neighborhood uses have occurred. As the population has moved out of the center of the cities, new neighborhoods have been created in many previously rural communities on the outskirts of metropolitan areas. The process of transition has resulted in considerable corruption, extensive developer pressure on local government, widespread public antipathy toward developers, and general disrespect for zoning law. Richard Babcock reflected the general attitude with the title of his book, *The Zoning Game*. While some of these problems of suburban transition have resulted from zoning practices designed to protect the community as a whole, the largest share of the responsibility lies in the failure to provide any effective mechanism for needed transfers of neighborhood zoning rights.

There is an extensive literature describing the problems of suburban transition. Few of its authors, however, have considered the culprit to be the inherent inability of zoning to accommodate change without severe stresses. Most observers have instead blamed some particular guilty party—profit-hungry developers, extorting local officials, or greedy landowners.

Developers have become favorite targets for public dislike because their role in the process of neighborhood transition is that of undermining existing neighborhoods. The author of a recent book, *Mortgage on America*, saw the profit-hungry developer as the villain in the problems of land development:

Even with strict and complicated zoning laws almost everywhere in the country, real estate speculators are able to do what they please by making the zoning laws work for them.

Realtors and developers turn up on local zoning boards and local governmental bodies and consistently rule in favor of themselves and their buddies. Or they steer campaign contributions and, sometimes, bribes to officials who decide zoning cases their way. . . . [2]

William Whyte, who, after writing *The Organization Man*, has concentrated his literary efforts on conservation and land-use problems, has described the severe conflicts among neighbors during a transition in the Brandywine Valley west of Philadelphia during the 1950s:

All this time the main body of developers and new people moving out from the city was getting closer. Somewhat in advance of them, moving at the rate of about half a mile or a mile a year, was a sort of greed line, and once touched by it an owner's fealty to the land was put to sore trial. The majority of landowners did resist it; some turned down extraordinary offers. Unfortunately, however, only a handful have to fall from grace to spoil things for others. One landowner, for example, might decide to sell a piece of meadowland for a drive-in theatre. This would be intolerable to the abutting landowner, and his property would go on the market. Then the next one.[3]

A number of investigators have found local officials willing participants in corrupt practices involving sale of zoning changes. A 1966 article in *Harper's Magazine* reported:

Dennis O'Harrow, Executive Director of the American Society of Planning Officials bluntly told his Society's annual convention last year, in all too many instances zoning has failed because it has become a "marketable commodity." He cited a respected planning official who assured him that "you can buy with money any kind of zoning you want in half the communities in the United States." Another consultant described gatherings of shopping center developers who "go upstairs for a drink and start comparing the prices they have to pay for zoning."[4]

The article concluded that in many localities "zoning is little more than an exclusionary, publicly condoned racket, perpetuated by short-sighted, squabbling communities out of individual greed and indifference."[5] Marion Clawson, past director of the land and water use and management program of Resources for the Future, suggested in 1966 that perhaps the best way to clean up corrupt zoning practices would be to face squarely the need for many zoning changes and to have fair and "open, competitive sale of zoning and zoning classifications."[6] More recently, Bernard Siegan commented: "It is most distressing to speculate how many major developments may have come about only as a result of the payment of graft or fees to certain parties."[7]

In the places where planners have had a role in land development, they have not been immune from strong development pressures. In recent decades, Fairfax County, Virginia, in the Washington, D.C., suburbs, has been one of the fastest-growing counties in the United States. As is not particularly unusual in places of rapid transition, in 1967 a major scandal broke out in which six of seven members of the board of supervisors, three planning department employees, and several developers and their attorneys were indicted for corrupt actions in obtaining zoning-change approvals. A 1973 speech by County Supervisor Audrey Moore reflected the general cynicism that the current informal mechanism for transfer of zoning rights tends to produce:

How many times have you seen the planner with his beautiful plan on the wall, all colors of the rainbow. Red is where your high intensity uses go, yellow is where people live in their single family homes and green is the land that is going to be left open. What the planner doesn't tell you is that when he paints that plan red, in Annandale where I live, he paints it at at least $90,000 an acre; and when he paints it yellow, it decreases to about $18,000 an acre and when he paints it green, you've just won the booby prize. As anybody in real estate can tell you, the name of the game is to maximize the profits on land. You get a little green or you get a little yellow and you turn it into red. If you don't believe it happens, just come to Annandale and look at the old master plan and see what took place.[8]

In Los Angeles, another fast-growing area, a 1968 citizens' committee study described how transition has occurred there under zoning:

Piecemeal or spot zoning is resorted to in place of zoning on an area-wide basis. Individual rights are sometimes restricted or privileges granted on the basis of personal circumstances and pressure, rather than on the basis of serving the public interest. . . .
The Zoning Code lags, rather than leads, City development. There has been no comprehensive, overall review of the Code since 1946. Since then there have been over 300 amendments to

the text of the Code and several thousand changes in the Zoning Map, mainly as a result of individual requests and specific
problems.[9]

Partly because developers first take the suburban land most
easily obtained, a widely scattered pattern of development—
suburban sprawl—results. Its aesthetic unattractiveness has long
been decried. In 1958, William Whyte observed in *The Exploding
Metropolis*:

The problem is the pattern of growth—or, rather, the lack of
one. Because of the leapfrog nature of urban growth, even within the limits of most big cities there is to this day a surprising
amount of empty land. But it is scattered; a vacant lot here, a
dump there—no one parcel big enough to be of much use. And
it is with this same kind of sprawl that we are ruining the
whole metropolitan area of the future. In the townships just
beyond today's suburbia there is little planning, and development is being left almost entirely in the hands of the speculative
builder. Understandably, he follows the line of least resistance
and in his wake is left a hit-or-miss pattern of development.
Aesthetically, the result is a mess. . . . [10]

Besides suburban fringes, a second area of substantial transition has been old neighborhoods in big cities, in many cases
the areas vacated by immigrants to the suburbs. The Douglas
commission was critical of the failures of inner-city zoning to
protect these neighborhoods:

Such failure is particularly serious in so-called gray areas, older
neighborhoods that are not slums but where signs of deterioration are beginning to show. Market demand for compatible development may not exist in these areas, and pressures develop
to allow the introduction of formerly prohibited uses that often serve as blighting influences. Examples include junkyards,
garages, filling stations, bars, liquor stores.
Gray areas seem to be especially vulnerable to these pressures. Where rapid transition is taking place in the population
of an area, political influence and interest may be on the wane.
Residents may lack the means and sophistications to insist on
tight enforcement of regulations and to oppose requests for rezonings and variances. Persons anxious to move out may, in
fact, encourage zoning changes to widen their potential market.
With admission of a few of these uses, the floodgates open,
pressure continues to mount, and the justification for resisting
that pressure gradually disappears.[11]

As happens frequently in circumstances of transition, the
Douglas commission did not perceive the root cause of virtually

unavoidable long-term social and economic trends. While the process might be better guided, neighborhood decline in some central-city areas becomes unavoidable, and to some degree even desirable, when there is a massive exodus of middle-income residents. Declining neighborhoods can serve basic needs: cheap housing (albeit of lower quality) within the means of the lowest-income groups, for whom it may actually represent a substantial improvement from previous housing quality; places for garages, filling stations, and other such uses that have to be located somewhere. In fact, given rapid immigration to suburbs, if there were no economically sustainable use of vacated neighborhoods, even of a lower quality, the alternative would be for some neighborhoods to end up abandoned altogether (as has happened in some places). Just as it has bowed to the long-term trend of suburban development, zoning could not have halted the trend of inner-city decline. In failing to provide a structured means of transition, more control over ultimate development than necessary was lost.

It has now become almost commonplace to assert that "the system is to blame" for many of our social problems. But zoning institutions do seem to contain features that lead almost unavoidably to severe problems for neighborhoods in transition. And as often occurs when an institution is faulty, the criticism tends to be misdirected to particular parties within it who have conspicuous and unpopular roles. Many developers and local officials are, of course, neither sinless nor blameless, but their efforts to undermine zoning arise from basic problems in zoning itself. The consequences of zoning rigidity have been very similar to the consequences of laws that aim to suppress abortion, prostitution, gambling, and other services that grow out of some basic human need. In the case of zoning, of course, the need is for new housing and other socially essential facilities. As Bernard Siegan asked: "Can one justify an institution where consumer demand can frequently only be satisfied by resorting to illegal or morally and socially questionable tactics?"[12]

These morally questionable tactics have been necessary because zoning has created a collective property right without providing an adequate formal mechanism for its transfer. In the absence of such a mechanism, a highly informal, and in many aspects unsatisfactory, mechanism for transfer of zoning rights has been brought into being.

The Basic Problem of Community Transition

Neighborhood zoning controls the uses to which individual properties can be put in an existing neighborhood, while community zoning controls the types of uses in entirely new neighborhoods. Community residents thus effectively exercise important property rights to the land in undeveloped neighborhoods. In the typical suburban example, because few uses are allowed without community approval, the collective property rights of the community residents include most of the development rights to undeveloped land.

But, unlike most holders of property rights, community residents cannot sell their development rights. Instead, if community zoning becomes less restrictive, and thereby effectively transfers some of the community development rights to some private party, the profits from the transfer of those rights go to the individual landowners in the undeveloped neighborhood. Predictably, the residents of communities have frequently chosen to hold on to their development rights for long periods, allowing transfer of the rights to private parties to permit new development only in quite limited circumstances.

A community obtains several benefits by keeping neighborhood land in an undeveloped state. Some property taxes can be collected on the land, yet the community has no public-service obligations. The congestion and density of the community are held down. If the land is in an attractive setting, keeping it undeveloped may significantly enhance the quality of the community environment. On the other hand, the gains to the community residents from development will often consist mainly of increased property taxes collected on new neighborhood properties. Balancing the costs and benefits, many communities have concluded that, unless new development is of unusually high quality, capable of generating high property taxes and of being an asset to the community environment, they will be better off without it. The consequence has been that in numerous undeveloped areas throughout the suburbs, the only development permitted is that for high-quality uses designed for a limited number of well-off people.

If suburban communities had had the ability to sell their zoning—i.e., development—rights, and thereby to capture the revenues from transfer of these rights to private parties, the consequences almost certainly would have been much different. For any ordinary goods or service, it is obvious that separating the rights to control the use of the goods or service from the ability to receive revenues for the transfer of these rights would have very undesirable consequences. These consequences would include inefficiencies when goods or services were not transferred to more valuable uses and inequalities when those wanting to pay the going price were blocked from purchase of the goods and services.

In the United States since World War II, the automobile and highway construction have opened up huge suburban areas for new development. In this period, many inefficiencies in the use of suburban land and social inequalities resulting from suburban exclusion of low- and moderate-income groups have been consequences of the ill-conceived separation of property rights to control use of undeveloped suburban land from the ability to obtain the profits from transfer of these rights. The resulting problems of community transition could best have been avoided by not allowing communities to acquire most of the development rights to undeveloped land in the first place, but once that acquisition had taken place, the error was probably compounded, and the social consequences made worse, by denying to the community the ability to sell its acquired rights.[13]

The Course of Recent Community Transitions

The typical course of transition in suburban communities since World War II can be illustrated by a hypothetical example of a community consisting of only two neighborhoods. For the purposes of the example, conflicts among property owners within each neighborhood are assumed somehow to have been resolved so that their residents speak with a united voice. The two hypothetical neighborhoods are located in a rural community on the edge of a metropolitan area. While farm owners and other long-time community residents may have initially resisted development, they are now welcoming the high land and property values and other economic gains that it will bring.

Largely for reasons of public-facility installation, it makes sense, and often happens, that development proceeds in one neighborhood at a time. Hence, one of our two hypothetical community neighborhoods will be filled up first with a fairly homogeneous, well-off population occupying housing of high quality. When this happens, political control in the community shifts from the farmers and whatever other sparsely settled old residents remain to the more numerous residents of the newly developed, high-density neighborhood.

The incentives of these new residents differ substantially from the incentives of the old residents, many of whom own considerable property. Because they have gained political control, the new residents will almost certainly change the zoning of the still sparsely settled neighborhood to suit their wishes. They are very likely to allow development only for a use of equal, or higher, quality than the high-quality use of their own recently developed neighborhood.

A problem arises if there is no great demand at that point for development of such high quality. This is especially likely to be the case if many other undeveloped neighborhoods in nearby suburban communities have been similarly zoned. The land may simply lie idle or be used for farming or some other low-value use. In the meantime, the residents in the recently developed neighborhood bear few of the costs of waiting for a suitable, high-quality use for the second, still undeveloped neighborhood. A change in zoning to permit higher-density uses—effectively a transfer of development rights from the community to a private party—brings the community no profit. Largely because communities bear little or no waiting costs, they may be willing to delay for long periods, perhaps indefinitely if necessary, to obtain high-quality development regarded as being compatible with their neighborhood. They may well even prefer no development at all.

While this two-neighborhood community is hypothetical, it has many real-world suburban counterparts. Residents of the same neighborhood seldom speak with a united voice, and most communities have more than two neighborhoods. But these differences only complicate the political relationships in a community, and do not essentially alter the factors that can cause large areas of sparsely developed land to sit idle for long periods in communities in transition. (One might note that, in the private sector, condominium and other large-scale private developers face a similar problem, but deal with it by retaining exclusive control over the whole area until its development is virtually completed. Only then do the incoming residents acquire broad powers of control.)

During the process of suburban expansion in the post–World War II period, it has frequently been the more affluent individuals who have been the first to move to the suburbs, settling in a widely scattered pattern. Once settled and as soon as they are able to obtain sufficient political influence, they typically zone the rest of the community for compatible higher-quality development. There has often been little or no immediate demand for those uses. Many other nearby communities at the same time might be similarly zoning undeveloped sections for high-quality uses. Overall demand for such uses is limited by the small number of high-income individuals in a metropolitan area; in most places there are not nearly enough of them to utilize the total supply of land thus made available. On the other hand, the total supply of suburban land made available for higher-density development suitable for individuals with low and moderate incomes has often been drastically reduced by community zoning.

Beyond political factors internal to communities, interactions among the communities in a metropolitan area also create pressures to deny entry to low- and moderate-quality uses. Most communities recognize some social obligation to accept change. If a number of communities were to coordinate zoning, each might be willing to accommodate a certain amount of low- and moderate-quality development. But when each community has an independent policy, there is always a significant economic incentive and a hard-to-resist temptation for some communities to show greater zeal in keeping out the development than others, which results in driving it to the communities with less restrictive zoning. Some of those communities will be unwilling to bear the resulting burdens, and will increase the restrictiveness of their policies in self-defense. Remaining communities that do not follow suit may find themselves facing a flood of development, much of it of lower quality, virtually compelling them to take defensive action as well. The net result of these chain reactions is that all communities are eventually put under strong pressure to be restrictive in the uses they will accept. These pressures were described by, among others, Charles Haar, in the Wayne Township case in 1953:

Perhaps the most harmful tendency of such restrictive ordinances would be to stimulate protective movements on the part of neighboring communities, each anxious to avoid excessive immigration and the danger of absorbing those to whom neighboring towns refuse to grant building permits. . . . If one community can rule out some elements, so can others. . . . [14]

An Example of Restrictive Zoning Policies

Neighborhood transition is highly disruptive for many of its residents, and this often leads them to resist it. Unless the proposed development is of high quality or fiscally advantageous, transition of underdeveloped neighborhoods is often opposed by other parts of the community as well. The greatest benefits usually go to persons outside the community who would like to become residents, and to a few large owners of property who hope to profit from its sale. Prospective residents, of course, have no vote, and resident property owners wanting to sell are often a small minority. As a result, in large numbers of suburban communities, especially surrounding the older central cities, the political influence of residents who stand to lose from development has been sufficient both to delay transition for long periods and to require that it occur only when higher-quality uses are feasible.

Courts have overturned large-lot zoning requirements on only a few occasions. In 1965, however, in a widely noted case, the Pennsylvania Supreme Court overturned the requirement of four-acre minimum lot sizes for a section of Easttown Township, a community in transition on the fringes of the Philadelphia metropolitan area. [15] The case offers a classic example of the political and economic pressures that can cause community development to be delayed for long periods and suburban land supply to be tightly restricted.

The primary instigator of the court suit was a landowner who wanted to develop his land right away by selling it for a more profitable use. The court commented on the lack of demand for the zoned use: "Although there was some evidence in the record that lots of four acres or more could eventually be sold, it is clear that there is not a readily available market for such offerings."[16] The landowner's intentions brought him into conflict with the determination of many of his neighbors to preserve the neighborhood unchanged; the court described its old homes in a generally desirable rural setting: "The photographic exhibits placed in the record by appellants attest to the fact that this is an area of great beauty containing old homes surrounded by beautiful pasture, farm and woodland. It is a very desirable and attractive place in which to live."[17] In such a setting, new development would be disruptive to the nearby residents: "There is no doubt that many of the residents of this area are highly desirous of keeping it the way it is, preferring, quite naturally, to look out upon land in its natural state rather than on other homes. . . . "[18] The threat to the neighborhood which caused the old homeowners to resist transition was entry of cheaper, higher-density housing: "What basically appears to bother interveners is that a small number of lovely old homes will have to start keeping company with a growing number of smaller, less expensive, more densely located houses. . . . "[19]

The court also dealt with the various interests of the neighborhoods. The residents of a small, more intensively developed part of the township were numerous enough to exercise political control over the zoning of geographically much larger but sparsely settled parts. As the court commented:

At present, about 60 percent of the township's population resides in an area of about 20 percent of the township. . . . Of the total 5,157 acres in the township, some 898, or about 17 percent, have been restricted by the new zoning ordinance to minimum lots of two acres. Approximately 1,565 acres composing about 30 percent of the township are restricted by the zoning ordinance to lots of four acres minimum area. About 5 percent of the population live in the areas zoned for two and four acre sites which together constitute about 47 percent of the township. . . . [20]

The township—largely representing residents outside the immediate neighborhood in question—justified its four-acre zoning partly on the ground that higher-density development in undeveloped areas would overburden local sewer, water, and highway systems—in effect saying that higher public-service expenditures would be required. Easttown also argued the need to preserve its general character from four threats posed by the new development: "Involved in preserving Easttown's 'character' are four aspects of concern which the township gives for desiring four acre minimum zoning. First, they cite the preservation of open space and the creation of a 'greenbelt.'"[21]

The court then described the second threat Easttown saw: "Next, the township urges us to consider the historic sites in the township and the need to present them in the proper setting." The third and fourth were described as follows:

Closely related to the goal of protecting historic monuments is the expressed desire to protect the "setting" for a number of old homes in Easttown, some dating back to the early days of our Commonwealth. . . .

[Finally,] the fourth argument advanced by appellants and one closely analogous to the preceding one, is that the rural character of the area must be preserved. . . . [22]

In its decision the court also clearly recognized that the cumulative consequences of many community zoning policies, not simply the effects on the one community at issue, were of critical concern: "It is not difficult to envision the tremendous hardship, as well as the chaotic conditions, which would result if all the townships in this area decided to deny to a growing population sites for residential development within the means of at least a significant segment of the people."[23]

The court took note of the conflict of interest existing between the politically dominant majority already residing in Easttown and the minority who were seeking to become residents. The court's conclusion was that the interest of the majority that lived in Easttown township at a particular stage in its transition could not be allowed to restrict further development so severely as to forbid the accommodation of a substantial number of the people who wanted to locate there. As the court described its decision in a later case:

The implication of our decision in National Land is that communities must deal with the problems of population growth. They may not refuse to confront the future by adopting zoning regulations that effectively restrict population to near present levels. It is not for any given township to say who may or may not live within its confines, while disregarding the interests of the entire area. . . . [24]

While few land-use students have described the matter as such, the decision in this court case amounted to a determination of the holdings of development rights to the site at issue. The four claimants were the individual landowner, the neighborhood residents, the community residents, and the residents of the wider society. In the more common situations described earlier, the residents of a stable neighborhood or community have secure rights for controlling matters that primarily affect them alone. But in areas of transition, such as Easttown, both the division of property rights into its personal and collective parts and the control over those collective rights that are exercised become much more uncertain.

The basic complaint of the landowner was that zoning had taken away too large a portion of his development rights, turning them into collective rights of neighborhood and community residents. Neighborhood residents were anxious to keep their existing collective rights undiminished in order to maintain the high attractions of their neighborhood environment. A rezoning to a higher-density use would in effect have been a transfer of certain accustomed neighborhood rights back to the individual landowner. While this transfer of rights would benefit the landowner handsomely, it would not benefit other neighborhood residents, but instead would lead to the neighborhood's becoming significantly less attractive. Community residents were generally sympathetic to the wishes of the neighborhood residents, and they also preferred to keep the neighborhood in an undeveloped state. In addition, they feared higher public-service burdens from the new development. In the end, the court ruled, in effect, that the legitimate claims of the individual landowner combined with the claims of the wider society were sufficient to compel a redistribution of some development rights back to the landowner. This redistribution would make possible a more efficient use of community land than the use represented by four-acre lots.

Not surprisingly, the courts have frequently felt uncomfortable with the responsibility to determine the distribution of property rights among contending parties. The determination of such a distribution has often not been governed by any clear rules, nor in many cases has there even been a very clear understanding of what was involved. One of the most straightforward characterizations of zoning was that by Chief Justice Bell of the Pennsylvania Supreme Court made during a 1970 case involving issues similar to those of the 1965 Easttown Township case:

For over a century it was the law of this Commonwealth that every person in the United States of America had a Constitutionally ordained right to own, possess, protect and use his property in any way he desired, so long as it did not injure or adversely affect the health or morals or safety of others. . . . Then along came "zoning" with its desirable and worthwhile objectives. The result was that all the aforesaid basic fundamental rights of an owner of property were restricted by a Judicially created higher right, namely, the general welfare of the people of that community. No one knows, and the Courts have been unable to define what is meant by "general welfare." . . . To some, it means what the Zoning Board or a Court believes is best for the community or township or county involved. To others, it means the right of our expanding population to live in any county or place in our Country they may desire. To still others, it means the right to have the Government set aside millions of acres of open land for the benefit of our Country. These rights are sometimes indefinite, sometimes overlapping, and sometimes conflicting.[25]

The Inequality and Inefficiency of Suburban Zoning Restrictions

Although the Pennsylvania Supreme Court ruled against Easttown Township, few other comparable court decisions have been made. In most suburban areas, the cumulative result of many communities' following restrictive zoning policies is a severe limitation on the overall supply of land available for other than high-quality uses, most of which are of low density. The Douglas commission regarded this limitation of land supply as a fundamental zoning problem when it commented that "the regulatory powers of local governments in a number of metropolitan areas are being used to bar vast land areas to apartments,

mobile home parks, and other dwellings that can meet minimum standards of health, safety and amenity. . . . ''[26] A national survey made for the commission showed that 25 percent of
metropolitan communities of more than five thousand population had no provision in their zoning ordinances for lot sizes of
less than one-half acre.

A more recent 1971 study examined the relative supplies of
land available for various uses in four New Jersey counties in
the New York and Newark metropolitan areas.[27] These counties
contained more than 400,000 acres of vacant land zoned for residential use. The study reported that multifamily housing was
permitted on only one-half of 1 percent of all the vacant land
that was zoned for residential use. No land was zoned to allow
mobile homes. Floor spaces of 1,200 square feet or more were
required on 77 percent of the available land and of 1,600 square
feet or more on 13 percent of that land. Lot sizes of one acre or
larger were required on more than 75 percent of the land zoned
residentially, and in two counties lot sizes of three acres or
larger were required on more than 20 percent of the land. Finally, lot sizes of 5,000 to 7,500 square feet, adequate space for
many of the homes of earlier generations of Americans, were
allowed on only 1 percent of the residentially zoned land.

To demonstrate the seriousness of this situation, consider the
following: suppose that new government regulations were proposed requiring overall automobile production quotas of 10 percent Rolls Royces, 25 percent Cadillacs, 30 percent Chryslers, 25
percent Fords, and 10 percent Volkswagens; it would be so inefficient and inequitable as to be unthinkable. Far fewer than 35
percent of automobile buyers need or want expensive luxury
cars such as Rolls Royces or Cadillacs. Volkswagens and Fords,
cars that could satisfy the automotive needs of most people at
far lower cost, would be limited by government regulation to 35
percent of the automobile supply. Many people would probably
no longer be able to afford any automobile at all.

Yet, partly because of the confusion surrounding them, the
zoning ordinances in metropolitan areas that have been widely
supported cumulatively establish quotas for metropolitan land
use that are quite comparable to our hypothetical supply quotas
on automobiles. While exact figures are generally not available,

in a number of metropolitan areas probably as much as 10 percent of undeveloped land is set aside for two-acre, or larger, lots, 40 percent for one-to-two-acre lots, 40 percent for quarter-to-one-acre lots, and 10 percent for smaller lots and for multifamily housing. Zoning regulations create major inefficiencies and inequities in use of land, as would a set of supply quotas for any product so far out of line with existing needs and demands.

Because of these metropolitan land-supply quotas, prices for the limited amount of suburban land that is available for high-density uses are often driven above $100,000 per acre, while prices for nearby land zoned for low-density uses may be one-fifth that amount, or even less. Translated into the final consumption item—housing—the price of high-density housing is forced to rise both in the suburbs and in the central-city areas because of the extra demand for high-density housing pushed back into the central cities by high suburban prices. In contrast, the price of low-density suburban housing is held much below levels that unregulated supply-demand forces in land markets would produce, in effect subsidizing the rich. The system of suburban land-supply restrictions is highly discriminatory not only against low- and middle-income groups, but also against the elderly, childless couples, single people, and anyone with a preference for high-density housing. It also, of course, is an extremely inefficient way to use land.

As do most attempts to ration or otherwise restrict sale of widely demanded goods and services, zoning has created a black market in the form of zoning corruption that has provided badly needed relief to the most serious supply distortions caused by overall metropolitan zoning quotas. Zoning limited supply quotas for higher-density uses result largely from prohibiting the sale of neighborhood and community zoning rights. In effect, through the evolution of highly informal mechanisms for transition, often involving illegal activities, the sale of zoning rights nevertheless occurs. The market for zoning rights has even occasionally functioned so well that some developers thought they had little need to complain. In the mid-1960s, one developer confided: "We know where we stand now

—$25,000 for zoning for a trailer park in this country. Why upset things by talking about it?"[28]

New Mechanisms for Transition

The severe problems of land development in the United States have generated several proposals for new mechanisms that would govern transitions in basic use. These proposals generally start with the assumption that the foremost objective should be to provide for a transition that does not occur in a piecemeal fashion. Under the informal transitional mechanisms that have evolved under zoning, a rezoning occurs at one location, an unrelated change takes place somewhere else, a third unrelated change at a third location, and so forth. This manner of transition has made it impossible comprehensively to plan and develop whole neighborhoods or larger areas.

Coordinated development of an entire neighborhood or larger area offers major advantages. A private (or public) developer can take account of interdependencies among properties that are neglected when development occurs piecemeal. Economies of large-scale building come within reach. Because a development schedule can be prepared in advance, close coordination with school, sewer, and other public-facility installation is possible. Large-scale development may also make it possible to avoid the inequitable treatment of different property sellers under piecemeal change. At the very least, each seller of property would receive, if not an equal price, at least a more equal bargaining opportunity in dealing with agents trying to acquire all the properties in an area.

Representative of the conclusions arrived at by other study groups, a 1972 task force on national growth policy of the American Institute of Architects gave top priority to the following recommendation:

The building and rebuilding of American communities should be planned and carried out at neighborhood scale (ca. 500–3,000 residential units along with a full range of essential facilities and services) and in a form appropriately called a "Growth Unit."
The Growth Unit does not have fixed dimensions. Its size

[is] . . . enough in any case to require an elementary school, day care, community center, convenience shopping, open space, and recreation. Enough, too, to aggregate a market for housing that will encourage the use of new technology and building systems. Also enough to stimulate innovations in building maintenance, health care, cable TV, data processing, security systems, and new methods of waste collection and disposal. Large enough, finally, to realize the economies of unified planning, land purchase and preparation, and the coordinated design of public spaces, facilities and transportation.[29]

The greatest obstacle to development at neighborhood scale is assembling a large enough open block of land. While large tracts are sometimes available, in most places land ownership is highly fragmented. Initial purchases may be easy, but as more land is assembled, progress becomes more difficult. The last parcels to be assembled have frequently become extremely valuable to an assembler, because if he cannot purchase those parcels, his whole effort may be for naught. If they exploit their advantage fully, the last holdouts can in effect capture a significant share of the profit. Finally, a few owners in an area may be so attached to their property that they refuse to sell at any price.

Intricate strategies have often been employed in the past to assemble land privately in big cities:

The actual process involved making unobtrusive and carefully camouflaged offers to owners, using a series of intermediaries to conceal the identity of the actual assembler. He might use dozens of agents and record titles in many different "straw" names. His devout hope was to bamboozle the public and especially the "old" owners, until he had control of the parcels he needed.[30]

In a more recent suburban example, before developer James Rouse could build the planned community of Columbia, Maryland, he had to assemble 15,000 acres. To try to prevent discovery of the scheme, a number of dummy corporations (with names such as Serenity Acres and Potomac Estates) were created and various ruses employed by purchasing agents to explain the heavy buying activity. One hundred and forty purchases were ultimately made and five landowners holding 850 acres eventually refused all offers.[31]

Private land assembly is both inequitable to land sellers, often benefiting sharp (or lucky) traders who hold out until the last moment with huge gains, and risky and costly to developers, in time and effort as well as in money. Most developers avoid the problem, either by finding a single large tract or, more likely, by developing at a number of locations and on a smaller scale. To solve these problems, public assistance in land assembly through use of condemnation powers has been widely proposed in recent years. The Model Land Development Code contains provision for public land assembly for neighborhood-scale development. The Douglas commission also recommended

that State governments enact legislation authorizing local governments of general jurisdiction to use the eminent domain power for the assembly of land needed for large planned-unit developments. Such legislation should include a procedure whereby such power can be used to assist private developers to assemble land for approved development. . . . [32]

Public assembly of neighborhood land might occur prior to any expressed developer interest, after negotiation with a developer for a proposed project, or after the developer has already assembled by himself a certain minimal percentage of the neighborhood area.

Public assistance in assembly of neighborhood-size blocks of land could solve many of the problems of neighborhood transition. But the problems of regional planning involving coordination of development among different neighborhoods would still remain. Public purchase of much larger areas than neighborhoods in advance of their development has also been widely advocated. Public acquisition of land for recreational and environmental purposes such as national parks, forests, wildlife refuges, historic sites, and seashores is an old and continuing practice in the United States. In the 1930s, public acquisition of large metropolitan land areas was prominently advocated as a means of improving control over development. In 1941, the National Resources Planning Board commented that "public acquisition of land is a powerful tool in controlling the development of new areas,"[33] and also noted that "one objective of land acquisition in new areas is the development of . . . self-contained neighborhood units."[34] Little more was heard of the idea through the 1940s and early 1950s in the United States, though it has been employed in a number of European countries (with the greatest fanfare in Sweden and Holland) in recent decades.

Extending the principles of the recently initiated inner-city urban renewal programs to suburban areas, in 1957, Charles Abrams suggested that:

State-land renewal agencies should be organized for the main function of acquiring vacant land outside city boundaries. The state agency would have power to acquire large areas, improve them with streets and utilities, and resell them for private development according to a prearranged plan. Land essential for schools, parks and other public uses would be preserved. The state and federal governments would contribute the essential subsidies for acquisition and improvement, and the land would be resold at market value.[35]

In 1960, Marion Clawson similarly recommended that a major part of future growth be accomplished in "suburban development districts."[36] Through ordinary purchases and through condemnation, specially created public authorities would acquire all lands in areas of up to ten, or possibly more, square miles. Development would be undertaken by private builders on the basis of low bids for projects specified by the district plan. On completion, the special development authority would be self-liquidating, turning responsibilities over to local governments.

Public-acquisition proposals generally involve similar features. A public agency would acquire land areas that seemed likely to be developed within the next decade or two, probably using funds obtained from the sale of bonds. Some of the acquired land would be held back for greenbelts and other public uses. The development itself in some cases might be placed in the hands of public corporations, but most of the land would probably be either leased or sold to private parties for development in accordance with publicly prepared plans.

Experimentation with large-scale public land acquisition (sometimes called land banking) has been widely recommended. The Douglas commission, the Task Force on Land Use and Urban Growth, and the Model Land Development Code are among those that have proposed this transitional mechanism. But despite the virtual consensus of expert views, there is no sign that either proposals for public neighborhood assembly or for land acquisition over larger areas will soon be adopted. These proposals have been made by study groups since at least the 1930s. Their failure to receive much support is largely a consequence of the prevalent attitudes toward property rights in the United States. The American property owner strongly favors as decentralized a system of control over use of property as it is possible to have. Originally, he preferred that all property rights be retained as his personal rights alone. Only grudgingly, out of clear self-interest, has he conceded property rights to his fellow neighborhood and community residents under zoning. But, without a similarly strong perception of self-interest, property owners are likely intensely to oppose establishment of any right given to metropolitan and state agencies to acquire properties according to the policies of these agencies.

At least to date, the general public has not perceived the aesthetic and economic advantages of large-scale development to be sufficient to balance off the disadvantages of allowing central government agencies to employ eminent-domain powers to obtain neighborhoods and other large areas of land prior to development. The one experience with such powers—under urban renewal in inner cities, where they were applied mainly to evict the poor—has not improved their prospects for a new trial. One of the objectives of the new metropolitan tenure system that will be introduced later in this book will be to provide a transitional mechanism better than the current system without having to make use of eminent-domain powers.

5 Zoning Evolution in Historical Perspective

The introduction of zoning in 1916 and its subsequent spread are typically explained as constituting the establishment of public control over use of private property that was made necessary by the increasing complexity, congestion, and density of modern urban life. In fact, however, early zoning is better explained as being a new resolution of a conflict between two private rights, the personal right of each individual property owner to use his own property as he wishes and the collective right of residents of neighborhoods to have the neighborhood environment they want to have. Neighborhood zoning was thus not an infringement on private property but a reassertion of its importance on a collective plane.

Contrary to standard views, perhaps the most important factor in shifting the balance in favor of collective rights of neighborhood residents was the onset of less congested and less dense suburban living patterns that accompanied the automotive age. The likelihood that housing for people with low incomes could be built in high-income neighborhoods represented a much greater threat to these better neighborhoods when they were built at low suburban densities. For people with lower incomes and much to gain from living in a good neighborhood, occupancy of significantly higher-density housing could bring the price of land in such neighborhoods within their reach in the suburbs. Previously, entry into high-quality neighborhoods in older and more congested big cities had not been possible to the same degree because the good neighborhoods there were typically already built at moderate or higher densities and thus tended to have high land values.

Another basic misconception concerning neighborhood zoning has been that it is a form of public regulation having a justification comparable to those for the regulation of banking, securities, food and drug, and other industries. Traditionally, public regulation in the United States has been justified as a necessary corrective for private-market failings. The private market is the basic determinant of the allocation of resources, but where there is an excessive concentration of economic power, where economic activity creates large external costs, or where other factors cause the market to misallocate resources, public intervention is necessary. Land-use regulation has generally been justified in this traditional manner. Nuisances create large burdens for others, for which the responsible party bears little or no cost (an "external" cost). Public regulation is the needed market corrective. Most land-use students have also maintained that, while the external costs are less than those of a classical nuisance (such as a stockyard), neighborhood zoning only extends the nuisance-control principle. It protects neighborhood environments from uses which, while not so damaging as to constitute nuisances as legally defined, do impose external costs sufficient to justify public regulation.

However, one critical difference is generally overlooked. New uses are often attracted to desirable neighborhoods precisely because of their desirability. While they create external costs for existing neighborhood residents, these new uses receive substantial external benefits that must also be entered into an accounting of overall social costs and benefits. There is often no reason for necessarily supposing that the external costs they create are larger than the external benefits they receive—quite the opposite could be the case. For example, a few new poor residents might value the attractions of a good neighborhood environment more than enough to offset the losses experienced by existing neighborhood residents.

If zoning were regulation in the traditional—"market corrective"—sense, it would attempt to balance external benefits and costs in each case in order to determine whether a new use should be allowed in a neighborhood to overall social advantage. However, zoning generally excludes all uses that would create any significant external costs, without giving any weight to the size of external benefits that might have been received by the excluded uses. Rather than a traditional form of regulation, neighborhood zoning has in fact represented a change in property-right institutions, with the purpose of creating the collective incentive to establish and maintain high-quality neighborhoods.

The historical antecedents of neighborhood zoning protection lie, not in the various forms of industry regulation created in the United States in the last one hundred years, but in much

older historical changes in land tenure. Some of the most important changes in English land tenure took place under the enclosure movement, an essential element in

a profound revolution, both social and technical. The most fundamental change was the supersession of open by enclosed
fields. The enclosure of fields and of common land had been
going on steadily from the fifteenth century, but the face
of England had hardly been changed. Between 1750 and 1780
the English countryside became the countryside we know, a
countryside of hedges, fields, and scattered farms. The technical
case for enclosure was exceptionally strong. It made each farmer
independent of his neighbor, free to introduce improvements in
crops and breeding without fear that his efforts would be wasted. Before, with land held in common and with herds mixing on the common pastures, improvement had been wellnigh
impossible. . . . [1]

Modern neighborhood zoning protection is a close urban
counterpart to the English enclosure movement. In early-twenti-
eth-century urban areas in the United States, the absence of
barriers to the mixing of different quality residential uses was a
threat to the achievement of high-quality residential neighborhoods. Efforts to create high-quality neighborhoods might well
not have been made in the absence of assurances that low-
quality uses would subsequently be excluded, for fear that the
efforts would be wasted. In rural areas of Britain, the earlier
solution to almost the same problem was to establish well-
defined private-property rights to the land, replacing common-
law rights of universal access. In urban areas of the United
States, the solution has been to give neighborhood residents a
collective right to control neighborhood uses, replacing the traditional open access to anyone who could afford to buy a plot
of neighborhood land. Whereas the enclosure movement established individual property rights, zoning created collective
property rights exercised through local legislatures.

By converting common rural lands to private lands, or open
urban neighborhoods to restricted neighborhoods, the rights
created by enclosure and zoning have both often been highly
damaging to the interests of the poor. Enclosure was strenuously—if unsuccessfully—opposed for three hundred years by
many Englishmen disturbed by its social consequences. Ulti-

mately, the rapid spread of enclosure in the eighteenth century had a major role in creating a large class of mobile poor and the necessary labor supply to fuel the English industrial revolution. Zoning has, of course, also stimulated wide opposition among those concerned with its consequences for the poor. It is not even inconceivable, although of course impossible to predict confidently, that zoning could ultimately play a significant part in a social upheaval as profound as that produced by the industrial revolution.

The extension of zoning protection from the neighborhood to the community was originally explained as being necessary for the achievement of the important benefits of public land-use planning. Implementation of public plans required control over broad development patterns. The hope and aim of public planning were better to plan and coordinate regional development. The result was that community zoning has given the small-to-medium-size suburban community an ability to insulate itself from regional pressures for housing, commercial facilities, industrial sites, or other uses of regional importance. Without zoning, such pressures would have generated rising land prices in the uses demanded, and eventually a willingness to sell for development of those uses on the part of some community landowner. Pressures of this nature can now be checked by community zoning. To a significant extent, community zoning thus has had the practical effect of diminishing regional coordination.

With its zoning powers, the small-to-medium-size suburban community has become an instrument by which the better-off avoid the redistribution burdens of having to make local tax payments to cover the cost of local public services for the poor. Better-off communities are also able to provide high-quality public services closely tailored to the demands of a fairly homogeneous higher-income population. The effect has been to make the small-to-medium-size suburban community, while nominally a public institution, closely equivalent to a private club. In this manner, as in the case of the neighborhood, zoning has created a new collective property right. Its purpose is to create incentives to establish and maintain high-quality community environments and public services. Such an incentive requires that residents be protected from future sharing and any loss of the benefits derived from their efforts to establish and maintain the community attractions.

The failure of community zoning to assist in coordinating regional development is easily explained in this light. A property right that is open to frequent breach of its defenses would not provide the security of use that is the essential purpose of such a right. Effective regional coordination would have required regular intervention by a regional or other central agency in community land-use affairs.

When zoning is employed to protect community character, its closest historical antecedents are found in feudal land tenure. As under zoning, feudal tenure divided the authority to control the use of land. Feudalism was

a state of society in which the main social bond is the relation between lord and man. . . . This personal relation is inseparably involved in a proprietary relation, the tenure of land— . . . the lord has important rights in the land, and (we may say) the full ownership of the land is split up between man and lord. . . . Jurisdiction is regarded as property, as a private right which the lord has over his land. . . . [2]

During the feudal period, most of the European countryside was divided up into numerous small fiefdoms that were at least nominally the creations of the king. Feudal tenure combined governing responsibility and landownership under the same authority, the feudal lord. As the historian R. G. Hawtrey, puts it: "Feudalism is in principle the identification of sovereignty with land ownership."[3] In modern times, numerous small suburban communities are legally the creation of state governments. The effect of community zoning is to transfer a significant portion of traditional landownership rights from the individual landowner to the community. As under feudal tenure, ownership rights and governing authority are joined, though in the modern case exercised collectively through local government instead of individually by the feudal lord.

Zoning has thus had fundamental social consequences never anticipated or even imagined by its architects, many of whom would certainly have regarded them as undesirable. On the whole, the intentions of zoning architects have borne little relationship to the results. This wide divergence between zoning

theory and actual result has been accompanied by the employment of fictions such as the justification of neighborhood zoning as a way of protecting health, safety, and morals, or the
justification of community zoning as an instrument for achieving comprehensive public land-use planning. In order to maintain such fictions, courts and others have had regularly to evade
or deny the obvious evidence before them. While the form of
zoning has remained little altered, major changes in the practical substance of zoning have occurred without much acknowledgment.

In all these respects, the development of zoning institutions is
consistent with the long previous history of land-tenure evolution. In his classic study, *The Land Laws*, Sir Frederick Pollock
described the numerous fictions, subterfuges, and other characteristics similar to American zoning experience throughout the
long history of English land-tenure evolution. As Pollock put it:
"The history of our land laws, it cannot be too often repeated,
is a history of legal fictions and evasions, with which the Legislature vainly endeavoured to keep pace until their results . . .
were perforce acquiesced in as a settled part of the law itself. . . . "[4] Although the substance changed radically, the form
of English land tenure generally resisted major change from the
thirteenth to the late nineteenth century. Over this period,

the system underwent a series of grave modifications. Grave as
these were, however, the main lines of the feudal theory were
always ostensibly preserved. And to this day, though the really
characteristic incidents of the feudal tenures have disappeared
or left only the faintest of traces, the scheme of our land laws
can, as to its form, be described only as a modified feudalism.[5]

In the history of English tenure, the intended and actual results of legislative enactments have often differed greatly. While
the legal issues are, of course, far different from those of modern zoning, the descriptions of English tenure change given by
Pollock, including the important role of efforts and devices of
ingenious land lawyers aiming to satisfy the practical needs of
their clients, exhibit a remarkably close resemblance to the
twentieth-century development of zoning:

These changes have not always been such as the Legislature
intended; in one or two material instances the effect has been
the very opposite of that which was aimed at. One celebrated

measure of Henry VIII's reign, the Statute of Uses, was passed in order to restore the ancient simplicity and notoriety of titles to land, though more in the interest of the Crown and other great lords than in that of the public. The object of the statute was almost at once defeated by judicial construction. But it did not remain inoperative; it had other and quite unexpected results. The first was to make the transfer of land, without any act or ceremony for securing publicity, far easier than it had ever been before. The second, worked out in the days of the Commonwealth and the Restoration by the ingenuity of two or three lawyers, was to introduce the method of strict settlement of landed property which is practised by a great proportion of landowners to this day. Thus, as we shall see more fully hereafter, a measure intended to compel notoriety and simplicity became the chief instrument of secrecy and complication. . . . [6]

The explanation for the common characteristics of traditional English and modern American land-tenure evolution, despite vast differences in historical setting, seems to be that major changes in land tenure have typically been a response to basic practical needs and strong popular demands for their satisfaction that came well in advance of intellectual and philosophical developments that were able to justify them. Feudal tenure featured a control over land that was based on a person's place in the social order. The lord of the manor, for example, by virtue of his responsibilities, received rights to control the land of the manor from the king, and in turn had compensating obligations to provide the king with certain military and other support in specified circumstances. He could no more sell the manor than today an army general could sell his command or the king or queen of England could sell the rights of the Crown.

As feudalism declined, the principal changes in land tenure were the substitution of regular rents and taxes for previous military and other customary feudal obligations, the spelling out of formal rights of inheritance to land, and the establishment of the formal right to sell land and property at the full discretion of its owner. From the perspective of the twentieth century, these changes can easily be seen as leading to the modern concept of personal private property and, more broadly, as essential elements in the development of a capitalist economic system. But to the people of the time such changes seemed very radical in nature, contrary to their basic concept of feudal society—as in fact they were. Hence, to meet practical requirements, modern

property concepts typically could evolve only through subter-
fuge and only slowly.

In the twentieth century, social processes have speeded up to
the point that the sixty years since the introduction of zoning probably corresponds to several centuries of development of
land tenure in earlier English history. If tenure evolution is still
the accurate indicator of changes to come that it was previously,
there is the intriguing possibility that, by examining the significance of zoning, a good prediction of future society can be
obtained. On this admittedly rather speculative basis, we can
conclude that in future social systems personal rights may be
increasingly superseded by collective rights. But far from the
doctrinaire socialist version of collective rights, they will be exercised by many small groups and organizations, making them
private collective rights for all practical purposes. The nineteenth-century concepts of free-market economic systems and
personal property dealt with the individual entrepreneur and
the personal-property owner as the basic units for social and
economic activity and analysis. Perhaps, in the social and economic systems of the future, the small collective will have increasing importance relative to the individual.

In addition to zoning, the other fundamental property-right
change of the past one hundred years in the United States,
probably even more far-reaching in its consequences than zoning, has been the creation of collective property rights to
business property under corporate ownership. New zoning and
corporate forms of collective ownership of land and business
property have greatly influenced a major part of the American
experience during the twentieth century. Both now also appear
much in need of reform. In both cases, progress toward reform
has been inhibited by an attempt to deal with these new property rights using social and economic theories created at a time
when the individual was the primary unit for both business-
property and landownership.

While the long-range social significance of zoning cannot be
predicted with any certainty at this time, it is not hard to understand why the creation of collective property rights brought
about by zoning could not have originally been described explicitly. The collective rights created by zoning are inconsis-

tent with basic American beliefs. Americans have traditionally placed a very high value on individual freedom, and they have sought to keep to a minimum government or any other collective infringements on personal independence. Nowhere has that belief been stronger than with respect to personal property. In the law, the only valid justification for society's interfering in the use of personal property has been for the strictly limited police-power purposes of protection of the health, safety, or morals of other people.

In contrast with this view, zoning has imposed tight collective controls over use of personal property that have borne little relationship to ordinary police-power purposes. Equally radical, when zoning was first introduced, its new requirements for collective approval of uses were imposed on existing neighborhoods. Until then, all property owners had acquired their property with the full and entirely reasonable expectation of continuing to have a long-guaranteed personal right to determine its use in all respects (subject always to genuine police-power concerns). Newly enacted zoning ordinances suddenly imposed collective controls on many unwilling property owners who, with good reason, could regard their fellow neighborhood and community residents as having changed the basic rules right in the middle of the game without even offering any compensation for their consequent losses.

Since World War II, the ideal of a highly homogeneous society has had a great intellectual and moral influence in American life. Increased social equality has been a prime national objective. The result of the collective property rights created by zoning has been to distribute the advantages of neighborhood and community environments and community public services as ordinary private goods are distributed. Aside from its purely income-distributional consequences for the poor, zoning has also created widespread economic segregation of living patterns. Given the relatively low incomes of a large proportion of blacks, it has also contributed significantly, if not always intentionally, to racial segregation.

In short, since its inception, zoning has had consequences that were in direct conflict with basic American principles. On the other hand, zoning has effectively met strongly felt, if poorly understood and inadequately explained, needs. Instead of dealing directly with the resulting conflict between its philosophical views and its strong practical needs, the American public has preferred to avoid acknowledging that the conflict exists. Zoning has been supported by fictions, evasions, contrived arguments, and other dodging of the fundamental issues it has raised. In this respect, society as a whole has acted much as persons behave in rationalizing or in other ways avoiding difficult conflicts between their personal goals and philosophies.

As with individuals, however, society may have to pay a high price for insisting on maintaining its illusions. For the basic zoning purposes of protecting the quality of neighborhood and community environments, this price has probably been small. Protection has usually worked fairly well. But largely because of the many misunderstandings and confusions that have surrounded zoning, it has proven impossible to develop satisfactory mechanisms for accomplishing transitions in the type of basic use of areas. The failure to deal with problems of transition has been a grave defect in the American system of land-use regulation.

There may be one last parallel between the evolution of zoning and the earlier history of land-tenure evolution. Personal-property rights to land evolved from the feudal period in response to the strong practical need for a formal mechanism by which socially beneficial transfers of personal property from one user to another could be easily accomplished. In the process, land became a normal market item—in the current popular phrase, a commodity. In order to introduce a better mechanism for neighborhood transition, zoning may also reach the point where zoning rights become salable. If this should happen, it would repeat the earlier example of evolution of rights to sell personal property, although now at a collective level, in response to the same practical need for a transitional mechanism.

II Feudal Tenure Trends under Environmental Land-Use Regulation

Introduction to Part II

Although it has not been widely characterized as such, much of the environmental legislation of recent years has represented a new wave of reform in land-use regulation. Partly to avoid tired debates and controversies, a new vocabulary and institutional framework have been introduced to deal with some old and familiar regulatory concerns. Federal air and water quality controls, for example, are an application of traditional principles of nuisance control, although now applied on a far broader scale than ever before. New state environmental legislation aims to regulate land along the coastline, in the mountains, and in other areas that are particularly vulnerable to new development. The local anti-growth movement, which is an offshoot of the environmental movement, has many of the same purposes as traditional community zoning. Environmental impact statements are meant to improve the design and location of major federal and other projects.

The most basic principle of the environmental movement has been its opposition to the private-market verdict. Environmentalists point to the failure of market decisions to take account of all social costs and conclude that there is little sacred about the market verdict. They are among the chief proponents of more public planning that would substitute administrative decisions for market forces. Lawyers for environmentalists argue that the needs of society should increasingly supersede the property rights of the personal owner in determining use of land, even when large land-value losses may result. On moral grounds, environmentalists argue that the land is a sacred trust for future generations, and that its use should not be determined by motives of private profit. Such views lie behind one of the most popular statements of the environmental movement, that land should not be treated or regarded as a "commodity."

The decline of feudalism was accompanied by the rise of the market institutions of a capitalist economic system. In the case of land, this decline was accompanied by the rise of—as Sir Frederick Pollock put it in the late nineteenth century—"something thoroughly opposed to feudal ideas—namely, the modern economical conception of land as an article of commerce which, like any other commodity, is bought, sold and hired for prices regulated by competition."[1] In the view that land should not be

treated or regarded as a normal market commodity, the environmental movement proposes to revive a concept of land tenure
that is basically feudal in nature.

A society's concept of land closely reflects its fundamental
beliefs and organization. Current trends toward a feudal concept
of land are compatible with other recent trends toward a much
stronger localism and regionalism in the United States, sacrifices
of economic efficiency for personal security and stability, less
willingness to accept private profit as a legitimate personal mo-
tive, and less confidence in the possibilities of social progress.
In these respects, despite several centuries of regarding feudal
as being synonymous with backward, feudal ideas and social
organization have recently acquired much greater appeal.

Feudal tenure trends under environmental land-use regulation
are still largely incipient. It is necessary to examine the likely
future consequences of current developments to see these trends
more clearly. How far matters will proceed is uncertain and will
depend on a number of unpredictable factors. As the implications of current tenure trends become better understood, that in
itself could well generate substantial resistance.

Fully in keeping with the history of land tenure, the proponents of new environmental land-use controls have attempted
—probably unconsciously in most cases—to avoid acknowledging the degree to which their proposals would depart from
American traditions of land tenure and, more broadly, social
and economic organization. A new set of fictions and misunderstandings has arisen which has effectively prevented most people from recognizing the broader social implications of tenure
trends under pressures from the environmental movement.

6 New Regulatory Protection of Regional and State Quality

Zoning was first introduced as a reform of nuisance law; because of the growing complexity of modern urban life, the problem of nuisances was said to require a new method of land-use control. Today, "environmental danger" has replaced "nuisance" as the object of concern. The most critical difference between the two is the geographic scale of their impact. While a traditional nuisance affected only a neighborhood, a source of air or water pollution or other environmental danger affects a whole region. To control them, much as zoning was introduced to protect neighborhoods from nuisances, new federal and state land-use regulations have been introduced to protect regions from environmental threats and dangers.

In early zoning theory, regional planning was required to provide coordination among many neighborhood zoning controls in order to assure that their cumulative consequences were not damaging to the region as a whole. For those who regarded public planning as a much more positive force, one of the primary motives in creating zoning was to introduce an instrument of land-use control that could help implement comprehensive public land-use plans. Today, state and national land-use planning is said to be a necessary means of providing coordination among regional land-use controls in order to assure that their cumulative consequences are not damaging to a whole state or nation. Also following zoning history, in the view of many current planning proponents, new regional controls are to be an instrument for implementing state land-use plans and a national land-use—or growth—policy.

A 1976 *New York Times* editorial echoed countless earlier proclamations of the necessity for land-use planning, then aimed at the regional level to ensure that local zoning and other local controls were exercised responsibly:

Environmental concerns are now implicit in practically every aspect of government policy. They are basic in any consideration of the country's transportation. . . . Indeed, underlying all else is the question of land-use planning, without which execution of sound policies with respect to parks, plant siting and the preservation of farmland are hardly possible. The enactment of national land-use planning legislation is a basic "must" for the environmental future of this country.[1]

Although zoning was justified as a method of nuisance control and as an instrument for implementing public plans, both of these justifications were largely fictions that camouflaged zoning's actual purposes. The need for protecting our environment from such dangers as industrial pollution is indisputable. There are probably also benefits to be gained from greater state and national land-use planning, although these are less clear. Nevertheless, both of these justifications for new regional land-use controls could well turn out, as traditional zoning justifications have turned out, to be largely fictitious. Just as the real purpose of zoning has been to protect the overall quality of neighborhood and community environments, the most important purpose of new regional land-use regulations may well ultimately be to protect the general quality of regional and state environments. While this purpose may sound laudable, it in fact has radical implications, which can be seen by considering the consequences of establishing relationships among regions and states in the United States as a whole that parallel relationships for which zoning has been responsible in metropolitan areas among neighborhoods and communities.

That protection of the overall environmental quality of regions and states might not be either the intended or the stated purpose of new regional controls is not particularly important. Based on historical experience, it seems almost a rule that new land-use controls will eventually be employed for purposes never intended by their designers. Court interpretations, practical economic needs, popular pressures, and other factors tend to be just as important, perhaps even more important than designer intent in determining the fate of land-use controls. New regional land-use regulations are recent enough that their eventual role is best predicted by examining the authority they create, the potential uses to which such authority might be put, and the economic needs and popular pressures likely to influence the future administration of this authority.

New Federal and State Authority to Protect Regional Quality

Zoning has long been available to protect the quality of the environments of individual neighborhoods and communities in a region. Protection of the quality of a regional environment requires a new authority to regulate development in circumstances where regional interests diverge from neighborhood and community interests. Such circumstances generally involve two types of development: single major facilities with significant impact outside the community in which they are located, and many individually small projects whose cumulative effect creates a pattern of development that affects the whole region.

In 1965, it would have seemed highly improbable that federal land-use regulation would occur in the near future. Yet, because of new environmental pressures, the federal government in the following ten years acquired broad authority to regulate land use. This authority includes control over both large individual facilities and overall patterns of development.

The instrument used to regulate land use is the authority to grant or withhold permission to develop. Under the Clean Air Act Amendments of 1970, the federal Environmental Protection Agency (EPA) designates classifications of development that are major sources of air pollution—so-called stationary sources. Authority is provided for EPA (or states under EPA-approved programs) to withhold permission to develop such uses "at any location which . . . will prevent the attainment or maintenance . . . of a national ambient air quality primary or secondary standard."[2] Under the Water Pollution Control Act Amendments of 1972, industrial or municipal facilities that directly discharge water wastes into rivers, lakes, or other water bodies must obtain a discharge permit from EPA. The power to grant such permits can often effectively control where and whether such new facilities can be built.

EPA is also concerned with broad patterns of development. In the first years after enactment of air- and water-quality legislation, the top priority was to clean up the most offensive single sources of pollution, such as oil refineries, power plants, and refuse dumps. In a few years, these steps brought considerable improvement. But in many metropolitan areas, the improvement has remained short of air- and water-quality targets that EPA has established and that it has had a legislative mandate to achieve. Substantial additional improvement requires dealing with a different kind of problem—pollution that results not from a few serious offenders but from many small, individually minor sources such as homes, automobiles, and small commercial facilities. Solutions are, first of all, long run and are most economically—and perhaps only—achieved by changes in overall land-use patterns. Because of this, the EPA has been authorized to exercise control over broad patterns of land use.[3]

For example, in many major metropolitan areas where existing controls on emissions from buildings and automobiles cannot achieve air-quality targets, major changes in land-use patterns are necessary. EPA has required states to prepare plans for such changes, including proposals for constructing mass-transit facilities and employment of new land-use controls. While it is not always clear how to enforce them, EPA also has had the authority to set timetables for the implementation of these changes.

Similarly, the 1972 Water Pollution Control Act Amendments give EPA broad authority for regulation of patterns of development. In metropolitan areas, EPA can control agricultural, recreation, construction, or other uses or activities that produce water runoff or in other ways contribute to water pollution. In fact, through mandated state programs, which EPA must approve, EPA is in effect granted the power to regulate the "location, modification and construction of any facilities within such areas which may result in any discharge in such area."[4] If this congressional language is taken literally, it creates the authority for comprehensive federal regulation of virtually all aspects of regional land use.[5]

In the public mind, land-use regulation has been closely identified with zoning, which federal environmental regulation has thus far employed very little. In the future, however, as the problem of cleaning up existing pollution recedes into the background, federal environmental controls could well increasingly adopt direct zoning approaches. In a sense, the zones already exist. For example, in some geographic areas, it is possible to obtain development permission for a use that creates a certain amount of pollution, while in other geographic areas that permission would be denied. Over time, delineation of geographic areas should become more exact, with greater refinement in prescribing acceptable levels of pollution emission in different areas. EPA has already commissioned studies of formal systems of air-emission zoning.[6] When zoning was first introduced, problems of nonconforming uses in newly created districts were similar to the current problems with existing heavy polluters, and there were only a few use classifications, much as there is now not much refinement in emission standards by area.

Perhaps the biggest difference between zoning and air- and water-quality regulations is in the standards for acceptance in a district. Whereas traditional zoning has employed standards such as building height, lot size, and type of use, air and water regulations employ standards of acceptable quantities of polluting emissions. Moreover, because there is a significant correlation between type of use and type and level of emission, pollutant-emission zoning has the potential for substantial direct control over the types of uses permitted in a geographic area.[7]

Recent federal environmental legislation thus creates the authority for comprehensive federal control of regional land use. However, Congress has shown that it will not support EPA when its administration runs into too much opposition from the residents of a region. EPA's proposals for major programs to reduce automobile traffic and pollution have not been in harmony with the value that most people place on automobile use. Attempts by EPA to force adoption of bridge tolls, regulations on parking, and controls over major shopping centers and other "indirect" automotive sources of air pollution have largely been defeated by popular opposition. EPA's experience in this regard is reminiscent of efforts of early zoning administrators to zone neighborhoods according to standards of "good planning" when such zoning was opposed by the neighborhood residents. In time, zoning administrators gave up such attempts and routinely zoned neighborhoods as their residents wished. If, as seems likely, federal administrators learn the same lessons, newly created federal environmental controls will generally be administered in accordance with the wishes of regional residents. Much as zoning serves neighborhood residents, federal environmental controls may then provide protection for the environments of regions only insofar as they are desired by their residents.

Some regions cross state boundaries and may require federal

authority to protect regional environmental quality. For the majority of regions, those that lie within states, state governments are probably best suited to administer regional protections. In the last few years, new state authority has been introduced to regulate both single major facilities with unusually wide impact in a region and broad patterns of regional development.[8]

The American Law Institute began work in 1964 to develop its Model Land Development Code. Although a final version was not approved until 1975, preliminary drafts were published and widely circulated after 1968 and were the inspiration for a number of state land-use enactments. The Model Land Development Code provides for a major new state regulatory role. A basic feature of it is state review of local decisions concerning permission for "Development of Regional Impact." Such development could include projects of public agencies other than the local government; development by educational, religious, or charitable institutions; public-utility projects; low- and moderate-income housing projects; or any other sufficiently large development. The designation of developments that are considered to have regional impact is left to the state, and it can vary according to the size of the state, its population, the part of the state in which the development is to be located, and other considerations. Local regulatory agencies are to approve development with regional impact if they determine that "the probable net benefit from the development exceeds the probable net detriment." This criterion is obviously subjective, and the model code specifies that local decisions can be appealed to a state board, the State Land Adjudicatory Board.

Florida, in 1972, was the first state to create a system of land-use regulation based on the guidelines of the model code.[9] Among other provisions, the Florida legislation requires that newly created regional planning councils review development considered to have "a substantial effect upon the health, safety or welfare of citizens of more than one county." For each such development, the regional councils are to prepare comprehensive statements that analyze, among other matters, the development's consistency with regional planning objectives. These reviews are then passed on to local governments, which make the final decisions as to whether development permission will be granted. Decisions by local governments can then be appealed by the parties involved to a state review board, consisting of the governor and his cabinet (the six members of which in Florida are each separately elected).

A number of other states have introduced less comprehensive programs for state regulation of certain types of major facilities. In Maine, after 1970, when residents were stirred by the threat of an oil refinery's being built along the coastline, state permission from the Environmental Improvement Commission was required for any development of greater than 20 acres or 60,000 square feet of floor space. In 1973, the Oregon legislature enacted the Land Conservation and Development Act, which authorizes a state commission to declare public construction of any transportation, sewer, water, solid-waste, or educational facilities as "activities of state-wide significance" requiring commission permission.[10] On the approval of the Oregon legislature, additional development categories can be added. Energy facilities are the type of project most often subject to state regulation. In California, the Energy Resources Conservation and Development Commission was established in 1974 with state-wide authority to regulate permission to develop power plants. Between 1969 and 1975, more than twenty states had enacted some form of energy-facility-siting legislation.

These state controls affect individual projects that have a particularly wide impact. Some states have also established an authority for control of broad patterns of development. These controls tend to be much more controversial than is regulation of individual large facilities. Local citizens often fear that state authority might be exercised to override their interests, for example, by intervening in the zoning policies of suburban communities. Because of these apprehensions, state authority over general patterns of development has been adopted mainly in nonmetropolitan regions.

The most comprehensive state effort at regional land-use control is found in Vermont.[11] In the late 1960s, new highways and Vermont's desirability as a recreation, especially skiing, area had caused rapid development, much of it in rural areas with few land-use regulations. In 1970, state control was established over most kinds of development throughout the state, including residential development of more than ten units; commercial and industrial development of more than ten acres, or of more than one acre where the local government does not have zoning and subdivision regulations (only a few communities do); and all mountain development above 2,500 feet in elevation. To administer the Vermont controls, the state was divided into seven regions. Within each region, a district commission must approve uses within the categories listed. Decisions by district commissions can be appealed to the Vermont Environmental Board, which consists of nine members appointed by the governor for four-year terms.

Comprehensive regional controls were also established in 1974 by Massachusetts for the island of Martha's Vineyard.[12] The new Martha's Vineyard Commission includes members designated by the boards of selectmen of local Vineyard communities, members directly elected by Vineyard residents, one member each from both the local county commissioners and the Massachusetts cabinet, and four nonvoting summer residents. Closely following the Model Land Development Code, the commission has the authority to regulate all individual facilities that it determines will have island-wide impact and to approve local regulations in currently undeveloped areas where future development could affect the whole island ("districts of critical planning concern").

New state controls over regional land use have typically been regarded as the establishment of state rather than regional authority. In practice, the administration of new controls will be determined by the relative political influence of the residents of a region versus the rest of the state. In many cases, existing regional residents will effectively determine regulatory policies, as is explicitly provided for in the new Martha's Vineyard controls. However, in many other cases, new regulatory authority may be exercised for state rather than regional purposes.

New Federal and State Authority to Protect State Character

When zoning was introduced, its purpose was to protect the environmental quality of neighborhoods. As a political entity, and frequently lacking proper boundaries for achieving land-use objectives, the community was not of much concern to zoning architects. Nevertheless, zoning gave communities important new authority, and it did not take long before communities began to employ zoning to protect the existing character of the community.

Neighborhood zoning has been employed to protect a fully, or at least considerably, developed neighborhood. By contrast, a characteristic of community zoning has been its concern with undeveloped sections of the community. In sparsely settled neighborhoods, community zoning policies are often opposed by the majority of the existing residents—most of them landowners. But the more densely populated sections have had the political power to zone undeveloped areas in the community to suit their wishes. The objective of community zoning has been to control changes in the type of basic use these undeveloped areas may be put to, thereby assuring that new neighborhood uses in these areas would be beneficial to the whole community, if not always to the existing residents.

New environmental land-use regulations have been designed to protect the environmental quality of regions. Their principal architects have not intended to use them to protect the existing character of states. States, like communities, are political entities whose arbitrary boundaries in many cases greatly complicate the problems of achieving desirable overall land-use patterns. Nevertheless, new federal and state land-use controls also create the authority to protect the existing character of states. Following the example of zoning, the key to that authority is the ability to control land uses in largely undeveloped regions.

Under the 1970 Clean Air Act Amendments, the federal government has acquired comprehensive authority to regulate major new development in sparsely settled regions. By a tie four-four vote, the United States Supreme Court in 1973 affirmed a lower-court ruling to the effect that states were prohibited from allowing any "significant deterioration" of air quality in those areas of the country already at, or above, certain national air-quality objectives established under the 1970 Act.[13] If followed literally, industry, high-density development, and other intensive land uses would be effectively prohibited from those large areas in the United States that are still underdeveloped and thus still have high air quality. Future intensive development would instead have to be channeled to areas that already have poorer air quality. As the federal Council on Environmental Quality noted:

A nondegradation policy is not neutral between developed and undeveloped areas. A literal nondegradation policy could severely curtail or even prevent growth in areas with clean air and require instead that growth be accommodated, if at all, in developed areas that may already have severe air quality problems. . . .[14]

The EPA realized that a literal nondegradation policy could have many undesirable consequences and has, in effect, therefore proposed only a partial implementation of the Supreme Court ruling. States would be allowed to divide their land into three categories. On Class I land, air quality would have to be maintained at existing levels; on Class II land, some air quality changes could occur; and on Class III land, air quality could deteriorate so long as it did not fall below national minimum standards. The Sierra Club, which brought the original suit, has gone to court to try to compel EPA to drop the Class III category. As of this writing, Congress is rewriting the air-quality laws and the future of nondegradation regulations has yet to be determined. But the existing EPA proposal for three land classes would create ample authority to institute tight regulatory control over all sparsely developed areas.

State governments have also been instituting their own state controls over undeveloped areas—often called "critical areas." The Model Land Development Code includes provisions for state designation and regulation of "Areas of Critical State Concern." In such areas, the state must prepare general principles and guidelines for regulation. Local governments are then to prepare regulations and submit them to the state land-planning agency for review to ensure that they are consistent with the state guidelines. Once approved by the state, the local government bears the subsequent administrative responsibility. If local governments do not submit regulations for approval, the state land-planning agency can prepare its own; if there is no local regulatory body, the state agency can establish or designate one.

The 1972 Florida land-use legislation based on the Model Code provided for the Florida cabinet to designate areas of

"critical state concern" and for state review of local regulations in these areas. As of 1975, two critical areas, the Florida
Keys and parts of the Green Swamp, had been designated by
the cabinet. (Another critical area, the Big Cypress, was specially designated by the legislature.) The Oregon legislature in
1973 considered a similar plan, but ultimately rejected state-
executive-agency designation of critical areas. Under the law
enacted, the state legislature will individually approve each
critical area proposed to it by the Oregon Land Conservation
and Development Commission. By 1975, Colorado, Maryland,
Minnesota, Nevada, and Wyoming had also enacted laws under
which the state is to designate critical areas, with widely varying subsequent state roles.

In the last decade, acting on an ad hoc basis, a substantial
number of states have established controls over particular areas
of the state. These areas usually have environmental characteristics considered especially vulnerable, including wetlands,
bayshores, lakesides, mountains, islands, riverbanks, and coastlines. For example, California has created new agencies to regulate land around Lake Tahoe (jointly with Nevada), along San
Francisco Bay, and for its entire Pacific coastline. Under the
California Coastal Zone Conservation Act, enacted by referendum in 1972, virtually all development within a thousand yards
of the coastline has required state permission.[15] (A new law for
coastal regulation was enacted in California in 1976 to replace
the interim 1972 commission.) Since 1965, more than ten states,
including Massachusetts, New York, New Jersey, Maryland, and
Georgia, have enacted state permit systems for development in
wetland areas. Thus far, the largest critical area is Adirondack
Park in New York State, a recreational area larger than some
states, which contains large private landholdings and a number
of towns.

Much as residents of undeveloped areas in communities have
often reacted in the past, residents have sometimes strenuously
resisted imposition of new regulations in newly created critical
areas by the rest of the state. With respect to state regulation of
the Adirondack Park area in New York State, one report noted
that the "plan represents a strong assertion of the environmental
and recreational interests of the state as a whole over the local

interest in economic development."[16] Similarly, on the island of Nantucket, where critical-area controls have been under consideration, the permanent residents have opposed their imposition:

The islander's needs clash inevitably with the desires of the well-heeled summer people who want Nantucket preserved as a refuge from the mainland hells where they normally domicile. Having acquired what they regard as a piece of Paradise, the summer people tend to conservationist schemes aimed at stopping development, and thus become political enemies of the islanders who often view them as fat interlopers insensitive to the needs of the year-round people.[17]

Although state critical-area controls have thus far not been employed to protect the character of a substantial part of any one state, the instrument is nevertheless available for that use. Many proponents of critical-area controls in fact advocate the placing of major parts of undeveloped areas of states in the critical-area category.

In examining the potential uses to which new authority contained in federal and state land-use regulations can be put, the terms under which this authority is to be exercised will be an important consideration.

Broad Discretion in Federal and State Land-Use Regulation

New environmental land-use regulation has discarded some traditional aspects of zoning that had become little more than formalities. By making decisions on applications for individual zoning changes the critical element in zoning administration, community zoning for practical purposes has been a discretionary system for some time. Because of the weight of tradition, however, the form of rigid zoning-use classifications has been preserved. Under environmental land-use regulation, broad administrative discretion is explicit.

Because of its obvious impracticalities, Congress made no effort to legislate zones with predetermined air and water waste-emission standards. Instead, in a major break with the traditions of land-use regulation, the Environmental Protection Agency received broad administrative discretion. New state regulatory systems have almost all followed the same approach. The granting of development permission is generally left to the discretion of a state or regional agency, often an independent board or commission. Although administrative decisions must follow certain legislative guidelines, in practice the guidelines are usually so general that the effect (if not always the legislative intent) is to allow wide flexibility and discretion.

The Model Land Development Code recommends as the primary standard for granting permission for development a calculation of whether the "probable net benefit [of the project] . . . exceeds probable net detriment." The model code then attempts to be more specific by enumerating a number of factors that administrators might take into account. Finally, for practical purposes conceding the futility of exact specification, the model-code authors provide an illustration of how a decision might actually be calculated:

Illustration . . . [a Code provision] requires a Land Development Agency to use benefit-detriment analysis in considering a metropolitan waste disposal agency's proposal to locate a sanitary landfill on land within the boundary of a particular municipality. The development will remove land from the tax rolls and thus will adversely affect the revenues of the municipality. The traffic and odors generated by the facility will cause annoyance and discomfort to some nearby residents. On the other hand, the only other available sanitary landfill sites are so far from populated areas that the increased cost of waste disposal would be a substantial burden on taxpayers throughout the metropolitan area. The only other feasible method of waste disposal is incineration which at any available site would create air pollution problems. Balancing the costs and benefits the Land Development Agency concludes that the permit should be granted.[18]

In the New York State wetlands law, the administering agency has authority "to carry out the public policy set forth in this act," which is "to preserve and protect tidal wetlands and to prevent their despoliation and destruction, giving due consideration to the reasonable economic and social development of the state."[19] Under the 1972 California coastal-zone law, permission required that development be "consistent with the findings and declarations of the Act," which said little more than that:

The California Coastal Zone is a distinct and valuable natural resource belonging to all the people and existing as a delicately balanced ecosystem; that the permanent protection of the remaining natural and scenic resources of the Coastal Zone is a paramount concern to present and future residents of the state and nation. . . . [20]

Attempts to be more specific about the reasons for granting development permission are not likely to have much success in describing the actual basis for decisions. The Vermont Environmental Control Law identifies ten requirements that must be met before development is permitted, including that the development "will not result in undue water or air pollution"; "will not cause unreasonable highway congestion"; and "will not place an unreasonable burden on the ability of the local government to provide municipality or governmental services."[21] The effect is to leave matters essentially to the discretion of the district commissions and the Vermont Environmental Board.

Some state legislation is naive in its seeming declaration that only environmental and certain other factors explicitly mentioned should enter the calculations of the state administering agency. For example, the Maine site-location law states that only "financial capacity" of the developer, effects on "traffic movement," "adverse effects on natural environment," and suitability for "soil types" are to be considered in deciding whether to grant development permission.[22] Clearly, when refineries, port facilities, and any large commercial or residential development are subject to the regulations, the social and economic value of the development to Maine is a major consideration that any sensible administrator will take into account.

In sum, legislatures have granted wide discretion in the administration of new federal and state land-use regulations. The actual use of the authority will thus depend on court interpretations and, most of all, on economic needs and the political climate within regions and states. Both economic and political factors are currently contributing to strong pressures for much greater regional and state autonomy. If these pressures are accommodated, new federal and state land-use controls will be key instruments.

Pressures for Greater Regional and State Autonomy

Demands in the United States for greater regional and state autonomy are a part of worldwide pressures that have recently emerged for greater independence of areas considerably smaller than the modern nation-state. In Canada, the Parti Quebecois, which advocates independence for Quebec, was elected in 1976. A number of observers have recently described an increasingly influential regional separatism within Western Europe. Major economic and defense pressures are still felt for forming groups of nations such as the Common Market or all Western Europe. But within the traditional nations, new strong centripetal pressures have raised issues that would have been totally unlikely only a few years ago and that in some cases have not been major public concerns for centuries. For example, Scotland and England have been joined under the same crown since 1707, but within the past few years, partly attracted by the riches of their offshore oil, Scottish separatism has become a major factor in British politics. One British political figure commented:

If and when "Scottish oil" comes on stream, one cannot help wondering whether Scotland will be content with a "state" legislature, or whether it will not insist on total independence from England. If in the end this does take place, Wales will demand similar treatment. If London is more understanding in its approach to regional affairs, things may never reach this point, but owing to the long history of reluctant concessions to the "Celtic fringe," it is not impossible that the United Kingdom, as we know it today, will cease to exist.[23]

Regional pressures of a similar nature have been reported all over Western Europe. According to a 1975 *New York Times* article:

Western Europe is still a quilt of nation states. But the ancient ethnic groups that were beaten, bullied and cajoled over the centuries into forming the map of nations have been trying to revise that map of late. . . .

Independence that would change the map of Europe into many more little states is a rare demand, but some Basques, some Corsicans, some Scotsmen are making it. Many more argue for a degree of autonomy that runs from mere cultural rights to learn and live in old languages as well as modern ones, to social and economic self-government that could probably only be achieved in a federal Europe.[24]

Similar pressures exist in the United States. But the supporters of greater regional or state autonomy have been much more circumspect in their demands and have attracted less attention. A principal reason is that in the United States there are no traditions of ancient regional languages, culture, and sovereignty. The long history of Scottish culture and independence make it much easier for a Scot lured by oil wealth than, say, an Alaskan to demand greater autonomy or even political independence. Pressures for greater state and regional autonomy in the United States thus have been formulated in much more moderate terms. The main vehicle for regional and state aspirations here has been the environmental movement, especially its advocacy of greater regional and state control over growth.

For example, in 1974, the Washington state government commissioned a task force of 167 prominent state citizens to prepare a guide for the state's future. Governor Daniel Evans saw the objective of the task force as being an examination of the ways by which the residents of Washington State could control their own future. The task force regarded finding ways to enable residents to resist outside pressures for change as being one of its principal tasks:

The pace of technological and social change is rapid, and continues to increase. Decisions are being made, inside and outside of Washington, that will have long-range impacts upon our future. The questions we must answer are, . . . do we want to be carried along in the wake of change and "progress" as it's imposed upon us? Or, do we wish to exercise our freedom to choose, to enter into the process of public dialogue necessary to decide what our future *should* be, and then to work together to make it happen?[25]

The most threatening was the pressure of immigration from other areas of people attracted by Washington's environment. To discourage it, the state task force recommended that tight controls over employment opportunities be maintained, providing sufficient jobs for residents but discouraging new residents from entering the state:

In large measure, the people's choice of a moderate rate of economic growth was based on the hope that such growth would not induce heavy migration into the state from other areas. If this is to be the case, we perceive some additional constraints upon the way in which we pursue economic development. First, such development must be carefully *timed*, in order to provide job opportunities for both those presently unemployed and underemployed and for our young people as they enter the state's labor force. Additionally, we must coordinate our policies relating to the desired economic "mix" of the state with the activities of our vocational and professional educational systems, in order to assure that the appropriate skills and talents will be available to Washington employers without recourse to substantial recruitment of workers from other areas.[26]

Citizens of other attractive states also feel threatened by sizable immigration. In Oregon, California, and Colorado, among other states, there has been widespread discussion in recent years regarding the desirability of limiting future state development. A 1973 article on a conference of sixty-five of Florida's "top scientists, educators, conservationists, economists, land planners and urban experts" reported that the participants concluded that Florida should "discourage all in-migration" until it could devise a planned growth strategy.[27] In 1974, the Hawaii Department of Planning and Economic Development published a state growth plan which recommended "an overall policy of slowing growth by one-third."[28] In his 1977 State of the State Address, Hawaii Governor George Ariyoshi bluntly acknowledged the radical character of his aims when he announced plans to seek a constitutional amendment allowing Hawaii to establish its own state immigration controls. He expressed hope that "some of our sister states such as California, New York and Florida, which attract a large number of migrants, would join us in this effort."[29]

Reflecting a reemergence of issues of federal-state sovereignty, one of the key provisions of proposed national land-use legislation, which has twice passed the Senate but has been defeated in the House of Representatives, would have required a wide variety of federal actions to be "consistent" with the state land-use programs that the legislation aimed to stimulate.[30] Such a consistency requirement was included in the 1972 Coastal Zone Management Act. Location of major energy facilities is another area in which states are raising new questions of sovereignty. Resistance by the Western states to coal and other energy development and the terms they propose before allowing it have been characterized by opponents—if with some exaggeration— as an attempted formation of a new "little OPEC." One University of Montana professor complained about sacrificing small local interests for larger national ones:

A comparison of local with regional or national costs and benefits always, by its very nature, makes the local area lose. What does it matter if a few score or a few thousand people in an impacted area have to suffer a severe messing up of their lives so long as (the) cost-benefit comparison leads to the confident prediction that the many thousands or millions of people in the region or nation will enjoy the benefits which the impact was designed to produce. This sort of comparison merely encourages and sanctions a tyranny of the majority. . . . Ultimately this kind of comparison leads to the loss of any real prospect of security for small businessmen, small communities, small industries, small governmental units, small anything. An ongoing consequence of all this is that the big are being given license to gobble up the small. In process of being lost is our fundamental concept of civil rights.[31]

Fiscal considerations have also entered into state resistance to new development. In past years, suburban communities have exhibited a well-known liking for "clean" industry, such as research parks, which pay high taxes and cause few environmental problems. In an interview before leaving office, former Oregon Governor Tom McCall described what his concerns would be in administering state regulatory protections. His calculations were strikingly similar to those of suburban communities, even to the analogy with private clubs:

Now we are at the point where we can look at some tremendously good firms and maybe we can let a limited number into the state. I'd like to get, maybe, an electronics industry or two, if we could move them around. Nice clean industry that doesn't use much power and pays pretty good money. We could have a little more of that. Not that we want to hurry. We are in a position to pick. We can go down to Los Angeles and say, "If you want to become a member of our club we'd like to have you, but we don't like rattle and bang and smoke and dirt and if you abide by our rules you can be a member of our club." That's our whole philosophy. . . . [32]

The basic incentive behind protection of regional and state environmental quality is much the same as that behind protection of neighborhood and community quality. Attractive regions and states such as Oregon face the problem of less well-off residents emigrating from regions and states that are not so desirable. If people from these less attractive areas are not excluded by government controls, the more attractive regions and states will eventually experience a decline in the quality of their environment.

To date, the total area under the authority of new state land-use regulations is small. Federal air- and water-quality controls provide authority to regulate land use over very wide areas. But thus far these controls have not been administered to protect the general quality of regions and states (although EPA nondegradation regulations are verging in that direction by acting to freeze future development over wide areas and thereby to protect state quality). Nevertheless, judging from the history of zoning and other land-use controls and from current pressures, new federal and state controls will eventually be used to protect the general quality of regional and state environments—at least it is possible and, in fact, it seems probable.

In neighborhoods and small-to-medium-size communities, zoning creates collective property rights. At the regional and state level, the authority provided by land-use controls creates the same collective rights. But on this level, these rights are better described as the authority of a sovereign state than as property rights. The creation of the authority for a much increased degree of regional and state sovereignty is a principal element in current feudal tenure trends.

The likelihood that current authority under new federal and state land-use regulation will be used to protect regional and state quality is considerably increased by the acceptance of certain ideas from the environmental movement.

Foundations for a Feudal Pattern of Land-Use Control

The decline of feudalism and the simultaneous rise of nation-states and market institutions was not coincidental. Markets provided a necessary mechanism for coordinating large numbers of distant and specialized activities within integrated national economies. The most basic principle of environmentalism is its opposition to the market verdict. This in itself could cause a major loss of central economic coordination, and a shift toward feudal patterns.

But a feudal trend cannot be concluded simply from the loss of market coordination. The market is not the only means of coordinating activities in large and complicated economic systems. Central public planning can also assume this role. Many environmentalists in fact propose the substitution of public planning for market decisions. Many would even assert that their basic objective is to increase the overall coordination of national land use through greater public planning.

In keeping with planning traditions, the question of whose interest shall be provided for in proposing greater public planning is generally not asked. Under most proposals, land-use plans are to be prepared by the region and the state. If regional and state planners act at all as past community planners have done, they will follow the wishes of existing regional and state residents in preparing their plans. A critical difference between market and planning decisions will be that the market result aims—however imperfectly—at improving the national—or even international—welfare, while the planned result is directed toward improving regional or state welfare.

The environmentalist opposition to the market verdict may thus have an altogether different basis than the need to remedy a classical economic situation of "market failure." Instead of an externality or some other classical market failing, the problem may be that the market is succeeding. But by the nature of market forces, market success many times provides for increases in national welfare at the expense of a region or state. For example, increases in the population resulting from immigration into a region will increase demands on the region's natural resources and attractions. From a national viewpoint, that increased use may very well indicate an improvement in the national welfare. But from the point of view of the existing residents of the region, it may be no improvement at all. They will be forced to share regional assets with many others and will probably suffer a loss of enjoyment. In short, from a regional perspective, greater planning may be needed so that the regional and state interests will not be submerged under market pressures that represent the interests of people throughout the nation.

Of course, the substitution of publicly planned for private-market decisions does not automatically favor state or regional over national interests. But the national interest is automatically reflected in market decisions even under a highly decentralized governing structure, while, in a publicly planned system, it is necessary to have national land-use planning and controls to guard the national interest.

Because it has few prospects, the methods that would be necessary to implement national land-use controls have not been much discussed. However, these methods can be ascertained from the principles that underlie most current proposals for state land-use legislation, including the Model Land Development Code.

First, the federal government would have to have a basic role in planning and land-use control in a system designed to provide for national interests. The federal government would have final responsibility for all land-use decisions of significance for more than one state. If such interstate concerns were defined as "greater than local" concerns in newly developed state regulation or in the Model Land Development Code, they would include certain large-scale and important categories of development—such as energy facilities, ports, dams, highways, large new communities—and development in certain limited geographic areas critical to the whole nation—such as coastlines, lakes, mountains, and historic sites.

However, although the federal role that would result from adopting such a definition of interstate concerns would be substantial, it would not include many matters that were also of major interstate concern. In constitutional law, for example, "interstate" matters are usually defined far more broadly. The national air- and water-quality improvement programs began with a focus on controlling large individual sources of pollution, but soon discovered that a major part of the problem was the accumulated output of many minor pollution sources. New legislation creating authority to bring small pollution sources under control was then enacted. Similarly metropolitan development patterns are the product of many small individual developments. Exclusion of the central-city poor from suburban areas is the result, not of a few conspicuous acts of exclusion of major development, but of the accumulation of many individually minor prohibitions. In short, federal review of the full content of state regulatory programs would be a necessary element in a comprehensive national system of land-use control that protected the national interest.

The same necessity is encountered in dividing responsibilities among state and local governments. Widely proposed state land-use legislation would limit state authority to particularly important categories of development and to "critical" areas. But, as suburban exclusionary zoning practices demonstrate, many of the most important features of state development patterns are the accumulated result of large numbers of individually minor decisions to grant or withhold development permission. Although a variety of explanations are given for the absence of proposals for state control over these small-scale decisions, it in fact simply represents an accommodation to the political fact of life that such a state role would have no prospect of enactment.

Aside from political considerations, the logic used to justify recent state regulation would require that each state be recognized in its entirety as a critical area. As is now the case in currently designated critical areas, local regulatory programs throughout the state would then be subject to state review. Perhaps without fully realizing the implications of its action, the Oregon legislature has in fact followed this logic. After approval of a state plan (a major hurdle that was left to be overcome later), the 1973 Oregon Land Conservation and Development Act required that:

All comprehensive plans and any zoning, subdivision and other ordinances and regulations adopted by a state agency, city, county or special district to carry out such plans shall be in conformity with the statewide planning goals within one year from the date such goals are approved by the commission.[33]

In brief, the principles of recent federal and state regulatory proposals lead one to the conclusion that in a system of comprehensively and publicly planned land use, states should directly review and approve all local controls and the federal government directly review all state controls. Through its authority over state controls, the federal government could then effectively supervise all local and state land-use controls in the United States.

For practical purposes, national land-use controls of this kind have no prospect of being enacted. Yet, substituting planned for market decisions without at the same time creating national administrative mechanisms to protect the national interest will have predictable results. It would be naive to believe that future administrators of state and regional controls will exercise these controls in a way contradictory to state and regional interests.

Such an eventuality is no more probable than the likelihood of local legislatures administering zoning laws contrary to community and neighborhood interests. Hence, to the extent that market coordination is eliminated, a general pattern of state and regional administrative decisions acting to advance intrastate and intraregional interests can be predicted.

Although direct national land-use control is not likely at present, if it were to be established, wide use of traditional zoning controls would be necessary. Within a specific geographic area, zoning applies a precise administrative rule specified in advance—the identification of each use classification as permitted or not permitted—to control development. The chief administrative advantage of zoning is that, once zoning is established, uses in an area are automatically known to everyone concerned.

Zoning methods are most needed where large numbers of development proposals are received in the same jurisdiction. In such circumstances, it is often clearly impossible for a single administrative board to examine the fine details of each proposal individually. While responsibility can be delegated, it makes sense to establish standards that are as clearly defined as possible for the granting of development permission. Otherwise, property in one part of the jurisdiction might be treated very differently from property in other parts, or the cumulative consequences of regulatory decisions in many small areas might differ from the overall objectives desired. It will also generally make sense to vary administrative rules by geographic area— hence zones are created.

Thus, if the final responsibility for land-use control were metropolitan, a traditional zoning system would probably be administratively unavoidable because of the large number of development proposals to consider. It would be virtually impossible for a single metropolitan review board to examine individually each proposal in a metropolitan area, requiring delegation of responsibility and the creation of administrative rules varying according to geographic area. While these standards might not involve minimum lot sizes, they would probably relate allowable project densities to the geographic location of the project, and would closely resemble traditional zoning in other ways as well.

All these considerations are far more compelling if national land-use control is the objective. The only way national control could be instituted would be to require that states and local governments establish clear administrative standards for granting development permission in their various areas. Such zoning standards could then be reviewed and approved by federal administrators. Any widespread assumption of broad administrative discretion in granting development permission would negate the possibility of effective federal review of state and local policies. Hence, if broad administrative discretion is available, the only practical way that federal control could be assured would be to have federal officials directly administer controls—a proposal that would be certain to cause a vast uproar in opposition.

Environmentalists are frequently strong proponents of a maximum of administrative discretion in land-use control. The Task Force on Land Use and Urban Growth—generally considered to reflect a moderate environmentalist viewpoint—recommended that: "Except for small projects with limited impact, discretionary review should be at the heart of development guidance."[34] Few, if any, proponents of wide discretion justify it on the grounds that it would eliminate the possibility of effective federal supervision of state and local regulation—or for that matter the possibility of state or metropolitan supervision of local regulation. Rather, the objection to zoning is that it has had major defects as a regulatory method. One failing results precisely from a feature of zoning controls that makes their use unavoidable in any highly centralized system of land-use control—the rigid rules specified in advance.

Like other administrative rules, zoning requirements can be rather arbitrary. Different uses are automatically segregated, even though some mixing may be desirable. Zoning applies the same standards to every location in a given district, even though locations may differ from one to the other in suitability for development. Finally, zoning does not offer flexibility with respect to the timing of new development. The rigidities of zoning have been criticized for years. The American planner, Clarence Stein, complained in 1924 in a speech to the American Institute of Architects' annual convention:

From the standpoint of the architect, zoning has imposed innumerable restrictions, many of them futile and unimportant, which tend to increase the complexity of his task in planning for the use of property, often preventing introduction of desirable innovations suggested by intelligent appreciation of his problem.

. . . the only rational end for which zoning can exist, namely, to promote better communities for living and working and bringing up children, is actually often hindered by the present applications of zoning.[35]

In addition to this zoning problem, it is frequently asserted that zoning is unsuited for guiding development. Because of uncertainty about proposed development pressures, it is said to be impossible to know in advance how to zone a particular area for development. Attempts to zone areas for specific uses are therefore likely to prove unsuccessful because demand for these uses is not likely to materialize at any time soon. In short, in a widely held view, the flexibility of administrative discretion is required as a practical matter because of the uncertainty governing development pressures.

The Task Force on Land Use and Urban Growth emphasized this uncertainty as a fundamental cause of the failure of zoning to provide coordination for development:

Developers and builders, not the town government, would be exercising development initiative, and you would know little about either the demand or the supply side of their development equations over time. How many people are likely to want to move into town? When? What kinds of homes will they want to live in and be able to afford? Will they be willing to live in that scruffy area by the highway, or will they insist on living somewhere in the country? Which landowner will be willing to make his land available for development at a reasonable price? When, if ever, will the legislature appropriate the state funds needed to build the highway? You could make some estimates but you could not be certain about them.[36]

Bernard Siegan offered the widely accepted conclusion:

The widespread adoption of "wait and see" techniques acknowledges the failure of traditional zoning concepts. The zoners have learned that it is simply not feasible to encumber the future of the land. There is no way to predict the future and exceedingly difficult to evaluate the present. . . . [37]

Such analyses of zoning are basically misleading. They do not take into account that the commonly experienced uncertainty about future uses is largely a result of those community regulatory policies in suburban areas that greatly restrict the range of development permitted. In many well-off suburban communities, there would be little question about the consequences of zoning an undeveloped district for high-density apartments, townhouses, or one-fifth-acre minimum-lot sizes. Within a few years, a large part of the land made available would be taken up by these uses. But the community is willing to permit only high-quality uses for which there is a limited demand. In essence, the policy of many suburban communities is to zone for uses for which there is already a large surplus of land and, as happens in any situation in which supply greatly exceeds demand, there is considerable uncertainty about the use of available supplies. Nevertheless, while it is mainly a myth, the idea of zoning inability to guide new development has contributed to the current disfavor in which traditional zoning methods are held.

In summary, the intellectual foundation for a future feudal pattern of land-use control includes the following main elements. First, the market verdict is no longer acceptable. Instead, administrative decisions are to replace market decisions in controlling land use. But there are to be only a few central rules established to guide administrative decision making, and a maximum of discretion should be allowed to each locality, region, or state in those aspects of regulation for which it is responsible. As a result, states, regions, and localities will each be free to determine their own future, according to their perception of their own interests.

We have already examined the consequences of independent local responsibility to determine regulatory policies in metropolitan areas. Neighborhood and community zoning policies have had effects that closely resemble the international consequences of protections of national environments—in large part through immigration control. Rich neighborhoods and communities deny entry to residents of poor neighborhoods and communities, who as a result are forced either to stay where they are or to move to other poor neighborhoods. Over time, large disparities in the quality of neighborhood and community environments and community fiscal resources develop. If use of cur-

rent federal and state land-use regulations becomes more widespread, there is reason to believe that much the same practices
will be employed on a larger geographic scale by regions and
states, for there is considerable evidence that regional and state
protections of their environmental quality would be administered in the future much as local zoning protections of environmental quality have been administered in the past. Existing
disparities among regions and states in environmental quality
and fiscal resources would be maintained and, to some degree,
broadened. Income segregation at a regional and state level
would arise. Regions and states would acquire increased powers
of sovereignty. The pattern of land-use control in the United
States could then well be described as feudal in its key features.

7 New Local Growth Controls

In addition to new protections of state and regional quality, the second important land-use regulatory product of the environmental movement has been the rapid spread of local growth controls. These controls are basically new applications of traditional community zoning principles. They thus represent much less of an innovation than do protections for regional and state environments. The closest historical antecedents to community zoning are found in feudal land tenure. New local growth controls make the resemblance between community land-use protections and feudal tenures increasingly explicit.

Local Opposition to Growth

In recent years, intense local opposition to further growth has sprung up in many communities, in substantial part as a result of the environmental movement. Environmental concerns have caused new development to be perceived as less beneficial (or more damaging) by communities; it is therefore less likely to be permitted. Communities have become much more concerned about avoiding air and water pollution, noise, and other adverse consequences of growth. Forests, fields, farmland, parks, and other open spaces free from development have become more valued. Attention focused on the general quality of the environment has stimulated new planning proposals. Because a community cannot build itself, it must depend upon development projects presented in accordance with its plans. The more exact and detailed the plans are, the longer they take to prepare and the longer the wait is likely to be before project proposals consistent with the plans can be expected.

The environmental movement has also directly challenged the traditional American regard for continual economic growth and the related willingness to accept the verdict of market demands. In the past, many communities accepted a certain amount of development that was to some degree detrimental. In many cases, communities realized that there were certain disadvantages, but because of the overriding consideration of economic growth, the detrimental consequences had to be significant—and there was always a substantial amount of that kind also—before it would be excluded. With the validity of market verdicts and the desirability of economic growth now in question, many communities have become much less willing to accept growth that involves even very minor fiscal and social disadvantages. The practical consequence is that large amounts of previously acceptable development are now unacceptable.

In England, there has been a long tradition of opposition to any growth that would alter the open countryside, perhaps because land is much scarcer there. In 1962, Delafons could observe (in something of an overstatement even then): "Despite . . . rampant growth, it is very rare in America to encounter any antipathy to new development. Quite the opposite is usually the case."[1] But, by 1973, the Task Force on Land Use and Urban Growth reported:

There is a new mood in America. Increasingly, citizens are asking what urban growth will add to the quality of their lives. . . .

Today, the repeated questioning of what was once generally unquestioned—that growth is good, that growth is inevitable—is so widespread that it seems to us to signal a remarkable change in attitudes in this nation.[2]

Under the influence of the "new mood," communities are now looking at the costs and benefits of growth with a skeptical eye. In the past, the consequences of development were often only very roughly evaluated. But with new questioning attitudes, a number of communities have introduced modern management techniques of analysis in order better to evaluate the impact of development.

The fiscal consequences of development are receiving close scrutiny under the formal procedures of fiscal-impact analysis. Such an analysis often shows that new residential development will cost a community more than the revenue it will generate. In some instances, even quite expensive residential projects have adverse fiscal consequences. One 1970 fiscal analysis, done for the suburban community of Barrington, Illinois, showed that the development of a fifty-acre parcel of land with $40,000 homes on one-half-acre lots would result in annual school costs to Barrington almost $100,000 more than would be generated in school revenues.[3] Even more surprisingly, the study asserted that the development of $100,000 homes on five-acre lots would fall just short of breaking even. The only residential development that showed a positive impact on education finance was apartment development. Mainly because fewer school children would occupy them, high-rise apartments with primarily one- and two-bedroom units could be expected to produce an annual educational surplus of $270,000. Another much noted fiscal-impact analysis showed that a proposed 800-unit residential development (with some commercial facilities) in a fast-growing suburban area outside of Charlottesville, Virginia, would produce an overall fiscal deficit for local government of more than $100,000 annually.[4]

To determine the overall desirability of development, a community needs a comprehensive environmental-impact analysis. In California, a 1971 Palo Alto–commissioned study attempted to estimate the overall impact of different kinds of development of the foothills section. Fiscal, social, ecological, visual, geological, hydrological, and other impacts were all considered. The study concluded:

> Development at 3 units per acre (the density proposed by Land Resources Corporation) would cost 10 percent less cumulatively over 20 years than City acquisition [by public purchase with funds from bond sales]; but when the bonds were paid off, the continuing cost of the residential development would be far higher. . . .
> Other factors weigh more heavily than [public] costs against development [of the area under study]. . . . none of the alternatives studied would have any great social utility except those that include low-moderate income housing (Alternatives 4 and 8) and these would have significant disadvantages in other respects. . . . Any of the development alternatives would do major ecological and visual damage to the area. . . .
> In light of all these considerations, it is strongly recommended that the City deny approval to all development proposals in the area below the park and be prepared to purchase the land when necessary to prevent development. . . . [5]

Instead of purchasing the land, Palo Alto chose a less costly and more traditional approach—rezoning the land to ten-acre minimum-lot-size zoning. Predictably, this action was contested in court by property owners in the area.

Communities are increasingly excluding growth for general environmental reasons. The Levitt Corporation was interested in building a $125 million planned community for over 10,000 people in Loudoun County, Virginia, on the outskirts of the Washington, D.C., metropolitan area. When it encountered difficulty in obtaining the required zoning approvals, Levitt offered to pay $900 per dwelling unit to the county to cover public-service costs. With fiscal burdens largely eliminated, Loudoun County, in 1972, still refused the planned community, primarily because of the effects that such a large influx of people would have on the environment of a little-developed county.

Under the new attitudes toward growth, only development for upper-middle or higher-income residents is likely to be welcome in existing moderate-income communities. In high-income, high-quality communities such as Palo Alto, virtually all development, except perhaps a scientific-research park, is likely to be considered undesirable. A 1973 article in the *Christian Science Monitor* reported on the growing inclination in communities across the United States to slow or stop development altogether:

New restrictive laws, zoning actions, moratoriums on building permits, density limitations, size or height limitations, or bans on septic tanks, are sprouting all over. They are accompanied by citizen lawsuits to prevent development. Once-tranquil city council or county commission meetings have become arenas of protest, overflowing with citizens seeking to block new subdivisions or factories or amusement parks.[6]

A 1974 *New York Times* article indicated an accelerating trend: "Growth controls have erupted . . . at a rate that has reached epidemic proportions."[7]

The most intense opposition to rapid rates of development is usually found in transitional communities that have been expanding the most rapidly. Nationally, population increase was 13.3 percent from 1960 to 1970, down substantially from the 18.8 percent between 1950 and 1960.[8] But the forces of growth in the United States do not distribute growth equally among geographic areas or in proportion to existing population; rather, at any moment, expansion is concentrated in areas that have reached a stage where they are ripe for it.

In the 1960s, the most rapidly growing sections of the United States were Florida (its population increased 37.1 percent from 1960 to 1970), followed by California and the rest of the South-west (26.8 percent), and, largely because of growth of the federal government, Delaware, Maryland, and the District of Columbia (21.2 percent). Given long-standing national trends toward greater metropolitan concentration of population, those metropolitan areas located in growing sections of the country are often faced with particularly rapid growth. The National Commission on Population Growth and the American Future projected that if recent trends were to continue, three major metropolitan areas in Florida could be expected to double in population between 1970 and 2000, the San Diego area would more than double, and the Los Angeles area almost double. Among others, the Denver, Houston, San Francisco–Oakland, Atlanta, Dallas–Ft. Worth, and Washington, D.C., metropolitan areas would each grow by more than 50 percent, compared with a likely national population increase of about 30 percent.

A third critical trend for growth patterns has been the massive population movement from the central cities to the suburbs. Between 1960 and 1970, while central-city population rose by 5 percent, the suburban parts of metropolitan areas grew 25 percent.

Much of suburban development has occurred on metropolitan fringes in communities where population increases of 100 percent or more per decade have been common. For example, in 1930, the Washington, D.C., suburb of Fairfax County, Virginia, had had a population of around 25,000 for many years. By 1973, its population had shot up to 530,000. During the decades 1940–50, 1950–60, and 1960–70, population had risen by 141 percent, 158 percent, and 83 percent respectively.

Communities that have introduced new methods of growth control include Ramapo, New York; Boulder, Colorado; Boca Raton, Florida; and Petaluma, California. All are on the fringes of major metropolitan areas and all have had very rapid population increases, rates of 119 percent, 77 percent, 310 percent, and 77 percent, respectively, for the 1960s. Except for Ramapo, all are also located in fast-growing regions of the United States, compounding pressures on metropolitan fringes even in slow-growing sections. Mount Laurel, the community involved in the recent and much-noted New Jersey Supreme Court decision on zoning, had grown 114 percent during the 1960s.

Local Growth-Control Methods

In response to strong popular pressures, many communities with rapid recent expansion have taken steps to restrict further growth.[9] The most widely used method has been to increase the restrictiveness of traditional zoning practices. Communities refuse applications for zoning changes necessary for development that would have been granted earlier, or they enact larger minimum-lot-size requirements. One example occurred in Sanbornton, New Hampshire, which received wide attention when a federal district court upheld the town's actions.[10] Shortly after a developer purchased a tract for five hundred vacation homes, Sanbornton rezoned the area to a combination of three- and six-acre minimum-lot sizes, and this prevented its development. With better timing, before any specific development proposal has been received, many other communities have similarly increased minimum-lot-size requirements.

While large lot sizes are an old fixture of restrictive zoning, in a few places these sizes have become astronomical. In 1971, in Marin County, just north of San Francisco, zoning requirements of sixty acres per dwelling unit were created in agricultural areas. Forty-acre minimum-lot sizes were required in Monterey County farther south of San Francisco. Other communities are more directly zoning areas for agriculture, forests, or simply as environmentally too fragile to allow development. Communities are zoning out development altogether throughout flood-endangered areas, confident that this action will be legally sustainable. (A 1973 consultant report on open-space preservation to the town of Medford, New Jersey, proposed extensive flood-plain zoning as the cheapest way of obtaining open spaces.)[11] Some communities are imposing higher minimum-quality standards in addition to minimum-lot sizes. Although eventually defeated in court, in 1970, the town of Glassboro, New Jersey, tried to require swimming pools, tennis courts, air conditioning, and garbage-disposal units, among other features, in apartment units.[12]

Under existing federal and state water-quality standards, a given sewage treatment plant can accommodate only so much development without violating standards for effluent discharge.

Many community plants currently fall far short of meeting these standards, a situation that ultimately must be rectified. In such communities, more development would cause a more severe violation. For this reason, a substantial number of communities have imposed restrictions on new development, ranging from limits on the number of building permits or sewer connections per year to total bans until increased sewage-treatment capacity is obtained. Some 1974 estimates of the number of communities with these "sewer moratoria" were 160 in Illinois and Ohio, 40 in Florida, and 74 in New Jersey.[13] A major part of the suburban areas surrounding Washington, D.C., have been under sewer moratoria at one time or another since 1970. While no one seems to have any exact figures, sewer moratoria are clearly being widely employed. In parts of the United States such as Florida, where water is in short supply, water availability limitations have also occasionally served as a reason for restricting growth.

Public control over the sequence and timing of development has been a longtime—although almost entirely unrealized—objective of planners. According to theory, communities should plan installation of roads, sewer lines, and other necessary public facilities according to a schedule for community development. Coordinated with public-facility installation, zoning or subdivision controls would prevent development in areas not yet ready. The pace at which areas are scheduled for development in effect establishes a maximum community-growth rate. In 1969, Ramapo, New York, enacted a controversial ordinance that scheduled areas in the community for development over an eighteen-year period. A number of other communities are considering similar controls over the sequencing and timing of development, and thus in effect over their rate of growth.

A small number of communities have considered, and at least three have enacted, regulations that explicitly propose to control their number of housing units. The main reason more have not done so has been the possibility that such controls might be declared unconstitutional as amounting to local immigration controls regulating community population levels. But if the courts permit direct housing-unit controls, many more communities almost certainly will adopt them.

In 1972, Boca Raton, Florida, voters enacted a limit of 40,000 to the total number of housing units that could be built in the community. Calculated on the basis of an average rate of 2.5 occupants per unit, that amounts to a total population limit of about 100,000 people. Also in 1972, Petaluma, California, adopted an ordinance that established a maximum limit of 500 new housing units per year, amounting to a maximum of about 1,250 additional people per year. In 1971, Boulder, Colorado, voters nearly enacted a maximum future population limit of 100,000. Then, in 1976 they approved a limit similar to Petaluma's of 450 housing units per year.

While thus far few communities have adopted long-term controls on numbers of housing units, many have enacted temporary moratoria—typically from six months to two years—on granting building permits, or on rezoning approvals. In Orange County, New York, on the fringes of the New York metropolitan area, at least seven of the twenty communities have imposed temporary moratoria of one kind or another on new building permission since 1970. Temporary moratoria have existed in thirty of the one hundred and twelve communities of New Jersey's Passaic valley. Some of these temporary moratoria are justified by the need for time to increase sewage treatment capacity, others by the need to take stock in order to plan better for future growth.

The Consequences of New Restrictions on Growth

On the face of it, new growth controls may seem more even-handed than zoning regulations in their treatment of rich and poor because they do not involve minimum-quality standards. This feature tends to obscure the reality that they have essentially the same purposes and consequences as traditional zoning. If more people would like to live in a community than are allowed to, the resulting supply-demand pressures will drive up the price of local housing. Prices will rise until there is no longer an excess demand for local housing. Housing prices will climb to a level where most individuals cannot afford them, bringing demand for community entry into balance with the tightly restricted supply. Thus, just as in the case of zoning, local growth controls exclude less well-off people by establishing financial barriers to entry that only the better off can surmount.

The results of such supply-demand workings were described in a city-sponsored, comprehensive 1973 study of future growth possibilities in Boulder, Colorado, which examined the implications of four alternative approaches to Boulder's future growth: continuation of current policies, no growth, emphasis on environmental factors, and emphasis on social, cultural, and economic aspects:

The effect of restricted growth (Model II) will probably redistribute income upward from the 1970 level. By 1990, Boulder should be much above the State in percent of high income residents. The unsubsidized poor and lower middle income persons will probably be pressured out of the valley, and, in some instances, possibly out of the county.[14]

Housing price escalations resulting from local growth controls have already begun to be experienced in some areas. In the period from 1970 to 1974, sewer moratoria were in effect for much of the Washington, D.C., metropolitan area. An article in the *Washington Post* reported:

Environmental restrictions, which have helped to reduce the supply of new homes to a record low in the Washington metro area, have finally hit the pocketbooks of consumers in an awesome way.

The average sales price of existing homes sold in Washington jumped to $63,700 in the third quarter of 1975. . . . [15]

New local growth controls add little to the ability to control land use beyond that already established by zoning. For example, in the many communities where discretionary zoning changes have been required to gain entry, it has long been possible precisely to control the rate of community growth. The most significant aspect of local growth controls may be that they have clothed traditional zoning practices in the more respectable language of environmental protection. Local growth controls have been adopted in a number of politically liberal communities where an "exclusionary zoning" policy might have been considered irresponsible but where local "control of growth" seems a more acceptable objective.

The increasingly restrictive administration of zoning and the rapid spread of local growth controls together threaten to create a severe shortage of housing in metropolitan areas of the United States. The children of the post–World War II baby boom are now entering the ages at which households are formed and families begun. Between 1975 and 1985, the number of persons aged thirty to forty will increase by more than 40 percent. Population composition is shifting toward growing numbers of aged and of single adults who will want their own housing units. Even though the birth rate has slowed down, population is still growing steadily, and the amount of metropolitan housing needed is sure to increase substantially. The Commission on Population Growth and the American Future projected in 1972 that metropolitan population would grow from 144 million in 1970 to 225 million in the year 2000—an increase of more than 50 percent.

Thus, at the same time that regulatory restrictions on the supply of metropolitan land are becoming tighter, housing demands are steadily growing. If reforms are not instituted, it is not only the poor who will suffer from the resulting shortage of housing. Large numbers of young middle-class adults and others who are seeking housing will be unable to find anything within their means in the areas they had hoped to live in. A Congressional Budget Office study found that, while median family income had risen by 39 percent from 1970 to 1975, the average price of purchasing a home had risen by more than 60 percent over this period.[16] The Federal Home Loan Bank Board reported that from February, 1975, to February, 1976, the average price of new homes in the United States rose from $38,000 to $43,000—a rate of increase in excess of 10 percent. The "continued rise in the price of buildable land in many metropolitan areas" was stated to be one factor.[17] A 1977 study by the Harvard-MIT Joint Center for Urban Studies indicated that if current trends continue the average house may cost an extraordinary $78,000 by 1981.[18] As law professor Arnold Reitze remarked of new restrictions on growth: "These attempts to protect the cultural and physical environment . . . in totality . . . threaten to leave the majority of Americans with no chance for home ownership; . . . much of the middle class is being added to the group priced out of the housing market."[19]

From 1970 to 1974, nonmetropolitan areas in the United States for the first time in decades grew more rapidly than metropolitan areas. Although a number of other influences are at work in this radical reversal of past trends, the fact that land for economical housing is increasingly unavailable over large parts of many major metropolitan areas is bound to force people to seek housing elsewhere.

Local Feudal Tenure Trends

New local growth controls offer communities an advantage in that they are less overtly discriminatory than zoning. However, these growth controls may give rise to even graver legal and intellectual challenges than zoning has thus far faced. New local growth controls can be objected to on the grounds that they openly limit personal residential mobility. The feudal quality of local growth controls is thus very explicit. In recent years, a new type of legal challenge has been mounted to both zoning and local growth controls which is based on a highly feudal-sounding concern. This challenge asserts that zoning and other growth controls unconstitutionally restrict the right of individual residential mobility—in legal terminology, the "right to travel." The 1973 Task Force on Land Use and Urban Growth concluded: "Clearly, the courts are going to be asked to draw, with some precision, the line between legitimate protective regulations and improper restrictions on growth and mobility."[20]

Although there was no specific mention of it in the Constitution, it had been assumed, and the United States Supreme Court agreed in 1941, that the Founding Fathers intended that states be prohibited from regulating movement of population among themselves. During the depression, California attempted to prevent migrants fleeing Middle Western dust bowls from taking up residence and possibly adding to welfare burdens. In overruling California's actions, the Court stated:

But this does not mean that there are no boundaries to the permissible area of the state legislative activity. There are. And none is more certain than the prohibition against attempts on the part of a single State to isolate itself from difficulties common to all of them by restraining the transportation of persons and property across its borders. . . . [21]

The prohibition on state regulation of population movement resulted from its infringement on what has come to be called the "right to travel," which the Court has said is a basic constitutional right.

The 1965 Pennsylvania Supreme Court decision, which overturned the four-acre minimum-lot-size zoning in Easttown Township, was the first to grapple directly with the conflict between land-use regulation and residential mobility. The court saw the four-acre minimum-lot size as an unwarranted infringement on mobility. The court acknowledged that the township took the position that:

It does not desire to accommodate those who are pressing for admittance to the township unless such admittance will not create any additional burdens upon governmental functions and services. The question posed is whether the township can stand in the way of the natural forces which send our growing population into hitherto undeveloped areas in search of a comfortable place to live. We have concluded not. A zoning ordinance whose primary purpose is to prevent the entrance of newcomers in order to avoid future burdens, economic and otherwise, upon the administration of public services and facilities can not be held valid. . . . [22]

In two later important cases, the courts have again dealt with the issue of restrictions on residential mobility. The cases involved the growth controls mentioned above of Ramapo, New York, and Petaluma, California. Petaluma proposed to limit the number of building permits per year to five hundred and Ramapo to schedule its future development by area over eighteen years. In a split 1972 decision, the New York State Court of Appeals, the highest state court, upheld the Ramapo ordinance. However, in dissent, Justice Charles Breitel emphasized the necessity of considering interests outside the community and noted that, if Ramapo's growth controls were adopted by all suburban communities, the cumulative restrictions on mobility might well prove disastrous. The controls were "a device that maybe a few more towns like Ramapo could adopt, but not all, without destroying the economy and channelling the demographic course of the State to suit their own insular interests."[23]

Ruling on the Petaluma ordinance in 1974, Federal District Court Judge Lloyd Burke for the first time accepted the argument that a local land-use regulation could too seriously infringe on the constitutional right to travel to let it stand: "Since the population limitation policies complained of are not supported by any compelling governmental interest the exclusionary aspects of the "Petaluma Plan" must be, and are hereby declared in violation of the right to travel and, hence, are unconstitutional. . . . "[24] Although Judge Burke's decision was later reversed on appeal, the reversal was based on other grounds and did not deal with the validity of the right-to-travel argument.

In 1976, the United States Supreme Court refused to hear a further appeal on Petaluma's growth controls. In the previous few years, the establishment of similar controls in other communities has been held up to await the results of court review. With this suggestion of possible future Supreme Court approval, the rate of introduction of new local growth controls could well escalate.

III A Proposal for a New System of Metropolitan Land Tenure

Introduction to Part III

Zoning has created a new system of land tenure in metropolitan areas. Prior to zoning, except for a limited number of nuisance restrictions, the single personal owner had full rights to the use of his own property. Zoning has in effect split the rights traditionally associated with property ownership into two components. One set of rights is held by the personal owner and another set is held collectively. Although nominally the collective rights are public rights, for most practical purposes they can be considered the private rights of either the neighborhood or the community residents.

Since zoning was introduced, the rights held by the personal owner have been steadily diminished, and those held collectively have increased. If zoning evolution were to continue along these lines, the final result would be the creation of collective rights to control virtually all matters affecting the exterior parts of properties. In already built-up neighborhoods, the collective rights created by zoning would be virtually equivalent to private collective rights under existing condominium ownership. The biggest difference would be that zoning rights concerning the neighborhood environment—the "common elements" in the legal terms of condominium agreements—would be administered by local governments rather than by a private condominium association. In undeveloped areas lacking existing structures, if zoning evolution were to continue along its present path, local governments would end up holding almost all the development rights at a site. In many communities, this situation has already been reached, in that these communities currently possess almost complete discretion in accepting new development proposals.

The creation of collective property rights under zoning has caused two major types of problems. The first is that a wide gap has been established between the actual substance and consequences of zoning and its formal appearance and intellectual justifications. Zoning could never have been introduced if its actual purposes—at least as they have turned out in practice—had originally been explicitly spelled out. Zoning fictions such as the police-power purpose of protection of health, safety, and morals, or the purpose of providing an instrument for achieving public land-use plans, may thus once have served a practical function. They were necessary for the establishment of collective environmental protections that the majority of neighborhood and community residents clearly wanted. But zoning is now well established. The tortuous justifications that once were necessary for its introduction are no longer needed. Rather, because they obstruct a realistic appraisal of the tenure system and the needs for change in it and because they involve other liabilities, these justifications have become superfluous.

There is a large intellectual cost associated with the wide failure to understand the genuine issues of zoning. Critics of zoning contribute little by pointing out obvious discrepancies between the standard theories of zoning and actual zoning practices. For example, the employment of public powers for zoning's private purposes is often condemned. But public powers are also employed for private purposes in just this sense to defend private property rights. If zoning is recognized as itself a collective property right, the important issue becomes not the use of public powers, but whether defense of this particular collective property right serves society's purposes. On the other side of the debate, when under critical attack the proponents of zoning also waste much time in formulating contrived defenses of traditional zoning theories.

Within the legal system, the continued employment of zoning fictions is costly. Significant amounts of lawyer time and client money are taken up in constructing legal arguments that have become little more than formalities. The confidence of the average citizen in the legal process is diminished by the absence of persuasive justifications for zoning and of clear explanations for judicial decisions. Finally, communities are required to make significant expenditures solely to comply with the formal requirements of zoning law. The great waste of money in preparing comprehensive community land-use plans over the last few decades has been primarily a product of formal legal requirements.

Although zoning has largely provided the protections sought by neighborhood and community residents, zoning fictions have impeded satisfaction of public demands in certain respects. In many neighborhoods, the great majority of residents would prefer to have expanded collective control over minor features of the neighborhood environment, such as landscaping, house color, signs, and fencing. Evidence of this demand is seen in the comprehensive regulations commonly established in large private developments, and also in the current movement for creation of historic-district regulations. But, except in the limited circumstances where historic district controls can be justified, even if neighborhood residents want it, the courts have ruled that public regulation of minor details affecting only the aesthetic quality of the neighborhood environment is not permitted under the police-power purposes that are said to justify neighborhood zoning.

In addition to these difficulties associated with zoning fictions, the second major problem area of zoning has been its effect on transitions in land use. Since the evolution of capitalist economic systems, the primary method of transferring property from one user to another has been by its sale. As stated, zoning has split property rights into personal and collective parts, but adequate provision was never made for transfer of the zoning rights held by neighborhood and community residents. As a consequence, the transfer of zoning rights has proved very difficult and has very often occurred only under intense financial pressures for new land uses. The informal mechanisms that have evolved for transfer of zoning rights have worked in piecemeal fashion and have been the main reason for the poor coordination and unattractive visual quality of much development in the United States. Developer strong-arm tactics and even corruption of public officials have been required to bring about transfers of the zoning rights needed to allow development of new land uses.

The next two chapters describe a proposal for a new system of land tenure in metropolitan areas. The proposal does away with the fictions surrounding zoning; it also includes provisions to satisfy the demand for more comprehensive control over neighborhood quality than zoning has hitherto provided; most important, it suggests a new mechanism for the transfer of the collective property rights created by zoning.

Many aspects of the proposal for metropolitan areas explained in the next two chapters can be applied to the problems likely to be posed for the whole nation by new federal and state land-use controls. The regulatory roles played by neighborhoods and communities within metropolitan areas are similar in many respects to the roles of regions and states within the whole nation. However, federal and state controls are still so new that it is best to await more experience with them before taking up questions of major reform.

8 Basic Principles for a New Tenure System

The new system of metropolitan land tenure proposed here is based on principles for dealing with four critical issues: the socially desirable degree of protection of neighborhood quality and the best way to provide it, the same issues with respect to protection of the quality of community environments, the role of private competition for land in determining land use, and the role of planning in the system.

Private Tenures to Protect Neighborhood Quality

There is little question that some institution will be maintained to protect neighborhood quality. Without that protection, the incentive to maintain existing attractive neighborhoods and to establish new high-quality neighborhoods would be diminished, probably resulting in a significant decline in overall environmental quality. It is also consistent with American notions of fair play that those who establish and maintain desirable neighborhoods should be able to retain the benefits of their efforts. On a collective plane, the issue is similar to that of whether the acquirer of desirable personal possessions should be able to protect them from use by others. In the United States today, there is little question of an affirmative answer.

The primary issue with respect to protection of neighborhood quality is the institution through which it will be provided. Currently, although condominium ownership and private covenants in large developments protect the quality of many neighborhoods, zoning provides protection for the great majority of them. But the availability of private means for accomplishing zoning purposes suggests that perhaps direct public regulation of neighborhood quality is not needed. It is often pointed out that zoning is anomalous in that public regulations are being employed in defense of private property. Given those private purposes of neighborhood zoning, its protections might best be provided through private institutions.

This possibility has previously been suggested. Although it did not explore the idea further, the Douglas commission remarked:

Another [reform] approach would be to create forms of land tenure which would recognize the interest of owners in what their neighbors do. Such tenure forms, which do not exist but which might resemble condominium tenure, might more effectively reconcile the conflicting interests of neighboring property owners than do conventional regulations. The objective of such tenure would be to leave the small scale relationships among neighbors for resolution entirely within the private sector, while public regulation would continue to apply to the neighborhood as a whole. In addition to giving neighborhood residents greater control over minor land-use changes within their neighborhood, such tenure could include provision for cooperative maintenance of properties where owners desire such services. . . . [1]

In making this suggestion, the commission noted the greater flexibility of private institutions for resolving conflicts among property owners within neighborhoods. There are also other major advantages to private tenures. Creation of new private tenures to provide the neighborhood protection now provided by neighborhood zoning is a principle of the metropolitan tenure system proposed.

First, there is little reason for not giving administrative control over neighborhood protections to the group in whose interest these protections are exercised. The traditional role of local government—effectively that of trustee for the rights of neighborhood residents—has created much unnecessary uncertainty within neighborhoods concerning the security of their protections. To provide solid assurance against arbitrary or unwanted actions by local community officials, neighborhood residents have believed it necessary to employ rigid zoning controls based on fixed use classifications. The resulting provision of greater security of zoning administration, however, has been gained at the expense of other objectives. Because of the rigidity of traditional zoning, desirable properties of the wrong classification have been excluded from neighborhoods and undesirable properties of the right classification have had to be admitted. These problems could be solved if neighborhood residents had direct responsibility for administering discretionary protections of their neighborhood environment.

If one must rely on the traditional justifications for public controls over use of personal property, neighborhood zoning literally has no intellectually respectable justification. Although long explained as an exercise of police powers, most applications of zoning laws clearly have little to do with protection of health, safety, or morals. The police power can also be employed for protection of "general welfare." But that term in its broadest sense is so unrestrictive as to place almost no limits on government police-power activities. Hence, as matters now stand, it is impossible to justify neighborhood zoning protections in a way that also specifies clear and understandable limits on the use of police powers. This highly unsatisfactory situation can be remedied if zoning protections are instead provided under private tenures. Protection of private-property rights is a very old and easily understood and accepted use of public police powers.

Because of the impersonality of modern society and the many failings of large-scale organizations, a number of people have reached the conclusion in recent years that small-scale institutions, such as neighborhoods, should have a much greater social role.[2] In a recent book, *Neighborhood Power: The New Localism*, the authors go further and assert that a greater role for neighborhoods may be not only desirable but imperative:

Yet the neighborhoods, many of them, persist. It is the contention of this book, throughout, that they do not persist merely as fossils, as sentimental areas, or as fortresses of special interest or prejudice. Most persist, and all could be revived, for the simply practical reasons of making life livable and resolving problems which have remained untouched by the movement toward huge, dehumanized scale in social organization, . . .

Neighborhoods deserve and are getting new attention for supremely practical reasons. . . . It may be necessary to revive and live in neighborhoods or face the possibility of having no place else to go.[3]

To the extent that others find similar values in neighborhoods, they could help to meet major social needs. Probably the most effective way to create strong neighborhood ties is to provide for collective exercise by residents of controls over their neighborhood quality.

But the most important reason for substituting private tenures for zoning is the great need for a mechanism for sale of neighborhood zoning rights. When the purpose is solely protective, administration of zoning rights by local government works tolerably well. Neighborhood residents usually agree on the aims of zoning administration, and other parties are not much affected or concerned. Local officials generally act in a manner consistent with neighborhood wishes. But when the neighborhood enters a transitional phase, the agreement disappears. Zoning administrators are subject to intense developer pressures, to conflicting pressures from individual neighborhood residents, and sometimes even to large bribe offers. There are few guidelines for their administration of zoning. Among other problems, widespread corruption and unfairness to neighborhood residents have resulted.

The problem of transition in existing neighborhoods is likely to grow rather than diminish in the future. For several reasons, future new development may have to be built at considerably higher densities than has been the case since widespread automobile use was first introduced. Economically, it will not make sense to locate moderate- and high-density housing far out in suburban fringes that are removed from existing centers of activity. Hence, a substantial part of new higher-density development may well have to be located within and among already existing neighborhoods—if it is allowed to occur at all.

The pressures for higher-density housing will be strong. Rapidly rising housing prices are threatening to cut off access to new housing for a large part of the population. The best—and perhaps only—answer to rising housing costs is to build at higher densities, thereby saving on land and building-material expenses. A 1974 federal government-sponsored study, entitled *The Costs of Sprawl*, compared the costs of building one thousand representative single-family conventional homes with the costs of representative higher-density housing.[4] At 1973 prices, the cost of the residential structure (excluding land costs) was estimated to be $32,146 for a representative single-family conventional home (1,600 square feet of floor space). The same cost for a townhouse unit (1,200 square feet) was estimated to be $16,263; for a walk-up apartment unit (1,000 square feet) to be $11,766; and for a high-rise apartment unit (900 square feet) to be $15,188. With higher densities, large savings can also be achieved in utility and in street and road costs per housing unit. Taking all costs into account, the total expenses for building one thousand representative new single-family conventional homes were estimated to be $43,337 per unit; for townhouses $22,447 per unit; for walk-up apartments $16,492 per unit; and for high-rise apartments $18,847 per unit. Although these cost figures were calculated under an assumption of a certain representative quality of housing and location for it, other housing-quality levels and locations would almost certainly show similar relative cost variations with density.

Other basic social and economic factors are adding to the demand for higher-density housing. Past government support for highway construction was a primary cause of decentralized low-density metropolitan living in the United States. But the American love affair with the automobile has been showing signs of cooling, and other forms of transit are beginning to receive increased government support. The energy wastefulness of the automobile seems likely to be an important stimulus for more intensive land use. A study by Resources for the Future and the Regional Plan Association in New York found that consumption of energy per capita for transportation in areas on the fringes of the New York metropolitan region, where densities are low and the automobile is almost the sole means of transportation, is almost three times that of the much more dense central areas of New York City.[5] Environmental demands for more open-space preservation could be another stimulus to higher land-use intensities. Existing low-density housing patterns are extremely space consuming. Each individual may have considerable private space available to him on his own lot, but if the objective is preservation of substantial open spaces available to the entire community, higher metropolitan intensities of use would be helpful.

The problems of neighborhood transition are most acute when neighborhoods try to employ zoning to resist economic pressures that are the result of long-term trends. The basic trend of the 1970s, the causes of which precede the energy and environmental crises of recent years, is toward higher densities. With time and a rapidly growing population, even the vast territories opened up by the automobile are no longer adequate to meet the high standards for private living space that characterized past suburban development. There is a boundary beyond which, even with new highway construction, a metropolitan area cannot extend and still preserve reasonable accessibility at an acceptable cost to other parts of the metropolitan area. And, although in most urban areas there is still a great deal of vacant land available, metropolitan boundaries are beginning to seem constricting.

As generally happens when fixed resources become shorter in supply, the growing scarcity of good accessible land has caused land prices to climb rapidly. Responding to the pressure of rising land prices, builders are taking the logical step and building condominiums and other higher-density housing to save on land. With energy and environmental problems offering an added incentive, government is responding by providing support for express-bus lanes and other new mass transit facilities, which make increasing economic sense as land-use intensities become greater. The long-run public interest lies in seeing that these developments continue. But, unavoidably, in the process many neighborhoods will have to undergo basic transitions in use. An important national problem is how and when these— for the most part desirable—neighborhood transitions will occur.

To aid in making such decisions, a new mechanism for neighborhood transition is badly needed. It should have several key features. Changes in use that represent the onset of transition should not be permitted at all in a neighborhood until a formal collective determination has been made by neighborhood residents that transition should proceed. In making such a determination, residents should be able to balance their own desire to stay in and maintain their existing neighborhood environment against the broader social needs for use of neighborhood property. As a practical matter, these needs will be shown by the value of neighborhood properties in new uses and the prices that developers are willing to offer for them. Procedures should be employed to ensure that the financial benefits of neighborhood transition will be fairly distributed among residents, presumably allowing gains in some reasonable proportion to the value of personal property owned in the neighborhood.

One approach that meets these requirements is to provide a way to offer zoning rights in a neighborhood to the highest bidder. If neighborhood residents voted to accept the high bid, proceeds from the sale would be divided among neighborhood property owners according to the formula adopted for this purpose. A better approach might be to assemble all property rights in a neighborhood in a single package, including all the rights that are now both personally and collectively held, and to offer this package to the highest bidder. Under such a scheme, any prospective developer of a neighborhood could make an offer for all the property rights in the neighborhood. Neighborhood residents would then make a collective decision whether or not to accept the bid. If the bid is accepted, residents would vacate the whole neighborhood within some specified period of time. A 75 percent neighborhood vote—or even higher—could be required for the offer to be accepted and for neighborhood transition to proceed. By law the minority that voted against acceptance of an offer would still be required to abide by the majority decision. A mechanism for neighborhood transition of this kind would be modeled on existing procedures for sale of other collectively owned properties, such as private business corporations.

A more flexible approach would be to allow site-by-site sale of zoning changes within the neighborhood. In order for a developer to build, he would have to purchase both the collective rights from neighborhood residents and the personal rights from owners for specific neighborhood sites he needed. Thus, neighborhood residents would be protected from undesired uses as under existing zoning, but if they received a financial offer sufficient to compensate them for any unattractive features of a proposed new neighborhood use, they could sell their zoning rights to allow the use at the site proposed. In this way, residents would be compensated to their satisfaction, and those now outside the neighborhood who placed a high enough value on gaining entry would be able to do so.

Although this approach is much more flexible than allowing sale of zoning rights only for whole neighborhoods at a time, it has other disadvantages. Although residents of many neighborhoods might decide on their own not to allow piecemeal redevelopment, residents of other neighborhoods would not. These neighborhoods would experience transitions to new basic uses one or a few new uses at a time. Society as a whole may have an interest in seeing to it that new neighborhoods are more comprehensively planned (if usually by a private developer).

The problems of neighborhood governance would be simplified by the greater homogeneity that would result from a prohibition of neighborhood transition in piecemeal fashion. Neighborhood stability and citizen participation in its affairs would similarly be promoted by avoidance of piecemeal change. Finally, public planning for schools, highways, sewage facilities, and other public services would be aided by the greater visibility and advance notice of new development where it occurred whole neighborhoods at a time.

Thus, there is a tradeoff required between the increased flexibility of piecemeal neighborhood change and the greater planning and other advantages of basic changes in use for whole neighborhoods at a time. Different choices might be made in different circumstances. For example, greater flexibility would be more important in smaller cities where sufficient demand for new housing to create a whole new neighborhood would take some time to accumulate. Even in large cities, certain areas would be needed with flexibility to accommodate new and unexpected demands for residential and commercial uses on short notice. Nonetheless, under the metropolitan tenure system proposed here, for all except perhaps a few neighborhoods, the zoning rights would be sold only in packages of all the property rights in the neighborhood.

If reform approaches involving sale of zoning rights were thought too radical, a less drastic departure would be simply to allow neighborhood residents to vote on whether transition should proceed through conventional piecemeal zoning changes (without any payments for the changes). No zoning changes to accommodate substantially new uses would be permitted until a neighborhood vote to allow such changes had been made. However, this transitional mechanism would still produce a piecemeal pattern of neighborhood redevelopment. Moreover, little gain in flexibility would be achieved. Because the first new uses to come into a neighborhood would offer financial benefits only to the owners of the sites they would occupy, neighborhood residents would probably resist any change until long after they would have been willing to accept it with suitable financial compensation through sale of zoning.

In summary, the preferable mechanism for transfer of neighborhood zoning rights would require that these rights be exercised under new forms of private tenure. They could then be exchanged, as are other property rights, when the demander is willing to pay the price that the holder of the rights—in this case the group of neighborhood residents—wants.

Substitution of private tenure for zoning would no doubt revive some of the issues that proved highly controversial when zoning was first introduced. In existing neighborhoods, the introduction of zoning required a use of public authority to compel unwilling residents to surrender certain of what, up to then, had been their purely personal property rights. Legally, this was justified as a necessary protection of health, safety, or morals. But in creating private tenures, the fictional quality of traditional claims of health, safety, or morals purposes is conceded. Nevertheless, if private tenures are to replace zoning, there will be neighborhood residents who will be required to accept private collective authority against their will. Despite the fact that zoning does the same thing, this might prove controversial. The controversy could be especially heated in situations where most of the neighborhood residents want comprehensive controls over even minor aspects of neighborhood property that zoning has not traditionally regulated and that a few residents oppose.

The proposal for sale of zoning rights involves an explicit acknowledgment of the supremacy of collective rights. In practice, a personal-property owner has had little individual ability to influence the transition in his neighborhood. If nearby properties were changing through rezonings granted by local government, there was not much he could do. Eventually, the changes in the neighborhood would force him to move. In conducting a vote of neighborhood residents to decide whether to sell collective rights, however, a decision requiring an owner to leave his neighborhood is made by his fellow neighbors in binding and explicit terms. Given the traditional American dislike of collective controls, this explicit subordination of personal to collective rights will also prove controversial.

In short, creation of private tenures along the lines proposed here will require some people to shed their illusions. Under the existing system of land-use control, the personal-property owner is already subject to many collective basic decisions concerning use of his property. The way to improve the system is to provide better institutions for making these decisions. This cannot be accomplished without an explicit and, for some, probably painful acknowledgment of the degree to which, in modern urban areas, collective decisions control the disposition of personal property.

Returning Full Development Rights to the Owner

The issues of community zoning are similar in a number of ways to those of neighborhood zoning. The biggest difference is that, instead of relations among individual properties, community zoning regulates relations among developed and undeveloped neighborhoods. The first question is whether a lower- or moderate-income neighborhood should have a preferential right to locate in an undeveloped area that is available in a higher-income community. Should public policies be adopted to promote or require economic integration of communities?

Community economic integration would to some extent constitute a form of income redistribution in favor of the poor. Some redistribution would take place indirectly in kind (for the poor, better public services and a better physical and social environment; for the wealthy, probably somewhat poorer public services and a less desirable environment) and some redistribution directly in income (lower property-tax rates for the poor; higher rates for the wealthy). Hence, in this one aspect, policies for community economic integration should be examined as a possible element in an overall national income-redistribution effort.

A recent three-year congressional study of the nation's income-assistance programs stated that a lack of planning and coordination among many of them is causing overall public income assistance to be both inequitable and much less efficient than it could be:

Uncoordinated governance has produced uncoordinated programs, with gaps, overlaps, cross-purposes, inequities, administrative inefficiencies, work and family support disincentives, and waste of taxpayers' money. . . .
We have concluded that public welfare programs must be consolidated and simplified. Programs will continue to grow,

and this growth must be controlled rather than haphazard. Small-scale changes here and there could right some of the more egregious wrongs. But the fundamental problems cannot be solved either by incremental change or a laissez faire approach. Fair and equitable treatment of all groups must be provided; . . . and funds must be distributed efficiently.[6]

The study was particularly critical of in-kind assistance programs on the grounds that they were often inefficient because the poor could spend the money more effectively if given broad discretion in its use. In-kind assistance was also regarded as inequitable in itself: "[The] limited availability of in-kind benefits like housing, medicaid and child care has meant that other needy families could receive no help at all. So in-kind benefits have established new inequities."[7] The study concluded, "For these reasons, the subcommittee recommends that the Nation not rely primarily on an in-kind approach to raise the living standards of poor families."[8]

Publicly required economic integration of communities would have two disadvantages as part of the national income-redistribution effort. First, it would be very difficult to coordinate with other redistribution programs. And second, to a large extent, it would provide in-kind assistance in the form of better public services and a better environment for the poor and would thus have the normal disadvantages of all in-kind assistance. Public services and environmental amenities received in better-off communities may not be very appropriate for the poor. Rather than access to a municipal golf course, the poor might prefer to keep their share of its construction cost and instead buy some to them more essential item. And while some poor would have the good fortune to gain entry into desirable community environments, others would have to continue to live in much less desirable areas. Transfers of small or moderate amounts of income directly to all the poor might be much more equitable.

Policies requiring community economic integration might also be an inequitable way of taxing the rich. Some wealthy individuals would have to sacrifice much more than others similarly situated, depending on the community in which they reside. The problem could be overcome only if each wealthy community admitted an equal proportion of poor. But existing availability of vacant land, different demands from commercial users for available vacant land, different accessibilities to jobs for the poor, and various other factors would make it difficult to achieve an equitable distribution.

Partly because of problems of this nature, it would be difficult to prescribe a set of reasonable criteria for distinguishing acceptable from unacceptable community economic segregation. Few people would claim that all instances are unacceptable—for example, when a community is no more than a neighborhood. A possible basis for determining acceptability might be the size of the community; economically homogeneous communities of larger than some maximum permissible geographic or population size might be judged unacceptable. However, this would produce quite arbitrary results: simply by dividing a large community into two or more smaller ones, the identical land-use pattern could be transformed from unacceptable to acceptable. And if the distinction were a legal one, there would be a significant incentive for large, wealthy communities to break up into smaller ones. Should the better-off residents of a large community contribute to support of public services for the poor, while an equal number of equally well-off residents spread around in smaller communities make no such redistributive payments? A concentration of the poor in small communities would require their assessing only other poor for revenues to pay for public services, while poor sharing large communities with other better-off residents would benefit from a much richer tax base per resident.

A second approach sometimes suggested for increasing economic integration of communities would require that communities make space available for all—or a sizable proportion of—those people whose place of employment was located within the community. But a significant degree of arbitrariness would again be involved, and some perverse incentives created. Communities of various sizes and suitability for development having no employment within their boundaries would be totally unaffected. Other communities, without much regard for the relative adequacy of their tax base, for the availability of vacant land, or for other determinants of relative capacity to absorb new development, would have widely varying and rather arbitrary

amounts required of them. Considerable low- and moderate-
income employment is now located in older, more densely populated, already poorer communities. If the addition of new poor
residents were required, the result would further economic segregation. Finally, substantial incentives would be created for
communities to refuse low- and moderate-income employment,
perhaps preventing it from materializing at all, forcing it into
other metropolitan areas, or causing it to settle in a poorly situated metropolitan location with respect to accessibility and other
needs.

Nevertheless, despite problems of this sort, there are some
significant advantages to redistributing income by increasing
the economic integration of communities. Most programs to redistribute income encounter the difficulty that increasing
income-tax rates to pay for them may reduce taxpayer work
incentives and, eventually, overall economic productivity. By
taxing land and property holdings of better-off individuals,
as community economic integration partly does, this problem
is reduced. Another problem with many income-redistribution
programs is that benefits to the poor decrease as earned income
increases and this tends to reduce work incentives for the poor.
But economic integration of communities, so long as entry of
the poor is not specifically tied to earned incomes, would have
no such work-disincentive effects. (However, this feature also
causes inequities because some of the best-off poor would be
treated more favorably than some of the worst off.) Proponents
of direct income-assistance programs generally assume that the
poor will spend the income they receive wisely. To the extent
that this assumption is not accepted, in-kind assistance would
be regarded as preferable. Finally, the better off might be more
willing to see income redistribution accomplished through economic integration of communities than through other more direct methods, such as cash grants.

With respect to this last possibility, it must be said that
almost all the evidence points in the opposite direction. The
strong challenges to suburban zoning policies stimulated by the
sense of urban crisis of the mid and late 1960s have generally
had little success. So far, they have produced almost no low- or
moderate-income housing in predominantly upper- or upper-

middle-income suburban communities in the United States. On the other hand, while direct zoning reform has been minimal, substantial increases have occurred in recent years in direct income redistribution to the poor by federal and state governments. The congressional study noted above reported that total federal expenditures for income support and maintenance rose from $50.7 billion in 1968 to $107.7 billion in 1973. Expenditures for direct "need-based" income-assistance programs rose from $11.4 billion in 1968 to $26.8 billion in 1973.[9] Over a longer period, federal grants-in-aid to state and local governments, which have a significant redistributive impact, increased from $3.3 billion in 1956 to $38.1 billion in 1972.[10] Because of transfers of revenue to them, local governments had available total revenues of $124.6 billion in 1974, although only $71.8 billion was raised from local sources.

The rapid past increases in expenditures for income redistribution combined with the simultaneous intense resistance to economic integration of communities provides a good indication of the current preferences of the American public. These simultaneous trends seem to say that there is wide support for policies to redistribute income but that the public also values a homogeneous living environment and would prefer that redistribution be achieved by means other than close residential integration of different income groups. In part, the strong support for federal and state redistributive programs of recent years may even have been designed as compensation for the adverse income-distribution consequences of trends toward greater economic segregation of living patterns.

In short, the case for economic integration of communities solely as a means of income redistribution is not a compelling one. The remaining reason for public policies to bring about economic integration is the view that integration is socially desirable for its own sake. While this view was widely accepted not long ago, support for it has been massively eroded in recent years. Community homogeneity—economic and in other, except racial, ways—offers major benefits that have begun to receive greater acknowledgment in recent years. A program aimed at increasing economic integration for its own sake would today have very little chance of broad acceptance.

These considerations suggest that economic integration of communities should not be a primary objective in a new tenure system. But this conclusion does not imply that major changes are not needed in community zoning. To the contrary, community zoning has had such a destructive influence on metropolitan land use that it calls for the strongest corrective actions.

The greatest problem of community zoning lies not in the objective of a homogeneous community but in the transitional means that many communities have adopted to achieve this end. Communities have very often held large supplies of land idle or in a relatively low-value use while waiting long periods for high-quality development to be proposed in accordance with their ultimate community design. The cumulative consequence of community zoning in a metropolitan area is a public rationing system for undeveloped metropolitan land. Under this system, a fixed total supply of metropolitan land is available for each type of use.

Because of community zoning practices, the supply of metropolitan land made available for high-quality uses has tended far to exceed the demand for these uses, and the supply of land made available for lower-quality uses to be far less than the demand for them. These large imbalances between supplies and demands have caused very serious social inequities and major inefficiencies in the use of metropolitan land.

Several courts have focused on precisely this problem in ruling against community zoning practices. The Pennsylvania Supreme Court ruled in 1965 against four-acre minimum-lot-size zoning in Easttown Township because of the immediate critical need to use Easttown's lands to meet metropolitan housing demands. In its widely noted 1975 decision, the New Jersey Supreme Court took a similar line of reasoning in declaring that the zoning ordinance of Mount Laurel Township violated the state constitution.[11] The court emphasized that Mount Laurel —which covers an area of twenty-two square miles—is a community in transition on the Philadelphia metropolitan fringe and that its decision applied particularly to such developing communities. Like many other communities, Mount Laurel had zoned substantial land areas for low-density and industrial uses considered beneficial for the community by its residents (in this particular case mainly for fiscal reasons). The court noted that in these areas there was no demand in sight for the uses allowed:

Akin to large lot, single-family zoning restricting the population is the zoning of very large amounts of land for industrial and related uses. Mount Laurel has set aside almost 30 percent of its area, over 4,100 acres, for that purpose; the only residential use allowed is for farm dwellings. In almost a decade only about 100 acres have been developed industrially. Despite the township's strategic location for motor transportation purposes, as intimated earlier, it seems plain that the likelihood of anywhere near the whole of the zoned area being used for the intended purpose in the foreseeable future is remote indeed and that an unreasonable amount of land has thereby been removed from possible residential development, again seemingly for local fiscal reasons.[12]

The basic conclusion of the New Jersey Supreme Court was that communities such as Mount Laurel could not hold such large areas of land idle or in farming for long periods, zoned for uses for which no significant demand was soon likely to materialize. Instead, land had to be regularly made available somewhere in the community for all the kinds of housing for which an immediate demand already existed.

The basic source of community-zoning inefficiency and inequity has been discussed: zoning separates property rights into personal and collective parts. Community zoning is primarily concerned with undeveloped areas and transfers to the community a major part of the development rights in these areas, but the community cannot legally sell its development rights. If certain development rights are transferred to a private builder through a zoning change, any legally authorized payment must go to the personal-property owner. The community incentive in such a situation is clear-cut. With little or nothing to gain, and often much to lose, many communities are reluctant to permit transfer of their development rights; they choose rather to hold on to them for long periods.

For any economically valuable item, a policy that grants property rights to one party and the right to receive payment for transfer of the rights to another party is certain to be a continuing source of serious difficulties. The best method for solving the problem is to reunite these two traditionally inseparable aspects of property ownership. In the case of zoning, one way to accomplish this would be to grant communities the authority to sell their development rights held under zoning. If communities could sell transfers of these rights—i.e., sell zoning changes—they would be far more disposed to make land available for development than they are at present. To avoid raising property taxes, or meet other financial demands, many communities would no doubt happily choose to sell some changes in zoning if they were allowed to do so.

But such a policy would amount to the outright expropriation of part of the personal owner's property. Because this might well be unconstitutional, as well as morally questionable, granting communities the authority to sell zoning changes, even though much preferable to the existing situation, does not seem to be the best solution.

Zoning was not at first intended for, and was not originally applied to, undeveloped areas. Community zoning of such areas became established practice only a number of years after zoning was introduced and after a series of court rulings had determined its legality. In hindsight, court acceptance of community zoning was a mistake. The problems of community zoning can best be resolved by returning the development rights held by the community under zoning to the original personal owner. In other words, the practice of community zoning of undeveloped areas—the essence of community zoning—should be abolished. If any collective land-use controls are exerted in undeveloped areas, these controls should be exercised by property owners in the areas under private neighborhood tenures as described above. In addition, the procedures described above for neighborhood transition should apply in undeveloped as well as developed neighborhoods. (In an entirely undeveloped area, the sole purpose of a private collective organization for a neighborhood would be to make transitional decisions.) The elimination of community zoning is a second principle of the proposed new system of metropolitan land tenure.

Determining Land Use by Private Competition

Land use can be determined in three ways: by the verdict of private competition for land, by public regulation, or by direct public assumption of building responsibilities. Among land-use experts, it has been the conventional wisdom that greater public control of land use is much needed. This control is to be accomplished mainly by regulation of private activities, but also to some extent by direct assumption of building responsibilities. The justification usually offered by proponents of greater public control has hardly varied for at least the past sixty years. In 1916, the committee that was responsible for establishing zoning in New York City argued in terms that could serve very well for the 1970s:

New York City has certainly reached a point beyond which continued unplanned growth cannot take place without inviting social and economic disaster. It is too big a city, the social and economic interests involved are too great to permit the continuance of the laissez faire methods of earlier days. . . . [13]

Despite the wide acceptance of such views, our analysis indicates that the truth of the matter is closer to the opposite. Public control of land use has worked so poorly that it has had to be regularly subverted by developer political intrigues, corruption, and other unsavory practices. The failure to eliminate these very widespread and widely recognized practices over fifty or more years must have reflected a considerable degree of tacit acknowledgment that they have served necessary functions. Where public controls have not been undermined by these devices, the results have often been very unhappy. A system of public rationing of metropolitan land supplies that is totally out of line with demands has produced major inefficiencies in land use and large social inequities.

One might point to zoning protection of the environmental quality of neighborhoods as an area in which public control has generally been well received. But the success of zoning in protecting neighborhood quality has been that of creating a collective property right. This property right provides an incentive to establish and maintain high-quality neighborhood environments through private efforts. In short, the success of neighborhood zoning is not that it has established public control of land use, but that it has created a new property-right institution to improve the workings of private incentives.

The greatest hope of those who have advocated strong public

controls has not been the protection of existing environments but the planning of new development to improve its quality. It is precisely in this area that public controls have failed almost completely. The severest deficiencies of zoning have involved its effects on transitions in land use. The biggest problem of transition has been that zoning has transferred important property rights to public agencies without making adequate provision for later retransfer of these rights to builders or other parties to allow development. Clearly, private incentives cannot be expected to produce satisfactory results when key property rights are removed altogether from the system of exchange. The greatest problems of new development in the United States are thus to a significant extent caused by just those public controls that have been established to improve its quality.

The long persistence of strong support for greater public control over land use and for a diminished role for private competition for land has several explanations. Clearly, one factor is the desire of many people—often upper-middle-class and politically influential people—who occupy or currently have special access to high-quality environments to reserve these environments for their future benefit. A less selfish concern of many people is that land use is too important to be determined by private profit motives. In this view, the public interest will generally be better served through controls administered by public officials than by reliance on private decisions based on self-interested profit motives.

But public officials themselves have their own private motives, and the political system exerts certain types of pressures on public decision makers. The history of public regulation in the United States shows a frequent reformer naiveté in assuming that public controls, once created, will be administered in the widest public interest. Political pressures have consistently produced land-use regulatory decisions—made mostly by local legislatures—with at least three general types of major deviations from the broad public interest: as would be expected, regulators have placed the interest of their own constituency above that of outsiders, even when the benefits to be gained by the latter might be much greater; regulators have shown a tendency to favor concentrated—and therefore usually better organized—interests against a greater public interest diffused among a large number of people each with a small individual stake; and regulators have shown a frequent willingness to sacrifice greater long-term benefits to avoid lesser short-term pains. To the extent that market mechanisms work as they are supposed to and maximizing profits furthers the broadest social welfare, private profit calculations are superior to publicly made decisions in each of these three respects.

Many of those who favor greater public controls are convinced that the overall coordination and quality of land use in metropolitan areas will be greatly improved by much greater use of comprehensive planning. In this view, strong public controls are required to achieve the goal of widespread implementation of public land-use plans.

But despite an enormous amount of literature and discussion, there still does not exist an adequate intellectual foundation for comprehensive land-use planning. Although years of effort and large public expenditures have been devoted to the preparation of plans, very few of them have ever been followed. The current optimism that there will be improvements in this respect in all likelihood only mirrors similar expectations for improvement in the past. The chronic failures of land-use planning efforts are strong evidence that there has been something fundamentally amiss in the thinking on which these efforts have been based.

The greatest problem is probably that comprehensive land-use planning, at least as it has been proposed in the United States, is incompatible with democratic processes. In fact, planning was very explicitly intended by its early proponents to take the place of political decision making for many areas of government activity. The idea was to avoid the many failings of the political process by removing key decisions from this process and putting them in the hands of technical experts, i.e., planners. For example, reflecting a general attitude of the time, one 1931 study of the Department of Commerce commented:

Planning should be designed to cover a long period of years, much longer than the term of office of any single city council. Legislation on the other hand is designed to meet pressing and immediate needs. . . . Although the two functions, planning and legislation, are both important, and essential to the efficient working of city government, yet they are quite different from each other and involve different considerations, differing points of view and different talents and interests. The two functions, therefore, need to be reposed in two separate bodies.[14]

For a number of government responsibilities, it makes good sense for professionals to decide how to carry them out. This is virtually inescapable for medical, engineering, and other activities that depend on knowledge of the physical sciences, or for other duties that similarly rely on specialized knowledge. But such responsibilities typically are fairly narrow. In contrast, land use reflects the basic qualities of a society and is significantly influenced by a number of important government policies, including transportation, housing, taxation, poverty, and environmental policies. To have given responsibility for determining land use to a particular profession would have been to give a small, not necessarily very representative group responsibility for basic decisions involving the nature of the whole society. This has never proved acceptable to most Americans.

The faith in the very broad applicability of scientific and technical expertise that was an essential element in the intellectual foundations of early land-use planning theory was characteristic of the decades just before and after World War II. That faith has lost much of its credibility by now, however, and most current planning proponents reject the anti-democratic elements of planning theory. In fact, planning has moved far in the opposite direction. Public land-use plans now are prepared with extensive public comments, meetings, and other forms of popular participation. Rather than a means of avoiding democratic processes, public planning is to be a principal instrument for implementing the popular will.

Although not much recognized, this trend toward wide public participation casts formal land-use planning in an essentially new role. Planning originally was to be a means of centrally coordinating land use. At least in theory, planning experts were to determine regional objectives and then to take the steps necessary to achieve them. Once established, the regional land-use plan was to be closely followed throughout the area and closely reflected in the plans of individual communities. But, under recent democratic trends, the common role of planning is to impede central coordination. Coordination of economic activities across large areas traditionally has been accomplished by market mechanisms. The functioning of market mechanisms is increasingly frustrated in the name of planning. However, no central planning authority exists or is being created to make up for the loss of market coordination. Rather, plans are to reflect state and local interests as interpreted by the citizens in these areas.

There has been a long tradition in the United States of local responsibility for land-use controls and of wide discretion in exercising that responsibility. Yet, there is also a clear need for regional and, beyond that, national coordination of land use. If development is to be coordinated over very wide areas, yet decision-making responsibility is to be both decentralized and highly discretionary, there is only one approach that seems feasible. It is necessary to structure the incentives faced by decentralized decision makers so that their decisions will advance the widest public interest. Under market mechanisms, decisions are decentralized and highly discretionary—left to the private developer—but the system is designed so that profit incentives will tend to produce decisions in the widest public benefit. While private-developer incentives have had many unsatisfactory consequences for land use, on the whole, land-market mechanisms have exhibited this tendency. By contrast, if decentralized and highly discretionary decisions are made publicly, the only assurance of actions in the broader public interest lies in the public spirit of the decentralized decision makers. As one would expect, and as experience of local zoning has very amply demonstrated, this is not a very adequate assurance.

Because of such considerations, a third key principle of the proposed metropolitan tenure system is that the verdict of private competition for land should be the basic determinant of land use. In this way, responsibilities can remain highly decentralized and discretionary, but central coordination can still be maintained, and national and other broad public needs adequately met.

Determination of land use by private competition would doubtless work poorly if all public controls were suddenly removed. New institutions are needed more closely to align private incentives with broad public objectives. The most critical need is to create instruments for land assembly in order to promote and facilitate development at neighborhood scale. In this way, the private developer determines the land use that will maximize the value of the entire neighborhood. His private incentive will ensure that the neighborhood is well planned and coordinated and that open spaces and other amenities that residents want are included. Large-scale development also offers other benefits. Among them, it allows economies of scale in installing public facilities, and it encourages fairer treatment of existing property owners during neighborhood transition to a new use.

The basic features of the needed instrument for land assembly were described earlier in this chapter. If private tenures were to replace neighborhood zoning, the collective private-property rights created in place of zoning could be sold, as ordinary private-property rights are now. By combining all neighborhood personal rights with collective rights in a single package, all the rights needed for development of a whole neighborhood could be assembled and sold to the highest bidder.

Besides a new mechanism for land assembly, additional institutional changes are needed to bring private incentives into closer alignment with social objectives. One of the most critical is to charge new development the full cost it incurs for installation of sewer, water, road, and other public facilities (except, perhaps, for schools). Currently, new development often pays significantly less than the public facility cost it generates. There is little justification for such subsidy; it simply creates an incentive for projects with large publicly paid elements. For example, new suburban construction would be favored, because many of the costs involve public infrastructure, while rehabilitation of existing properties would be at a disadvantage, because almost all costs are private. Residents of communities in developing areas rightly object to higher local property-tax payments that amount to subsidies for new development in their community. If all new development is charged its full public-facility-installation costs, public controls over the timing of development will not be needed. Developers will not engage in unwarranted "leapfrogging," and other activities that unnecessarily boost public-service-installation costs, if it is at their own expense.

On the other hand, it should also be recognized that a certain amount of vacant land within developed areas, and leapfrogging over such land, is not only unavoidable but desirable. Many past discussions of suburban development patterns have dwelt at length on their scattered quality and high public infrastructure costs, and scarcely seemed to recognize that there can also be major long-run benefits deriving from these same features.

To see how such benefits can occur, consider a metropolitan area experiencing fairly rapid growth. On the assumption that today's population and other characteristics will remain the same, a comprehensive metropolitan plan could be prepared for current circumstances. A second comprehensive plan could also be prepared for the year 2000, this one based on the assumption that metropolitan population and other characteristics expected in 2000 would remain the same thereafter. These two plans would obviously differ substantially. Because it had to accommodate a great deal of growth, the plan for the year 2000 would show the boundaries of the metropolitan area much extended. In many cases, roads, shopping districts, residential areas, and other land uses would be located in different places.

For the sake of discussion, assume that metropolitan development were being completely planned and controlled by a public agency. One might then ask which plan the agency should follow. Clearly it would not make sense to follow either. If the plan based solely on current circumstances were followed, residential properties might surround a site where a major highway interchange would be built by the year 2000 that would offer prime sites for high-value commercial facilities. Low-density housing might be built fairly close to the center at sites that, in 2000, would be much needed for high-density housing, possibly for low-income people. Generally, if uses were located solely to meet present demands most effectively, without considering future changes in needs, the result later on would tend to be a jumble of uses. As essential needs had to be accommodated, they would have to be located at many sites already occupied by different—often to some extent incompatible—current uses.

Rigidly following the plan prepared for the circumstances of the year 2000 would be even worse. Some types of uses might best be located on the metropolitan fringe in 2000, but to locate them there now would require a large leap beyond existing development and would thus require expensive and currently unnecessary infrastructure installation. Leaving other sites that are close to the center vacant in order to save them for the most appropriate uses for 2000 would be wasteful of scarce land. Generally, if the plan ideal for the year 2000 were rigidly followed, areas would only be filled in gradually, and, in the meantime, uses installed according to this plan would tend to be scattered amidst much vacant land. The overall result would be a great deal of leapfrogging of development over vacant areas and scattered development in the years up to 2000.

It is obvious that neither planning solely for current circumstances nor planning solely for the circumstances of the year 2000 (or any other future year) is the way to proceed. Rather, there must be a complicated attempt to balance competing social objectives to avoid losses due to installation of current uses that with changing circumstances will inevitably become inappropriate to their sites and to avoid losses due to leaving valuable land currently undeveloped or in a low-value use in order to keep it available for the most appropriate use expected at some point in the future.

It is indicative of the past large gulf between professional planning and actual land-use decision making that the question of how to accomplish this critical balancing has not received much attention in formal planning literature. In practice, land-market mechanisms have provided answers on a regular basis —even if not altogether satisfactory ones—through land speculation. Although much decried, land speculation actually serves a useful, and in fact necessary, social function. The speculator performs essentially the balancing just described. He must calculate whether, if he holds his land undeveloped, the increase in value over time as new future uses become appropriate will justify the losses he must take right now because he does not put the land to its most valuable current use. In making this calculation, the speculator takes into account the degree of his preference for returns sooner rather than later (through his choice of discount rate) and the various uses of his land that he expects will be demanded at future times and their expected values. These are essentially the same calculations that a central planner would have to make for sites throughout a metropolitan area in deciding how to compromise the various conflicting plans that he might prepare for the circumstances of various times in the future.

If speculation has sometimes had unhappy results, including excessive leapfrogging over vacant land and wide scattering of development, the biggest culprit has been the improper pricing of public services. Because developers have not borne the costs of public-facility installation, they have typically had little incentive to select locations that would economize on public costs. If this failing were corrected, a new problem might arise—that of excessively compact development patterns. If discount rates of private speculators are substantially higher than society's discount rate, as seems likely, speculators will tend to release land for development too early in order to obtain a high current return. Society might prefer to hold a site out of development a while longer, until a still higher-value use anticipated for the future could be located there. (It is sometimes similarly argued that energy resources are being exhausted too rapidly because private suppliers with high discount rates are not willing based on their private incentives to hold energy sources out of production as long as is socially justified.)

To give an example of how market forces can effectively balance competing current and future social needs, consider the matter of forming homogeneous communities. Homogeneous communities offer some significant benefits, but these benefits clearly are not so great as to justify every sacrifice. In the typical pattern of suburban growth, a certain number of well-off residents have been the first to move into newly developing suburban communities. To keep the community homogeneous, they have then zoned the rest of the land—which is still basically undeveloped—for uses that would maintain the desired homogeneity. Because these newcomers do not own this land, they have little or nothing to lose from requiring it to be left undeveloped for as long a time as they see fit. The end result is large blocks of valuable suburban land wastefully held idle while awaiting uses for which there will be no demand for some time.

Suppose, however, that the well-off newcomers in the same

suburban community were required to decide whether to float a bond issue and buy—instead of merely zone—the remaining land in the community. They would then have had to make a careful balancing of competing current and future needs. They would have to ask whether the goal of a homogeneous community was worth enough to justify the interest on the bonds and any other costs to them of holding the land idle for a considerable period while waiting for the preferred homogeneous use to materialize. In this way, by employing a market mechanism, a reasonable balance between society's need for land for current development and the desire of well-off residents to form a homogeneous community could be attained.

Generally, under the tenure system proposed, questions of the proper rate of growth or the timing of development would be answered through market balancing of competing current and future needs. But to avoid the serious problems of piecemeal land development, decisions to develop or not to develop currently would have to be made for entire neighborhood-size areas. Typically, there would be a number of owners of land within these areas. They would be required to choose between current and future development values—in effect, to speculate —collectively.

The Role of Planning

Although there would be little place for comprehensive public land-use planning under the tenure system proposed, any system requires some kind of planning, and this one would be no exception. However, if the verdict of private competition for land is to be the primary determinant of land use, then the role to be played by planning must be substantially rethought.

The average citizen finds it hard to understand planning issues because he is unfamiliar with important institutional details and intellectual debates of land-use policy. He is also too often impressed by the claims to professionalism of the planners. But there is a strong similarity between the problems of planning for an individual's future and for a community's (or city's or nation's) future. The lack of influence of formal comprehensive planning and the potential roles for future planning efforts should be more understandable if they are explained by analogy with the role of personal planning in an individual's management of his life.

A comprehensive personal twenty-year plan—prepared, for example, by a college student—might try to lay out his future education and career, when he hoped to marry, what kind of person, how many children, where he would like to live, where and how much he would like to travel, and other such matters. The college student could conceivably even seek the expert aid of a professional "life planner"—knowledgeable about the job market and experienced in personal counseling—who could be responsible for formulating his twenty-year plan.

While such a formal long-range plan would have its uses, few people would regard preparing one as being of much value —certainly not in its details. After a year or two, too many unexpected developments would probably have occurred—illness, unforeseen job opportunities, unexpected financial successes or failures—causing substantial changes in plan. After several years, so many assumptions of a long-range personal plan would probably have proved mistaken that the plan would be altogether obsolete. In addition, a formal planning document might never have contained the basic substance of personal hopes and expectations in the first place. Some personal goals might conflict in ways difficult to face, with rationalizations employed to cover over the conflict until an actual action had to be taken. Some of our most important personal objectives may be partially subconscious, or even consciously denied. Even if the individual has a good sense of his own objectives, with the best of intentions, he may not be able to articulate them either to himself or to a professional "life planner" for inclusion into a formal document. Finally, because no plan can cover all eventualities in detail, a formal planning document is likely to contain a variety of hidden implications that an individual does not recognize and that may in fact be inconsistent with his actual personal goals.

Largely because of such considerations, most people do not try to prepare comprehensive long-range life plans. People do, however, make many other kinds of plans. They plan short-term actions for the next few hours, or days; medium-term activities, such as vacation travel or Christmas shopping; longer-term steps, such as buying a house, deciding their education, their marriage partner, when to have children, and so forth.

A critical feature of longer-range planning is that it is focused around specific actions—education, marriage, children—which by their nature unavoidably exert a great influence on the future. In much the same way, actual metropolitan plans—as opposed to formal, comprehensive planning documents—are exhibited in connection with certain specific actions taken that exert a great influence on the future land-use pattern of the metropolitan area. In particular, the transportation system is the primary determinant of metropolitan land-use patterns. Any comparison of differences between older cities, such as New York, Chicago, and Philadelphia, and newer cities, such as Los Angeles, Houston, or Miami, reveals the huge impact of the highway and the automobile.

Neighborhood planning fits the traditional concept of land-use planning much better than metropolitan planning does, in that a comprehensive blueprint of future uses can be a useful product. Unlike the metropolitan area as a whole, the much smaller-scale, and smaller number of, interrelationships among uses make it feasible to construct comprehensive neighborhood maps with a reasonable chance of their being realized. (In this respect, neighborhood planning is similar to an individual's planning a two-week vacation trip, while metropolitan planning is similar to a personal twenty- or thirty-year plan.)

However, the fact that formal neighborhood planning can be worthwhile does not mean that plans for neighborhoods should be publicly prepared. Rather, under the proposal for a new tenure system made here, a large expansion of private neighborhood planning efforts would be called for. To meet this need, perhaps some of the resources now engaged in formal public planning could be shifted to the private sector.

But even though most neighborhood planning is, in this proposal, left to the private sector, there would still be major roles for public planning. Planning is most effective when focused on specific actions that require decisions. One important responsibility of the planner should be the design of the transportation system. Public planning would also be required to design the institutions of land tenure. The terms of collective-ownership agreements in neighborhoods, voting mechanisms, and other such tenure matters would have to be carefully designed and their operation monitored, especially to ensure against misrepresentation and fraud. The basic responsibilities for public planning should be met by state governments.

From Tocqueville on, many social critics have commented that the judicial branch of government in the United States assumes responsibilities that in almost any other nation would be borne by the legislative or executive branch. In some important respects, the planning role proposed here for state governments would take over responsibilities that are now lodged in the courts. As a practical matter, the courts have had a major planning function—perhaps *the* major function—for the system of land-use regulation in the United States. The courts first determined that zoning could become a fixture of American land tenure, and since then they have closely controlled the division of property rights between the personal-property owner and collective agencies. In allocating property rights among contending parties, the courts have had very little legislative guidance and thus have been given broad discretion to set their own policies.

The policy of the courts has generally been to avoid interfering in community zoning; in this sense, one could say that the courts have not played an active role in the system of land-use regulation. But the courts have had all the powers needed—including the necessary legal arguments if they wanted to use them—to change community zoning practices. Nevertheless, they have chosen not to. As a result, they have effectively determined that the community would hold a large share of the development rights to undeveloped land. This policy has had very important and undesirable consequences for metropolitan land use.

There are some significant advantages in the courts' playing a major planning role. The courts have provided a forum in which debate on land-use issues could be fairly conducted and decisions made by judges considerably removed from day-to-day financial and political pressures. (A principal reason for creating formal planning institutions had originally been to provide such a forum, made up of distinguished local citizens with indepen-

dent powers to supervise government conduct.) The structure of
state court review of local court decisions—and also potential-
ly federal court review of state court decisions—has provided
much needed lines of authority in land-use decision making
that have been lacking in the executive and legislative branches.
But the court's planning role has also involved major liabilities.
The formal structure of the law was not designed for determining basic policies, and even occasionally administering them, as
the courts have had to do in the area of land-use regulation. The
formalities of legal processes and reasoning can sometimes lead
to decisions that are far out of touch with basic economic and
social needs. The courts are forced to rely on litigants to develop
much of the information needed for decision making. In some
cases, neither of the contending parties has the resources or skill
to generate such information. The courts also have extensive
powers to prohibit, but little ability to create. When actions to
create new institutions are needed, as they are at the present
time with respect to means of land-use control, the courts face
many difficulties in designing and bringing them about.

Finally, as with the role long proposed for planners in community
planning commissions, the court planning role is essentially
undemocratic. Where special expertise is genuinely needed, or
where a decision maker can reasonably be regarded as neutral,
decisions by an impartial authority removed from political pressures of the legislative or executive branch may be appropriate.
But land-use issues are inherently highly political. The judiciary
is made up predominantly of men from the upper middle class,
who as a group have been the greatest beneficiaries of zoning.
Thus, even if he is not influenced by the fact, a judge very often
has a personal stake in decisions involving zoning. Consider the
explanation given in 1926 by the Chicago *Journal of Commerce*
for the Supreme Court's approval of zoning that year:

The Justices do their work in Washington. Most of them live
within the city limits. As they hold office for life, they regard
the place of their work as their permanent home. Many of them
own homes within the city and Washington has zoning . . . and
Washington is benefited by zoning.[15]

Similarly, it is very unlikely that consistent court support for
community zoning practices over many years is altogether unre-

lated to the fact that a large number of judges have lived in the attractive suburban communities benefiting most from them.

For these reasons, although it involves the considerable risk of introducing decisions that are too heavily politicized, the current major court role in the system of land tenure should be diminished, and a number of court responsibilities lodged within the state executive branch.

A Summary of Basic Principles

The basic principles for the proposed system of metropolitan land tenure are:

1. Private-tenure institutions resembling condominium ownership should be developed to replace neighborhood zoning in protecting neighborhood quality. These institutions would formally establish collective property rights to control matters affecting the neighborhood residents. When financial gains from a change in the type of neighborhood use became large enough to make it worth moving out, the neighborhood residents would determine as a group when and on what terms to make way for the new use.

2. Community zoning should be abolished. Communities should no longer hold most of the development rights to undeveloped land without possessing the ability to sell them. Unless the community is willing to purchase the land or its development rights outright, the full rights to use of undeveloped land should be returned to the private sector.

3. The verdict of private competition for land should be the primary determinant of future neighborhood use. To make this reliance on competition most effective, development should take place at full neighborhood scale to the maximum extent possible. To facilitate large-scale development, the tenure instruments for ownership of existing neighborhood property and land in undeveloped areas should allow basic changes in use only with transfer in one package of all the rights for a future new neighborhood to a single developer. To align private incentives more closely with social objectives, developers should be charged the full public-service costs of development, but no more than that.

4. Planning of neighborhoods should be carried out in the private sector, just as the architectural design of buildings is already. Public land-use planning—mainly at the state level —should be concerned with the installation of transportation and other public facilities, and design and operation of the legal framework for tenure instruments.

9 Steps in the Right Direction

Evolution in land tenure has typically been a process of gradual change, one of small steps at a time. Attempts to make radical shifts in direction have seldom succeeded. In recent years, a number of actions have been initiated or proposals made in the United States that are consistent with the basic principles for a new tenure system described above. Further steps in these directions ought to be encouraged.

Collective Neighborhood Tenures

There is a considerable history in the United States of collective property ownership on which to base new neighborhood tenures. A "homeowners association" is reported to have been formed in Boston as early as 1844; under it the property owners surrounding Louisburg Square maintain it as common property. Homeowner associations have been employed in recent years for the ownership of common areas in many large private developments.[1] The buyer of a home in such a development also becomes a member of the homeowners association—in most cases automatically. The association holds the actual title to the development common areas and assesses fees to provide for maintenance and other needs. It may also enforce architectural standards previously agreed to by covenant.

Collective property ownership in a condominium is in many ways similar to that under a homeowners association.[2] Legally, however, the condominium-unit owners are the direct owners of common areas. The condominium association is the administrative agent for the unit owners. The association assesses fees and regulates use of common areas, but does not, as it would in a homeowners association, hold legal title to the common areas. Condominium ownership is much more recent than the homeowner association, with the first state enabling legislation passed in 1961. By 1975, however, more than one million condominium units had been constructed.[3]

Collective property ownership in a cooperative differs substantially from either the homeowner association or condominium ownership. Legally, almost all cooperatives are corporations in which the unit occupants are stockholders or members. The cooperative corporation holds full title to all the property, and the stockholders or members receive from it exclusive rights to use of their personal unit. For several reasons, including the problem of large shared liabilities, even though of earlier origin, cooperative ownership has been largely eclipsed in recent years by condominium ownership as a means of holding collective property.

A public means increasingly being employed to establish collective property rights in a neighborhood is the creation of a historic or other special district. New York City now has more than twenty-five historic districts. In 1975, in the Boston suburbs alone, enactment of new historic-district ordinances was under consideration in ten communities. The new Model Land Development Code of the American Law Institute would encourage wider establishment of historic and other special districts.

Historic districts generally have the rights of control over even very minor changes in property that could affect neighborhood quality and appearance. Some public squares or other public areas in the district can also be included under historic-district regulation, analogous to common areas in private developments. As with zoning generally, the most distinctive feature of the historic district, as compared with private collective ownerships, is the means of establishing it and of administering the rights it holds. What is particularly important is that historic or other special districts offer the only practical means now available for establishing broad collective property rights in existing developed areas that already contain many individual properties under separate ownership.

Current trends toward greater collective possession of important neighborhood property rights could be significantly stimulated by the creation of a new, more satisfactory neighborhood tenure. Protection of neighborhood quality ought to be provided under private tenures. A new private tenure instrument—the neighborhood association—is proposed here for that purpose. The legal status of the neighborhood association would resemble in certain respects each of the already existing forms of collective property ownership. While extensive research would be required to specify the precise legal terms for neighborhood associations, the basic features can be described.

Under zoning, the local government effectively holds the rights to control new uses and major changes in property in a neighborhood. Under the tenure proposed, the zoning rights would instead be held directly by the neighborhood association. Hence, where a neighborhood association was formed, the first step would be to transfer to it the existing zoning rights now held by the local government. Or, alternatively, as a legal distinction, the zoning rights could be transferred directly to the residents themselves, with the neighborhood association only exercising those rights. While there would be little practical difference, legally these two alternative means of holding collective property rights would correspond either to the homeowners association or to the condominium model.

It would be necessary to establish boundaries for the neighborhood associations in some fashion. Under one approach, they could simply be imposed by fiat of the local government. It would seem preferable, however, for residents of large areas to try to work out among themselves a division into various neighborhoods. This might be accomplished by provisions that groups of residents within a contiguous area who desired to create a neighborhood association could propose to do so. After public approval of the proposed boundaries and other arrangements, the zoning rights in the area would be transferred to the neighborhood association.

The process of public approval of a proposed neighborhood association should probably include at some point a vote of its residents. If less than a certain percentage voted to approve the neighborhood-association arrangements, perhaps fewer than 50 percent, public approval would then be withheld and further negotiations would have to be undertaken.

Eventually, under this system, existing zoning would be abolished, and all collective property rights in neighborhoods would be exercised through a neighborhood association. This might involve a lengthy transition period, however, and local governments would continue in the meantime to exercise zoning rights for those areas.

In public examination of proposed neighborhood association boundaries, a number of considerations need to be taken into account. Boundaries should generally be drawn where mutual ties on opposite sides of the boundary are minimized. They should include areas of similar uses or social character. Neighborhood boundaries would be determined partly by natural features of the landscape—bodies of water, gullies, ridges, woods —and partly by man-made features of a similar character—highways, railroad tracks, changes in housing density, commercial districts. Neighborhoods should not be so large that their residents might begin to regard the neighborhood association as an impersonal institution that does not require their own participation. On the other hand, neighborhood associations should not be so small that they could not adequately control the environmental quality desired by most of their residents. In a big city, the area of an average-size neighborhood might consist of several blocks, in the suburbs, of several hundred homes, and in rural areas, of an entire small community.

Within a neighborhood association, some of the collective rights might be assigned to smaller clusters of units—formed into cluster associations. There could thus be two—or even more—levels of collective private-property ownership within the same area. This approach has, in fact, already been taken in some large developments with homeowners associations. In Reston, Virginia, there is a Reston Home Owners Association for the entire area of Reston and also a large number of small cluster associations of fifty to a hundred units to deal with more local concerns.

Like existing homeowner associations, condominiums, or cooperatives, neighborhood associations would have the authority to assess neighborhood residents to pay for common improvements. These improvements might include street cleaning, tending of common garden and lawn areas, tree care, and landscaping. The neighborhood association should probably also have authority to assess fees for neighborhood social activities, recreational facilities, special police protection, and certain other neighborhood services. It would typically adopt regulations for control of pets, speed limits on side streets, noise limitations, and other exclusively neighborhood concerns.

The proposed legal framework for neighborhood associations would allow one particularly significant type of action that is not available under existing condominium ownership, but is a basic feature of neighborhood rights under zoning (and is also possible to some extent under cooperative ownership). In existing condominiums, once they have been agreed to, it is generally impossible to redraw significantly the lines between collective rights and the personal rights of the individual-unit owners. For example, if house color, fencing, or landscaping were originally left as personal affairs, establishing collective controls over them later would be very difficult. Any major revisions in personal and collective rights would typically require unanimous consent, which in most cases is a practical impossibility. In contrast, in ordinary neighborhoods with zoning, if a large enough majority of the neighborhood wants them and enough political support is built up, zoning changes can be made that redraw the lines between collective and personal rights. As with zoning, under the proposed new neighborhood tenure, a favorable vote of a given majority of neighborhood residents (possibly 70, 80, or 90 percent) would be sufficient to redefine neighborhood-association collective and personal rights.

There would still, of course, exist some upper limit beyond which collective authority could not go under any circumstances. This would presumably involve matters relating solely to the interior of individual properties. If members of a neighborhood association wanted, they could also decide to reduce the scope of collective rights to less than the scope that has existed under zoning—perhaps, for example, in very low-density areas.

Residents of many neighborhoods might choose to give the neighborhood association extensive rights to control even minor changes in properties. Homeowner associations in many existing large private developments now hold such rights. For example, in Reston, the Architectural Board of Review is required to approve all changes as follows:

No building, structure, alteration, addition or improvement of any character other than interior alterations not affecting the external appearance of a building or structure shall be constructed upon any portion of the property . . . unless and until a plan of such construction shall have been approved by the Architectural Board of Review . . . as to quality of workmanship and materials, harmony of external design with surrounding structures, location with respect to topography and finished grade elevation, the effect of the construction on the outlook from surrounding property and all other factors which will in their opinion affect the desirability or suitability of the construction. . . .[4]

One of the more difficult decisions for the neighborhood association would be approving a use that would improve the whole neighborhood but would adversely affect the few immediately surrounding properties. Uses of this kind could include a gasoline station, a drugstore, a convenience store, or a restaurant. Zoning deals very rigidly with this problem by automatically excluding such uses. With the much greater flexibility that private tenures would offer, better approaches should be possible. One approach would be for the whole neighborhood that benefits to provide some type of compensation—financial or otherwise—to the few adjacent property owners who are adversely affected.

In a 1973 article, law professor Robert Ellickson offered one possible design for a system to provide such compensation. His aim was to establish a procedure under which "private nuisance remedies become the exclusive remedy for 'localized' spillovers —that is, those that concern no more than several dozen parties."[5] The basic principle behind his proposal is that mildly offensive uses should be allowed to remain at a site, but with regular compensation payments to adversely affected nearby properties. He would also give those parties a right to pay a certain fee if they wanted badly enough to force out or exclude the offending use (the fee would presumably be much higher to close down an existing use than it would be to exclude a proposed use). Ellickson gives an example of the proposed procedure:

The familiar example of a grocery in the Santa Monica Mountains can be used to demonstrate how a Nuisance Board could handle conflicts between residential and commercial uses. After examining metropolitan sentiment, the Board would probably classify groceries as an unneighborly land use. Nevertheless, because of the benefits of proximity to groceries, it is unlikely that more than a score or so of the grocery's neighbors could prove substantial harm from its operation. If the parties could not reach a private settlement, the uncompensated neighbors would take their case to the Nuisance Board either to collect damages or to purchase the closing of the grocery. This approach would be much more likely than the present system to assure the optimal number of groceries. . . . [6]

The greatest land-use problems in the United States have involved the poor procedures employed for transitions from a land use that is no longer appropriate for its particular location to a new use that fills a major need. To deal with this problem, an especially important feature of the proposed neighborhood associations would be provision of a system to allow for sale of all the property holdings in a neighborhood in one package. Under existing condominium ownership, little attention has been given to the means of transferring the collective property to others. Provisions usually do exist to dissolve a condominium, but very often they have the impossible requirement of unanimous consent. Although not a common practice, sale of all the property in a cooperative would be much easier. As a corporation, with a legal structure basically that of a business corporation, the stockholders could vote to sell all the properties in the cooperative.

The neighborhood association would follow the model of the cooperative in this regard. In a neighborhood association, on favorable vote of a sufficiently high percentage of the shareholders or members, but not requiring unanimity, the entire property holdings in the neighborhood could be sold in one block to a prospective developer. Carefully worked out procedures would be needed for receiving developer offers, analyzing them, and holding a vote.

It is quite possible that some subarea of a neighborhood association might be highly demanded for a new use, but not the entire neighborhood area. To deal with this situation, there could be provisions to allow such a change in use if two types of affirmative votes were obtained. First, the residents of the particular subarea would have to vote to sell all their property rights and holdings to the developer. Second, the rest of the neighborhood association would also have to approve the change. To facilitate such agreement on use changes that could be socially desirable but nonetheless adversely affect remaining neighborhood residents, financial or other payments might be made by the residents moving out to those remaining.

In existing condominiums and other private collective ownerships, several formulas have been used for assignment of voting shares to members. The most common arrangement is to assign shares in proportion to the value of individual unit holdings. Shares have occasionally also been determined on the basis of floor space. In other cases, equal shares are assigned to each unit owner, regardless of relative value. One, or a combination, of these approaches could be employed in neighborhood associations.

Another organizational concern is the status of renters. In existing private collective ownerships, renters generally have no vote. Under neighborhood zoning, a renter is likely to have a greater say in zoning administration than a property owner who lives outside the community. In neighborhood associations, some compromise might be needed. For example, on certain types of short-term or minor issues, such as neighborhood pet controls or noise limits, renters might have a significant voting role. On long-run issues, such as capital-expenditure decisions, they would presumably have no vote.

Different voting percentages might be required to make different types of collective decisions. In particular, a decision to dissolve the neighborhood association and sell all the neighborhood properties to some buyer might require an especially large favorable vote, say 70, 80, or 90 percent. On minor issues, a 51 percent vote should be sufficient to approve changes.

In order to provide for greater neighborhood stability and to economize on decision-making costs, the rules of the neighborhood association might require that certain types of neighborhood decisions could only be taken up every so often. Proposed small changes in the division between collective and personal rights—say, an increase in collective control over landscaping—might be considered every five or so years. More substantial changes—say, a change from collective controls similar to existing zoning to tight controls similar to historic districts—might be reviewed every ten years. Collective sale of the entire neighborhood association and all neighborhood property holdings might be opened for consideration no more often than every fifteen or twenty years.

As under existing condominium ownership, owners would be able to sell their individual units, together with their shares in the neighborhood association, with few restrictions. As in many existing condominiums, the neighborhood association might have a right of first refusal in any such sales.

Property Rights in Undeveloped Areas

A main theme in this book has been the different land-use concerns in stable and in transitional areas. Although it may be less true in the future, in the United States today the major areas of transition are still basically undeveloped. The problems of community zoning mainly involve such transitional undeveloped areas. These problems are caused principally by the transfer to local governments under zoning of most of the development rights to undeveloped land. This transfer removes these rights from the market system of exchange, and thereby greatly obstructs efficient utilization of suburban land.

A certain recognition of these problems is implicit in recent proposals for creation of systems of "transferable development rights." As a recent general description of such proposals explained: "In effect, TDR [Transfer of Development Rights] severs the development potential from the land and treats it as a marketable item."[7]

The transferable-development-rights concept thus far has been applied primarily in New York City as a tool for landmark preservation.[8] Under landmark ordinances, the designation of landmark status for a site in effect transfers from the owner to the city the rights to make major changes in the existing property or to tear it down for a new use. Because of the strong threat that courts will hold such an action to be an unconstitutional "taking," New York City has offered to compensate the developer by allowing him to transfer or sell his lost development rights for use at certain other sites.

A similar proposal has been made for undeveloped areas, where attempts to maintain open spaces or very low-density development also face a "takings" hurdle. Although specifics vary, the basic idea, as in landmark preservation programs, is to create a system whereby development rights at one site can be sold for use at another site. Landowners in areas where unusually tight public restrictions had been imposed would be allowed to offer some of their lost development rights for sale and use elsewhere. In this way, these owners would receive some compensation for the loss in value of their land.

Although the concept is simple, in putting it into practice there are a number of unclear points and potential problems. There is a basic conflict between the need to maintain the value of transferable development rights and the exercise of significant public control over the location of high-density and other high-value development. Transferable development rights would be of most value if highly restrictive zoning were maintained over broad areas and if any landowner in these areas were required to purchase some transferable rights to build a high-value—generally high-density—project. But this would leave little public control over the location of these projects. On the other hand, if specific sites for high-value projects were publicly determined (as would be the case for example if any substantial public planning were sought), the owners of these sites—necessarily limited in number—would be able to command a high price for their land. There is only so much total value for any given site. Hence, unless there were also a tightly limited supply of transferable development rights—unlikely since open spaces and very low density areas would presumably take up considerable total acreage—the bargaining position of holders of transferable development rights would be weak. Transferable rights thus might not be worth much and might not offer much of the intended compensation to holders.

As the systems would work in practice, the term "transferable development rights" would actually be somewhat of a misnomer. In open-space and very low-density areas, the specific development rights transferable would be those additional rights lost because of unusually restrictive public controls (that is, the rights lost beyond the normal transfer of development rights to the government under zoning). But these particular development rights would still be privately held in other areas with normal zoning, and hence there would be no private demand specifically for these rights. Rather, it would be necessary to convert the lost development rights in open-space and very low-density areas to some form of a salable credit, whose possession would allow greater development in other areas. In transferable-development-rights proposals, this credit is usually a density credit, which would allow increases in development densities elsewhere. Hence, the proposals do not really propose to transfer rights literally, but to create special credits that can be purchased to obtain a loosening of existing zoning at other sites. What is essentially being proposed is that the holders of the special credits would have the right to sell certain changes in zoning away from their own site.

Given the uncertainties of the market for such special credits, it would provide greater assurance of fair compensation if the government were directly to buy—perhaps at less than full value —the development rights at sites where unusually tight restrictions on uses were desired. It might also make good sense to pay for these purchases through direct public sale of zoning changes—in effect, sale of now publicly held development rights—at sites in other areas considered suitable for more intensive development.

A plan to do precisely that was in fact proposed in 1975 for the whole island of Puerto Rico. Although called a plan for a transferable-development-rights system, this plan does not actually propose to create any marketable density or other credits. Rather, in environmentally sensitive areas ("Protected Environmental Zones"), where uses of land were to be tightly restricted, owners could simply appeal to a board for compensation. In effect, they could ask for some public payment for their loss to the government of further development rights. The funds for these payments would be obtained by selling development rights to sites in other areas of Puerto Rico for which much more intensive development was planned. Under existing zoning, the government, of course, would already hold these rights. Although they do not describe it as such (historically, few land-use innovations have at first), the authors explain how their proposed plan for sale of zoning rights would work:

To illustrate: an urban area could be zoned to permit 50 density units per acre. . . . Upon the Planning Board's determination that planning and market criteria warrant further densities of, let us say, 8 density units per acre, developers opting to purchase the right to this premium would be authorized to build 58 density units per acre. The price paid for the premium would either be set in the open market pursuant to public bid proce-

dures supervised by the Land Administration or determined by
direct negotiations between developers and that body.[9]

The questions of possession of and payment for development
rights lie at the heart of current debate over the extent of public
compensation required for unusually tight land-use controls—
the "taking" issue.[10] The question most often raised has been
one of equity. Is it excessively unfair to establish public controls
on use of land that severely diminish its value, especially when
similar nearby properties may be permitted much higher value
uses? The equity issue is, however, only a transitional concern.
It could be disposed of, for example, by a once-and-for-all
determination that henceforth all land would be subject to public control without regard to the effects on land value. This
action would unambiguously transfer all development rights to
the government, and would cause many immediate large land-
value losses in a highly discriminatory manner. But thereafter,
equitable treatment of landowners would not be a concern
(although greatly increased incentives for political corruption
would create major new problems). The key consideration is
that the purchaser of land would know definitely in advance
that he was not also obtaining the development rights. To
obtain those rights, he would later have to pay for them, or
persuade the government to transfer them to him. The existence
of uncertainty about whether this could be done would generally tend to hold land values at lower levels. If a purchaser chose
to pay a high price in expectation of later receiving rights for a
high-value use, it would be at his own risk, and a claim for
compensation would have little grounds.

Basically, this type of situation now exists in England,
for example, where there is wide public discretion to control
development. As the above considerations suggest should be
the case, one report indicated little developer concern about
compensation:

None of the developers considered the limited availability of
compensation for planning law restrictions a detriment to land
development. Most of the developers agreed . . . that if property
had been purchased for development without planning permission, that would most certainly have been reflected in the
purchase price, and if not, then "someone has not done his
homework."[11]

If it were to be decided that development rights in the United States ought all to be held by public agencies, there are various transitional schemes that could be adopted. For example, following announcement of its intention, the government could gradually assume more and more development rights over a twenty- or thirty-year period. Because owner losses of development rights would occur well in the future, the present value (discounted) of those losses would be small, and little or no compensation might be judged to be needed. Or, a program of payments for landowner losses of development rights could be established, scheduled to decline as the losses would occur further in the future.

The many land-use students who now claim that public compensation is not required even for very tight controls are for practical purposes proposing public assumption of development rights.[12] The transitional mechanism they seem to have in mind is, in effect, a gradual court erosion of private claims to development rights (somewhat along the lines suggested above, except without prior formal announcement). The transferable-development-right concept is another possible transitional mechanism toward greater public assumption of development rights. Proponents of the approach explain that it is based on the view that "the development potential of privately held land is in part a community asset that government may allocate to enhance the general welfare."[13]

In short, the long-run-compensation issue goes beyond equity concerns to the fundamental question of who should hold development rights. The alternatives are either public or private holding of development rights. To prohibit the imposition of significant land-value losses without public compensation is basically to require that government leave development rights in the private sector (or, which it has very seldom been willing to do, purchase them). To allow large uncompensated land-value losses is effectively to say that most development rights can be transferred to the public sector.

With development rights in the private sector, land use would be determined by private competition in the land market. If development rights were publicly held, allocating them to the highest bidder in a competitive lease sale or auction would also result in land-use determination by private-market forces. However, many proponents of public assumption of development rights have traditionally had a different aim, comprehensive public determination of land use through public planning.

Despite such hopes, if publicly planned land use is the objective, public assumption of development rights has a critical practical drawback. Possession of development rights gives only the right to prevent development, and not the right actually to undertake it. To develop, the rights of the existing landowner must be acquired as well. This situation is likely to create major problems for public planning of new development. When the time comes to develop a site, the landowner will have equal control with the government over the ability to develop. Extended bargaining over the landowner's selling price and the time he will actually make his land available is likely to prove awkward and time-consuming. The uncertainties of the bargaining process and especially the timing are likely to prove disruptive to any hopes for major government planning of future land uses. Because of this, even full public purchase of development rights would be essentially a "negative" approach, as is zoning itself. It would be more suited to preventing development than to improving its future quality.

Even in areas where the current objective is to maintain open spaces and prevent development, public assumption only of development rights has this same undesirable feature. In fifty years, the area that now seems well suited for open spaces could well have become a prime location for intensive development. Previous designers of the regulatory system have shown little concern that the proper current use for the great majority of sites will not be so forever. Little attention has generally been given to providing procedures whereby eventually needed changes in the basic use of a location could be accomplished smoothly and fairly.

For these and other reasons, public discussion and debate are best focused on taking one of two directions, either full public acquisition of land in transitional areas or full private ownership, including the development rights. The tenure system proposed above is based on the principle of full private ownership. The basic reason is a preference for market, as opposed to political, decision making on issues involving such small details and made in such large numbers as the specific uses of land at sites across the nation.

The full development rights would therefore be returned to the private owners of the land. To avoid the problems of piecemeal land development and to assure fair treatment of small individual owners of land in areas undergoing transition, these owners would be required to act collectively in selling their land for new development. Collective ownerships would encompass undeveloped areas of a size suitable for a future neighborhood. To avoid complicating matters, the collective-ownership instrument would be the same as that for property owners in already developed neighborhoods, a neighborhood association.

To form new neighborhood associations in currently undeveloped areas, certain procedures would be needed. If a developer were interested in a particular area of undeveloped land, he could make an offer to the residents. At that point, through some mechanism that would involve local government, residents of the area, and the developer, two decisions would have to be made: whether the boundaries and other arrangements of the proposed development made sense as a new neighborhood, and whether the developer's offer had any reasonable chance of being accepted by the present owners. If both answers are yes, a neighborhood association composed of the owners of land in the area sought by the developer would be formed. Shareholdings in the neighborhood association would be allocated by a formula based on land area, value of property ownership, or other features. The shareholders would then vote on whether to accept the developer's offer. In undeveloped areas, the required vote for a neighborhood-association decision to sell all the property holdings might be less than in highly developed neighborhoods, possibly as low as a simple majority or two-thirds. Of course, once a collective, affirmative decision were made, each landowner would be legally obligated to accept it.

In the absence of a specific development offer, if there was enough demand, owners of undeveloped land could form a neighborhood association to advertise the availability of their lands among possible developers. Upon public approval of the proposed boundaries and other arrangements, the development rights to the land now held by the local government under zoning would be transferred automatically to the neighborhood association.

Remaining Public Roles

The basic approach of the metropolitan tenure system proposed here has been to diminish the role of public regulation, but some public roles will nevertheless still be needed. For example, close public scrutiny will be required to assure complete disclosure in all land-market transactions and to enforce strict laws against misrepresentation and fraud. A number of abuses of condominium ownership have received wide public attention. It can be expected that the new types of collective-property ownership proposed here will involve problems of a similar nature. The courts will no doubt have an important role in ensuring against arbitrary and capricious actions in the administration of neighborhood associations.

Projects in a neighborhood would still be subject to public control if they in fact represent a genuine nuisance to nearby neighborhoods. For example, a developer could not locate an oil refinery or paper-pulp mill in an area surrounded by residential neighborhoods. Guidelines would be needed specifying what impacts of one neighborhood on another are sufficiently adverse to constitute grounds for prohibiting the neighborhood development or requiring that the impacts be ameliorated on genuine nuisance grounds.

Although there would be little state and community regulation of the type of use or of aesthetic matters within new neighborhoods, regulations such as building codes and subdivision controls would probably still be necessary. While not specifically proposed, requirements that each neighborhood contain a certain percentage of housing for low- and moderate-income residents are also not precluded. Environmental standards for sewage treatment and air-pollution emissions would, of course, have to be met.

Because new development would pay its own public-facility costs, and could be regulated to the extent that it imposed large external burdens on other neighborhoods, a community might often have few reasons to prefer one type of development to another. Nevertheless, if a community wished to influence the type of development, a special means could be made available to do so. Communities could be given a right of first refusal on sales of the property holdings in a neighborhood association. Or, in a similar vein, if a community (or other government body) strongly preferred one development proposal to another for an area, it might be allowed to make a sufficient financial contribution of its own to boost the preferred developer's offer up to the level of the highest offer. For example, under these procedures, should a community want to keep lands in a certain area as open space, it could match the developer's offer for the area. Should the community not be willing to pay so much, the lands in the area would go to the developer.

Public approval of proposed boundaries for neighborhood associations would be needed, requiring some public-planning staff to fulfill this function. Nevertheless, the grounds for disapproval of a proposed neighborhood association would be limited. For example, control over the timing of new development would not be an accepted public regulatory objective.

In summary, of course, it is extremely unlikely that a metropolitan land-tenure system containing precisely the institutions proposed above will ever be created. But through gradual evolution, steps toward some of its main features are likely to be taken. The greatest obstacles to more rapid tenure evolution are emotional. The tenure system proposed above would be inconsistent with many strongly held personal attitudes and positions and would require a large number of people to change what are in many cases convictions maintained over a lifetime. Still, strong practical needs and the glaring contradictions between traditional regulatory theories and the reality of American land-use regulation make major change seem virtually inevitable at some point. If steps in the directions proposed are taken, the tenure system should be able much more effectively to meet two social objectives of major importance. First, the rapidly growing desire for strong local control and independence would be met at the most suitable level—the neighborhood; second, a much better balance could be achieved between society's need for continued large amounts of new development and the desires of residents in areas facing development pressures to be able to stay where they are in a stable environment.

Conclusion   The Future Lines of Social Conflict

10 The Struggle for High-Quality Environments

George Orwell and a number of other social critics have commented on the tendency in the twentieth century to misuse language for political purposes. The most conspicuous recent example in the United States has been the broad range of activities that have been justified on grounds of "national defense." Similarly, in recent years, numerous actions and policies have been justified in the name of "environmental protection" that also are radical departures from past American beliefs and bear little relationship to the traditional meaning of the term.

The principle of environmental protection originates with laws to protect the public from genuine threats to health and safety. The nuisance principle was later extended to apply to any activity that creates significant external costs. In economic theory, public protection can be justified when actions of one party impose costs on other parties, but the first party does not pay for these "external" costs. The preferred solution in economic theory is to impose a financial penalty equal to the costs. But, in the absence of the ability to take that step, recourse to public controls is justified.

Nevertheless, in economic theory, public controls are justified in curtailing activities that impose external costs only up to the point that greater benefits are not also thereby lost. If residents outside a neighborhood are included in the accounting of social benefits and costs, zoning violates this principle. Uses are excluded from neighborhoods that would impose any net costs whatsoever on the existing neighborhood residents. The benefits to the proposed user of entering the neighborhood or other benefits obtained by other people outside the neighborhood are not taken into account.

This new principle of environmental protection embodied in zoning has a purpose altogether different from traditional protections from nuisances or activities imposing significant external costs. The purpose of new environmental protections is the protection of the existing general standard of living in a particular area.[1]

Zoning is not the only public instrument used for this purpose. At about the same time that zoning was introduced, strict immigration controls were first employed in the United States to protect the nation's high standard of living. Continued acceptance of large numbers of immigrants, most of them poor, would sooner or later have caused this standard to decline sharply. As many local communities are doing today, the nation responded with what might be called an early no-growth policy. While the question is far from settled, there are numerous signs to suggest that new federal and state land-use controls will be used to create regulatory protections for the standard of living of regions and states.

For the past century, the most celebrated conflict in Western society has been the struggle among social classes for larger shares of income and wealth. In recent years, environmentalists and others have emphasized that personal well-being may depend less closely on levels of income and wealth, and more closely on the quality of one's environment in all its aspects. Like income and wealth, a high-quality environment is a limited resource; it can only be enjoyed by a certain number of people without causing a decline in its quality. It is thus not surprising that, as overall environmental quality becomes more important to personal well-being, people make greater efforts to secure for themselves areas that have high environmental quality and therefore offer high standards of living. Zoning and national immigration controls represent the first stage in that effort. It may well turn out that the greatest long-run significance of the current environmental movement will be that it represents a second stage.

Immigration controls and zoning have acted substantially to broaden disparities in the quality of life of neighborhoods, communities, and nations. As a general rule, the maintenance of environmental protections will act to widen these disparities. High-quality environments will be able to pick and choose among new residents and uses, while already lower-quality environments will be forced to accept less desirable residents and uses, further widening existing differences in environmental quality. At least in their effects, if not in their precise mechanisms, environmental protections thus follow in the tradition of other protections of private personal property.

New lines of social conflict thus appear increasingly to be competing with, and possibly even supplanting, the old class conflicts. Based on recent trends, instead of a conflict over shares of income and wealth, the bitterest conflicts of the future may be for control over the areas with the best environments and highest standards of living. Whereas, at least in theory, the poor throughout the world have been pitted against the rich; in the primary struggles of the future, all the residents of areas with higher-quality environments may be pitted against all the residents of areas with lower-quality environments. In the old class struggles, private property rights have protected the benefits of high personal income and wealth; in the future struggles, instruments of environmental protection will be the means to protect the fortunate of the world who occupy the environments with the highest standards of living.

In the new conflicts to secure control over high-quality environments, there will still, of course, be considerable overlap with the old struggles among social classes. Wealthier individuals will tend to reside in the more desirable areas, partly because they can afford the price of entry and partly because they have the resources to make areas more desirable. But, as instruments of environmental protection encompass very large geographic areas, poor people will find themselves sharing the greatest common interest with the rich who occupy the same areas. For example, currently the poor in the United States have far more interests in common with the rich in protecting the nation's high standard of living than they have with the poor in other nations in seeking a more equitable overall distribution of world income and wealth.

One of the most enduring human traits is the tendency to see personal well-being in idealistic terms. The strict protections of private personal property in the nineteenth century, for example, which allowed a few fortunate individuals to achieve huge wealth while far more suffered relative deprivation, were never justified on those terms. Rather, they were regarded by those who benefited from them—and by many who suffered, as well —as preordained, an attitude bolstered by the religious and moral beliefs of the time. Currently, instruments of environmental protection are often similarly regarded. Many of the strongest advocates of environmental protections are those who would also benefit greatly from them, but in their views they exhibit a conviction that is usually associated mainly with religious and moral beliefs.

Traditional private-property rights and new environmental protections can be justified in other than religious or moral terms. Both create socially valuable incentives for productive activities. Residency in a high-quality environment is often at least partly the result of efforts directed toward that end. Those who collectively make the effort to establish and maintain high-quality environments have a reasonable claim to the benefits of their efforts. Society may benefit from sustaining the incentive to establish and maintain high-quality environments, because overall environmental quality for all of society will then be higher. For example, success in world-population control may depend on a recognition by each nation that it will bear the consequences of a failure to control its own population.

Even when desirable environments are solely products of nature, society as a whole may benefit from the existence of a privileged and protected few occupants. Many of the finest works of literature, greatest scientific discoveries, and most celebrated works of art have resulted from the privileged status of a few that allowed the pursuits necessary for their achievement. On a more material plane, brilliant jewelry, beautiful country estates, the finest cuisines, and other luxuries require the presence of a privileged few. Most people derive at least some pleasure from the mere existence of a certain amount of very high-quality possessions. Similarly, if the world is to include areas of unusually high environmental quality, the residents of those areas will almost have to be highly privileged relative to the rest of the world.

Consider the consequences of a decision to stop all future growth and protect Alaska's environment from the patterns of development of the forty-eight mainland states. Such an action might well be desirable for preserving one of the last large wilderness environments left on earth. Yet, as population and congestion grew elsewhere in the world and ordinary economic goods grow more plentiful, the residents of the unusually attractive Alaskan environment will become better off than everyone else. If the few openings for residency in Alaska were determined by ability to pay, only a few rich would be able to move there—as is already the case in some unusually attractive local communities that strictly limit growth. Even if Alaskan residents were selected by lottery, they would still be a privileged few—although no longer determined by wealth—and large inequities would be maintained.

To put another perspective on the problem, if all environmental protections in the world were canceled, including national immigration controls, equality among the people of the world would be greatly increased. The high-quality environments of nations, such as the United States, would be shared by large numbers of new residents from poor nations, such as India. But the whole world would also tend toward a far greater uniformity of environments. Few, if any, unusually attractive environments would remain unspoiled by heavy pressures of population growth. The better-off nations would obviously be opposed to such a policy. But even from a world perspective, one might argue that the increased world equality would not be worth the loss of almost all high-quality environments.

Environmental protections thus pose a conflict between equality and other social objectives that is similar to that conflict long raised by private-property rights. Thus far, many attempts to deal with the conflict have been confused by a failure to perceive that connection and, more generally, to understand the nature of the issues raised. The common attempt of many of those who benefit greatly from environmental protections to justify them as moral and ethical imperatives, as defenses of health and safety, or as traditional controls on external costs is one of the causes of the confusion.

It is not difficult to understand the stances often taken by proponents of strict environmental protections. Many are liberals who have long vigorously opposed the inequities that have been established and maintained by protecting high personal income and wealth. The intellectual trend of the times has been strongly egalitarian. Yet, the justifications for many environmental protections are essentially the same as those for strict protection of personal property. Both justifications require defending the preservation of large inequities and of privileged groups. In short, many proponents of environmental protections hold beliefs that are inherently inconsistent. Rather than trying to reconcile conflicting beliefs, through myths and plain avoidance of the facts of the matter, proponents of protection of neighborhood, community, regional, state, and national environmental quality very frequently deny or ignore some of the most significant consequences of their views.

While protections of high-quality environments have their justifications, on balance one must conclude that the future strains that will be placed on the world will be immense if better principles are not established for handling the basic issues of environmental protection. Residents of the areas with highly desirable environments will come increasingly into conflict with residents of the areas with less desirable environments. In the international arena, the conflict among rich and poor nations could lead to war or to other less drastic protests against inequalities among nations. In metropolitan areas, zoning has already contributed to outbreaks of violence in the 1960s. Aside from principled concerns about achieving social justice, no social system that tends to establish and maintain very great inequalities is likely to produce a social order of lasting stability.

Three Options

The discussions in this and previous chapters show that the system of land-use control is not a narrow issue but one that is inseparable from the basic character of the social system. One distinguishing feature of feudalism was its form of land tenure. The creation of personal-property rights to land was a key element in the establishment of a capitalist social and economic organization. Zoning controls and corporate ownership of business property represent institutions for collective property ownership in a world in which collective organizations will probably play an increasing role. Thus, in proposing a future system of land-use control, one also proposes a vision of future social organization. Three options for the future social organization emerge from the analysis in this book.

The first option is a modern version of feudal social organization. Under it, the market verdict will be largely discredited and little central control established to take its place. Rather individual neighborhoods, communities, regions, states, and nations will be free to pursue policies to protect their own environments and standards of living. The larger social groups will mainly perform tasks that raise few conflicts among their parts. For example, the chief responsibility of the nation-state might be territorial defense. Perhaps to alleviate some of the tensions resulting from growing inequalities among its parts, the nation-state might also perform some redistribution of income from rich to poor areas. The advantages of this first basic option are that it would reward efforts to establish and maintain high-quality environments (for example, restraints on internal population growth), would foster strong community values in many small, self-governed areas containing fairly homogeneous populations, would allow much greater direct participation by citizens in government affairs, and would offer greater security and stability in a time when rapid social change is highly unsettling. By maintaining wide disparities among areas in environmental quality, areas of the highest environmental quality would be maintained and preserved for the future.

The second option is centralized planning and control. As in the revived feudal option, the verdict of market competition would generally be rejected, but, under this second option, international, national, and other centralized governing units would have the main responsibility for the planning and control of economic and environmental affairs. Comprehensive national land-use plans and controls would be instituted. At least in theory, these highly centralized planning and controls would produce much greater overall economic coordination. Because of the current broad acceptance of egalitarian views, the exercise of central authority could not allow inequalities in income and wealth or in environmental quality to become too great.

But the benefits of highly centralized planning and control seem to be far outweighed by some major losses. Private initiative would be eliminated in many areas of the economy. Large bureaucracies would replace market mechanisms in allocating resources. To maintain democratic control, the political system would probably have to be thoroughly restructured in ways that have not yet been much explored. In the United States at least, democracy has not thus far shown much capacity for central planning and coordination on the very large scale that would be required for the comprehensive and centralized management of economic and environmental affairs.

The third option would be to rely on market forces as the determinant of land use and other economic decisions. The biggest advantage of this option is that it would allow for decentralization of both government responsibilities and ordinary economic activity, while through the workings of the market mechanism, substantial central coordination would be maintained. One concern would be the highly equalizing effect of market pressures on environmental quality. It might well be that few very high-quality environments could withstand its pressures, resulting in a monotonous uniformity of environments and loss to the world of its most attractive places. There also, of course, exist the standard problems of externalities, and other market failings traditionally described in economic literature, and the tendency of market forces to lead to excessive concentrations of economic and political power.

In considering market approaches, it should be kept in mind that improved results may be achieved by making changes in market institutions. In particular, changes in property-right institutions can fundamentally influence the workings of markets. For example, however one regards it, the development of corporate forms of collective ownership for business property has had a vast impact. The gravest deficiencies of zoning are caused by a separation of the possession of certain property rights from the right to receive payment for their transfer. By designing new and better forms of land tenure to replace zoning, the greatest failings of the metropolitan land market can for the most part be corrected, without requiring that public decisions replace private ones.

I have described a proposal for a new system of metropolitan land tenure that largely follows the third basic option and emphasizes reliance on the market verdict for land allocation. In my view, the two options that do not include a large market role—the modern version of feudalism and comprehensive central control over the economy and environment—contain great dangers. In the long run, the revived feudal option promises large inequalities among areas, widespread social conflict, and possibly frequent outbreaks of violence in a nuclear age that makes conflict a threat to all mankind. The centralized option promises vast bureaucracies with loss of individual freedom and large-scale economic inefficiency. Inclusion of some elements of both these options will no doubt occur and is probably neces-sary. But unless Western society is to turn away from its basic orientation of the last few centuries—and that certainly can-not be excluded—market forces will have to continue to play a dominant role—although, it is hoped, through improved insti-tutions. It is, after all, the unique combination of centralization and decentralization found in market mechanisms that has been essential to the development of Western society.

Notes

Introduction

1. Benjamin Hibbard, *A History of the Public Land Policies* (Madison and Milwaukee: University of Wisconsin Press, 1965), p. 549. Original printing, McMillan and Co., 1924.

Part I   The Evolution of New Collective Property Rights

1. Richard Babcock, *The Zoning Game, Municipal Practices and Policies* (Madison: University of Wisconsin Press, 1966), p. 115.

Chapter 1

1. See the discussion in Fred Bosselman, David Callies, and John Banta, *The Taking Issue: An Analysis of the Constitutional Limits of Land Use Control*, prepared for the Council on Environmental Quality (Washington, D.C., 1973).

2. Welch v. Swasey, 214 U.S. 394 (1909).

3. Hadacheck v. Sebastian, 239 U.S. 394 (1915).

4. Alfred Bettman, *City and Regional Planning Papers*, Harvard City Planning Studies, XIII (Cambridge, Mass.: Harvard University Press, 1946), p. 171.

5. Edward M. Bassett, *Zoning: The Laws, Administration and Court Decisions During the First Twenty Years* (New York: Russell Sage Foundation, 1936), p. 97.

6. Ibid., p. 63.

7. Ibid., p. 97.

8. Village of Euclid v. Ambler Realty Co., 272 U.S. at 394 (1926).

9. Robert Anderson, *American Law of Zoning* (Rochester, N.Y.: Lawyers Co-operative Publishing Co., 1968), 2:47.

10. National Commission on Urban Problems, *Building the American City: Report of the National Commission on Urban Problems* (New York: Praeger, 1969), p. 219.

11. A similar argument has been made concerning the incentive to maintain the quality of existing properties in older city neighborhoods. It is argued that each property owner can maximize his gains by undermaintaining his own property. The end result of all owners' following that course would be a much less than socially desirable level of neighborhood quality and, in the worst cases, slums. See Jerome Rothenberg, "Urban Renewal Programs," in *Measuring Benefits of Government Programs*, ed. Robert Dorfman (Washington, D.C.: Brookings Institution, 1965), p. 300.

12. Hugh Pomeroy, "A Planning Manual for Zoning (Urban and Suburban)" (unpublished manuscript, American Society of Planning Officials, 1940), p. 57; available at the ASPO Library, Chicago, and the Avery Library, Columbia University.

13. Anderson, *Law of Zoning*, 2:48.

14. Village of Euclid v. Ambler Realty Co., 272 U.S. at 394 (1926).

15. John Delafons, *Land-Use Controls in the United States* (Cambridge, Mass.: Joint Center for Urban Studies of the Massachusetts Institute of Technology and Harvard University, 1962), p. 26.

16. National Commission on Urban Problems, *Building the American City*, p. 219.

17. Village of Belle Terre v. Boraas, 416 U.S. at 9 (1974).

18. Quoted in Delafons, *Land-Use Controls in the United States*, p. 23. See Borough of Cresskill v. Borough of Dumont, 28 N.J. Super 26, 100 A.2d 182 (1953).

19. Ibid., p. 31.

20. Donald W. Waesche, quoted in Martin Rody and Herbert Smith, *Zoning Primer* (West Trenton, N.J.: Chandler-Davis, 1960), p. 13.

21. Jane Jacobs, *The Death and Life of Great American Cities* (New York: Vintage Books, 1961), p. 153.

22. *A Model Land Development Code (Proposed Official Draft)* (Philadelphia: American Law Institute, 1975), p. 66.

23. Paul Goldberger, "Landmarks Commission Survives a Decade, But Road Ahead is Rocky," *New York Times*, April 19, 1975, p. 62.

24. Peter G. Brown, *The American Law Institute Model Land Development Code, The Taking Issue and Private Property Rights* (Washington, D.C.: Urban Institute, 1975), p. 10.

Chapter 2

1. Edward M. Bassett, *Zoning: The Laws, Administration and Court Decisions During the First Twenty Years* (New York: Russell Sage Foundation, 1936), pp. 47–48.

2. Ambler Realty Co. v. Village of Euclid, 297 Fed. at 316 (N.D. Ohio 1924), quoted in Seymour Toll, *Zoned American* (New York: Grossman, 1969), p. 224.

3. Rodgers v. Tarrytown, 302 N.Y. at 121, 96 N.E.2d at 733 (1951), quoted in Robert Anderson, *American Law of Zoning* (Rochester, N.Y.: Lawyers Co-operative Publishing Co., 1968), 1:66–67.

4. Robert Anderson, *American Law of Zoning* (Rochester, N.Y.: Lawyers Co-operative Publishing Co., 1968), 1:72.

5. Udell v. Haas, 21 N.Y.2d at 469, 235 N.E.2d at 900 (1968).

6. See *A Decent Home: The Report of the President's Committee on Urban Housing* (Washington, D.C., 1968), p. 140.

7. National Commission on Urban Problems, *Building the American City: Report of the National Commission on Urban Problems* (New York: Praeger, 1969), p. 7.

8. Advisory Commission on Intergovernmental Relations, *Urban and Rural America: Policies for Urban Growth* (Washington, D.C., 1968), p. 130.

9. Morris Beck, *Property Taxation and Urban Land Use in Northeastern New Jersey* (Washington, D.C.: Urban Land Institute, 1963).

10. One 1961 survey showed that housing expenditures fell from 15 to 6 percent of income as income rose from between $2,000 and $3,000 to over $15,000. See Advisory Commission on Intergovernmental Relations, *Financing Schools and Property Tax Relief: A State Responsibility* (Washington, D.C., 1973), p. 39. Census data are available for 1970 for renter payments by income class by metropolitan area. As a percentage of income, rent payments in almost every case decline rapidly as income rises.

11. Serrano v. Priest, 96 *Cal. Rptr.* 601, 487 P.2d 1241 (1971).

12. The court in *Serrano* refers to assessed value rather than actual market value. For effective tax rates as a percentage of actual value, see B. Levin, M. Cohen, T. Muller, and W. Scanlon, *Paying for Public Schools: Issues of School Finance in California* (Washington, D.C.: Urban Institute, 1972), pp. 7, 46.

13. *The Fleishman Report on the Quality, Cost, and Financing of Elementary and Secondary Education in New York State* (New York: Viking Press, 1973), 1:58.

14. The property tax may be significantly borne by landowners. When an owner of vacant land in an area with very high tax rates tries to sell his property, the high tax rates will reduce the value of the property. Although the eventual purchaser of the land and property pays high property taxes, he is not necessarily bearing the burden of high property taxes, because he may have been able to purchase his property at a price reduced by the capitalized future higher taxes. The final incidence of the tax thus may fall on the original landowner.

15. For discussion of these studies and references, see Henry Aaron, *Who Pays the Property Tax, A New View*, Studies of Government Finance (Washington, D.C.: Brookings Institution, 1975), pp. 27–32.

16. See Mason Gaffney, "The Property Tax is a Progressive Tax," *Proceedings of 64th Annual Conference on Taxation* (1971), pp. 408–26.

17. Aaron, *Who Pays the Property Tax*, p. 93.

18. Newton Baker, "Argument for Appellee," Village of Euclid v. Ambler Realty Co., 272 U.S. at 374 (1926).

19. Charles Haar, "Zoning for Minimum Standards: The Wayne Township Case," *Harvard Law Review* 66 (1953):1036, 1063.

20. Vickers v. Gloucester Township, 37 N.J. at 266, 181 A.2d at 147 (1962).

21. *The Report of the President's Committee on Urban Housing: A Decent Home* (Washington, D.C., 1968), p. 144.

22. National Commission on Urban Problems, *Building the American City*, p. 243.

23. *Equal Opportunity in Suburbia, A Report of the United States Commission on Civil Rights* (July 1974), p. 53.

24. Southern Burlington County N.A.A.C.P. v. Township of Mt. Laurel, 67 N.J. at 179, 336 A.2d at 727 (1975).

25. Michael N. Danielson, *The Politics of Exclusion* (New York: Columbia University Press, 1976), pp. 323–25.

26. Julius Margolis, "The Governance of Metropolitan Areas: Fiscal Aspects," Fels Discussion Paper No. 13, University of Pennsylvania, July 1971, pp. 19–20.

27. The seminal article for this economic school was Charles Tiebout, "A Pure Theory of Local Public Expenditure," *Journal of Political Economy* 64 (October 1956):416–24. For some recent discussions, see Edwin Mills and Wallace Oates, eds., *Fiscal Zoning and Land Use Controls* (Lexington, Mass.: Lexington Books, 1975).

28. See Robert Weaver, "Housing and Associated Problems of Minorities," in Marion Clawson, ed., *Modernizing Urban Land Policy* (Baltimore: Johns Hopkins University Press for Resources for the Future, 1973), p. 76.

29. Robert Nisbet, "The Decline of Academic Nationalism," *Change* (Summer 1974):28.

30. Peter Singer, "The Right To Be Rich or Poor," *New York Review of Books*, March 6, 1975, p. 19. See Robert Nozick, *Anarchy, State and Utopia* (New York: Basic Books, 1975).

31. Miller v. California, 413 U.S. 15 (1973).

32. Flora Lewis, "West European Nations Turning Inward," *New York Times*, March 23, 1975, pp. 1, 20.

33. James v. Valtierra, 402 U.S. at 142 (1971).

34. *Fair Housing and Exclusionary Land Use* (Washington, D.C.: National Committee Against Discrimination in Housing and the Urban Land Institute, 1974), p. 35.

35. For formal economic discussions of such an argument, see Bruce Hamilton, "Zoning and Property Taxation in a System of Local Governments," *Urban Studies* 12 (June 1975):205–11, and Bruce Hamilton, "Capitalization of Intrajurisdictional Differences in Local Tax Prices," *American Economic Review* 66 (December 1976):743–53.

36. See, for example, Dick Netzer, "Is There Too Much Reliance on the Local Property Tax?" in *Property Tax Reform*, ed. George Peterson (Washington, D.C.: John C. Lincoln and Urban Institute, 1973), p. 23.

37. Alfred Bettman, *City and Regional Planning Papers*, Harvard City Planning Papers, XIII (Cambridge, Mass.: Harvard University Press, 1946), p. 59.

38. National Commission on Urban Problems, *Building the American City*, p. 206.

39. *A Model Land Development Code (Proposed Official Draft)* (Philadelphia: American Law Institute, 1975), pp. 175–76.

40. City of Eastlake et al. v. Forest City Enterprises, decided by the United States Supreme Court, June 21, 1976.

41. National Association of Home Builders, *Transcript of the Second Legal Conference on Land Use and Growth* (Washington, D.C.: National Association of Home Builders, 1974), pp. 4–5.

Chapter 3

1. John W. Reps, "The Future of American Planning: Requiem or Renascence?" in *Planning 1967: Selected Papers from the ASPO National Planning Conference* (Chicago: American Society of Planning Officials, 1967), pp. 47–48.

2. Marion Clawson and Peter Hall, *Planning and Urban Growth: An Anglo-American Comparison* (Baltimore: Johns Hopkins Press for Resources for the Future, 1973), pp. 191–92.

3. Advisory Committee on Zoning, *A City Planning Primer* (Washington, D.C.: U.S. Department of Commerce, 1928), p. 14.

4. F. Stuart Chapin, *Urban Land Use Planning* (New York: Harper and Brothers, 1957), p. 276.

5. *A Standard State Zoning Enabling Act* (Washington, D.C.: U.S. Department of Commerce, 1924), sec. 3, p. 6.

6. For a good history of city planning, see Mel Scott, *American City Planning Since 1890* (Berkeley and Los Angeles: University of California Press, 1969). The figures on numbers of city planning commissions are found on pages 249 and 330.

7. Alfred Bettman, *City and Regional Planning Papers*, Harvard City Planning Studies, XIII (Cambridge, Mass.: Harvard University Press, 1946), p. 10.

8. National Commission on Urban Problems, *Problems of Zoning and Land Use Regulation*, Research Report No. 2, prepared by American Society of Planning Officials (Washington, D.C., 1968), p. 28.

9. Hugh Pomeroy, "A Planning Manual for Zoning (Urban and Suburban)" (unpublished manuscript, American Society of Planning Officials, 1940), p. 18. Available at the ASPO Library, Chicago, and the Avery Library, Columbia University.

10. Bettman, *City and Regional Planning Papers*, p. 46.

11. Charles Haar, "The Master Plan: An Impermanent Constitution," *Law and Contemporary Problems* 20 (1955):353.

12. Charles Haar, "In Accordance with a Comprehensive Plan," *Harvard Law Review* 68 (1955):1154.

13. Robert Anderson, *American Law of Zoning* (Rochester, N.Y.: Lawyers Co-operative Publishing Co., 1968), 1:21.

14. Norman Williams, Jr., *American Planning Law: Land Use and the Police Power* (Chicago: Callaghan and Co., 1975).

15. *A Model Land Development Code (Proposed Official Draft)* (Philadelphia: American Law Institute, 1975), p. 343.

16. Ibid., p. 139.

17. John Delafons, *Land-Use Controls in the United States* (Cambridge, Mass.: Joint Center for Urban Studies of the Massachusetts Institute of Technology and Harvard University, 1962), p. 9.

18. Haar, "A Comprehensive Plan," p. 1158.

19. Allison Dunham, "Property, City Planning and Liberty," in *Law and Land, Anglo-American Planning Practice*, ed. Charles Haar (Cambridge, Mass.: Harvard University Press and MIT Press, 1964), pp. 33–34.

20. National Commission on Urban Problems, *Building the American City: Report of the National Commission on Urban Problems* (New York: Praeger, 1969), p. 239.

21. Advisory Committee on Zoning, *A City Planning Primer* (Washington, D.C.: U.S. Department of Commerce, 1928), p. 12.

22. Bettman, *City and Regional Planning Papers*, p. 26.

23. Pomeroy, "A Planning Manual for Zoning," p. 18.

24. Village of Euclid v. Ambler Realty Co., 272 U.S. at 394 (1926).

25. Alan Altshuler, "The Goals of Comprehensive Planning," *Journal of The American Institute of Planners* 31, no. 3 (August 1965):190–91.

26. Bettman, *City and Regional Planning Papers*, p. 23.

27. Delafons, *Land-Use Controls in the United States*, p. 99.

28. National Commission on Urban Problems, *Building the American City*, p. 223.

29. Clawson and Hall, *Planning and Urban Growth*, p. 190.

30. Richard Babcock, *The Zoning Game, Municipal Practices and Policies* (Madison: University of Wisconsin Press, 1966), p. 65.

31. Donald Hagman, "Windfalls for Wipeouts," in *The Good Earth of America: Planning Our Land Use*, ed. C. Lowell Harriss, The American Assembly (Englewood Cliffs, N.J.: Prentice-Hall, 1974), p. 113.

32. National Commission on Urban Problems, *Building the American City*, pp. 244–45.

33. See Reps, "The Future of American Planning," and Charles Haar, "Wanted: Two Federal Levers for Urban Land Use—Land Banks and Urbank," *Papers Submitted to the Subcommittee on Housing Panels*, Part II, 92nd Cong., 1st session, 1971, p. 927.

34. Pennsylvania Coal v. Mahon, 260 U.S. 393 (1922).

35. Ibid. at 414.

36. Ibid. at 415.

37. This problem was described in Robert Walker, *The Planning Function in Urban Government*, second edition (Chicago: University of Chicago Press, 1950). See also T. J. Kent, Jr., *The Urban General Plan* (San Francisco: Chandler Publishing Co., 1964).

38. *A Model Land Development Code*, pp. 133–34.

39. Levine v. Town of Oyster Bay, 272 N.Y.S.2d 171, 26 A.D.2d 583, quoted in Arden H. Rathkopf, *The Law of Zoning and Planning*, third edition, 1973 Cumulative Supplement to Volume 1 (New York: Clark Boardman Co., 1974), p. 206.

40. Babcock, *The Zoning Game*, p. 62.

41. For a good early study of the limited influence of formal planning and a diagnosis of the causes, see Walker, *The Planning Function in Urban Government*.

42. Delafons, *Land-Use Controls*, p. 13.

43. William Whyte, *The Last Landscape* (Garden City, N.Y.: Doubleday Anchor Books, 1970), p. 168.

44. Babcock, *The Zoning Game*, p. 17.

45. See Rathkopf, *The Law of Zoning and Planning*, p. 206.

46. Golden v. Planning Board of Ramapo, 30 N.Y. 2d at 379, 285 N.E.2d at 303 (1972).

47. Haar, "A Comprehensive Plan," pp. 1157, 1171.

48. Whyte, *The Last Landscape*, p. 169.

Chapter 4

1. Leonard Downie, Jr., *Mortgage on America* (New York: Praeger, 1974), p. 90.

2. Ibid., p. 90.

3. William Whyte, *The Last Landscape* (Garden City, N.Y.: Doubleday Anchor Books, 1970), p. 20.

4. Alfred Balk, "Invitation to Bribery," *Harper's Magazine* (October 1966):18.

5. Ibid., p. 18.

6. Marion Clawson, "Why Not Sell Zoning and Rezoning? (Legally, That Is)," *Cry California* (Winter 1966–67):9.

7. Bernard Siegan, *Land Use Without Zoning* (Lexington, Mass.: Lexington Books, 1972), p. 196.

8. Audrey Moore, speech at the National Conference on Managed Growth, Chicago, September 1973.

9. *Citizens' Committee on Zoning Practices and Procedures: A Program to Improve Planning and Zoning in Los Angeles*, First Report to the Mayor and City Council, Summary Report 3, 5, and 6, Los Angeles, California, July 1968; quoted in Siegan, *Land Use Without Zoning*, p. 12.

10. William Whyte, "Urban Sprawl," in *The Exploding Metropolis*, the Editors of *Fortune* (Garden City, N.Y.: Doubleday Anchor Books, 1958), p. 116.

11. National Commission on Urban Problems, *Building the American City: Report of the National Commission on Urban Problems* (New York: Praeger, 1969), p. 220.

12. Siegan, *Land Use Without Zoning*, p. 196.

13. For a very similar analysis of community zoning problems and solutions, developed simultaneously and independently, see William Fischel, "A Property Rights Approach to Municipal Zoning," Dartmouth College Economics Department, working paper, August 1976.

14. Charles Haar, "Wayne Township, Zoning for Whom?—In Brief Reply," *Harvard Law Review* 67 (1954):992.

15. National Land and Investment Company v. Kohn, 419 Pa. 504, 215 A.2d 597 (1965).

16. Ibid. at 524 and 608.

17. Ibid. at 528 and 610.

18. Ibid. at 530 and 611.

19. Ibid. at 533 and 612.

20. Ibid. at 519 and 605.

21. Ibid. at 529 and 610.

22. Ibid. at 529 and 611.

23. Ibid. at 528 and 610.

24. Appeal of Kit-Mar Builders, Inc., 439 Pa. at 474, 268 A.2d at 768 (1970).

25. Ibid. at 480 and 771.

26. National Commission on Urban Problems, *Building the American City*, p. 243.

27. See Norman Williams, Jr., and Thomas Norman, "Exclusionary Land Use Controls: The Case of North-Eastern New Jersey," *Syracuse Law Review* 22 (1971):475.

28. Alfred Balk, "Invitation to Bribery," *Harper's Magazine* (October 1966):19.

29. The American Institute of Architects, *A Plan for Urban Growth: Report of the National Policy Task Force* (Washington, D.C., 1972), summary and p. 4.

30. A. M. Woodruff, "Recycling Urban Land," in *The Good Earth of America: Planning Our Land Use*, ed. C. Lowell Harriss, The American Assembly (Englewood Cliffs, N.J.: Prentice-Hall, 1974), p. 51.

31. See Edward Eichler and Marshall Kaplan, *The Community Builders* (Berkeley and Los Angeles: University of California Press, 1967), p. 61.

32. National Commission on Urban Problems, *Building the American City*, p. 246.

33. National Resources Planning Board, *Public Land Acquisition in a National Land-Use Program, Pt. II,* 1940, p. 17, quoted in E. F. Roberts, "The Demise of Property Law," *Cornell Law Review* 57 (1971):42.

34. National Resources Planning Board, *Public Land Acquisition,* p. 17.

35. Charles Abrams, "U.S. Housing: A New Program," speech at the National Housing Conference, 1957, cited in *A Model Land Development Code (Proposed Official Draft)* (Philadelphia: American Law Institute, 1975), p. 259.

36. Marion Clawson, "Suburban Development Districts," *Journal of the American Institute of Planners,* May 1960.

Chapter 5

1. J. H. Plumb, *England in the Eighteenth Century* (Baltimore: Penguin Books, 1950), p. 82.

2. F. W. Maitland, *The Constitutional History of England,* ed. H. A. L. Fisher (Cambridge: Cambridge University Press, 1908), 1963 reprint, p. 143.

3. R. G. Hawtrey, *Economic Aspects of Feudalism,* pp. 4–5, cited in Aaron Sakolski, *Land Tenure and Land Taxation in America* (New York: Robert Schalkenbach Foundation, 1957), p. 12.

4. Frederick Pollock, *The Land Laws* (London: Macmillan and Co., 1883), p. 62.

5. Ibid., pp. 51–52.

6. Ibid., pp. 2–3.

Part II   Feudal Tenure Trends under Environmental Land-Use Regulation

1. Frederick Pollock, *The Land Laws* (London: Macmillan and Co., 1883), p. 3.

Chapter 6

1. *New York Times,* December 28, 1976, p. 26.

2. *Federal Clean Air Act Amendments of 1970,* Section 110, 42 U.S.C. 1857c-5(a)4 (1970).

3. For a study of air-quality controls and land use, see George Hagevik, Daniel Mandelker, and Richard Brail, *Air Quality Management and Land Use Planning: Legal, Administrative, and Methodological Perspectives* (New York: Praeger, 1974).

4. *Federal Water Pollution Control Act Amendments of 1972,* Section 208, 33 U.S.C. 1288 *et seq.* (Supp. III, 1973).

5. For a discussion of water-quality controls, see *Toward Clean Water: A Guide to Citizen Action* (Washington, D.C.: Conservation Foundation, 1976).

6. See R. K. Brail, D. R. Mandelker, T. A. Sherry, and G. Hagevik, *Emission Density and Allocation Procedures for Maintaining Air Quality*, prepared for the Environmental Protection Agency, Research Triangle Park, North Carolina, 1975.

7. One might note that the question of sale of development rights has arisen with respect to air-quality controls much as it has for zoning as discussed in Chapter 4. Pollutant emission charges (sale of the right to pollute) have been widely proposed but thus far rejected by EPA. For many new land uses, purchase of pollutant emission rights could amount to purchase of development rights. EPA has already proposed that in some areas new uses will be allowed only if a corresponding reduction in emissions is achieved somewhere else in the same area. It would be only a small step further for a developer to pay an existing use to install new pollutant control devices or even to close down altogether in order for the developer to obtain a transfer of needed emission rights. Thus, although EPA formally rejects sale of emission rights, the practical effect of its actions is verging on such sale. Transfers of emission rights that may well result under EPA procedures are closely related to systems for transfer of land development rights ("transferable development rights") that have been widely proposed for historic and open space preservation in recent years and which are discussed in Chapter 9.

8. For examinations of new state land-use controls, see *The Quiet Revolution in Land Use Control*, prepared for the Council on Environmental Quality by Fred Bosselman and David Callies (Washington, D.C., 1971). See also Robert G. Healy, *Land Use and the States* (Baltimore, Md.: Johns Hopkins University Press for Resources for the Future, 1976); and Nelson Rosenbaum, *Land Use and the Legislatures: The Politics of State Innovation* (Washington, D.C.: Urban Institute, 1976).

9. For studies of state land-use controls in Florida, see Luther Carter, *The Florida Experience: Land and Water Policy in a Growth State* (Baltimore, Md.: The Johns Hopkins University Press for Resources for the Future, 1975); and Phyllis Myers, *Slow Start in Paradise* (Washington, D.C.: Conservation Foundation, 1974).

10. For a discussion of state land-use controls in Oregon, see Charles Little, *The New Oregon Trail* (Washington, D.C.: Conservation Foundation, 1974).

11. See Phyllis Myers, *So Goes Vermont* (Washington, D.C.: Conservation Foundation, 1974).

12. For background on the Martha's Vineyard controls, see Carla Rabinowitz, "Martha's Vineyard: The Development of a Legislative Strategy for Preservation," *Environmental Affairs* 3, no. 2 (1974):396–431.

13. Sierra Club v. Ruckleshaus, 344 F. Supp. 253 (1972); 4 ERC 1815 (1972); 412 U.S. 541 (1973).

14. Council on Environmental Quality, *Environmental Quality: The Fourth Annual Report of the Council on Environmental Quality* (Washington, D.C., 1973), p. 161.

15. For a study of the California coastal legislation, see Melvin Mogulof, *Saving the Coast* (Lexington, Mass.: D. C. Heath, 1975).

16. Healy, *Land Use and the States*, p. 151.

17. Russell Baker, "The Nantucket Trade-off," *New York Times*, December 28, 1976, p. 27.

18. *A Model Land Development Code (Proposed Official Draft)* (Philadelphia: American Law Institute, 1975), p. 327.

19. See "New York Wetlands Law," *Environmental Comment* (January 1974):2.

20. *California Coastal Zone Conservation Act of 1972*, Section 27001. See Mogulof, *Saving the Coast*, p. 115.

21. 10 Vt. Stat. Ann. Ch. 151 #6001 *et seq.*; see *Quiet Revolution*, appendix.

22. *Maine Site Location of Development Act of 1970*, C. 571, #2 (1970); see *Quiet Revolution*, appendix.

23. Terrence O'Neill, "The United Kingdom: Can It Survive?" *New York Times*, February 18, 1975, p. 29.

24. Flora Lewis, "West Europe's Minorities Are Getting Their Way," *New York Times*, November 23, 1975, sec. 4, p. 4.

25. *Alternatives for Washington: Pathways to Washington 1985, A Beginning; Citizen's Recommendations for the Future, Report No. 1* (Olympia, Washington: Office of Program Planning and Fiscal Management, 1975), p. 8.

26. *Alternatives for Washington*, p. 25.

27. Robert Cahn, "Mr. Developer, Someone is Watching You," in *Where Do We Grow From Here?* (Boston: Christian Science Publishing Co., 1973), pp. 6–7; reprinted from *Christian Science Monitor*.

28. See Phyllis Myers, *Zoning Hawaii, An Analysis of the Passage and Implementation of Hawaii's Land Classification Law* (Washington, D.C.: Conservation Foundation, 1976), p. 87.

29. See "Governor of Hawaii Seeks U.S. Constitutional Amendment to Limit Immigration; Fought as Possibly Racist," *New York Times*, January 30, 1977, p. 31.

30. For a discussion of efforts to pass national land-use legislation, see Noreen Lyday, *The Law of the Land: Debating National Land Use Legislation 1970–75* (Washington, D.C.: Urban Institute, 1976).

31. Report by Prof. Raymond Gold, quoted in Colman McCarthy, "Western Coal: Whose Boom?" *Washington Post*, April 24, 1976, p. 15.

32. Charles Little, interview; see Little, *New Oregon Trail*, p. 35.

33. *1973 Session Laws of the Oregon Legislative Assembly*, Senate Bill 100, Section 32; see Little, *New Oregon Trail*, p. 32.

34. Task Force on Land Use and Urban Growth, *The Use of Land: A Citizen's Policy Guide to Urban Growth*, ed. William Reilly, (New York: Thomas Y. Crowell, 1973), p. 210.

35. Quoted in John Delafons, *Land-Use Controls in the United States* (Cambridge, Mass.: Joint Center for Urban Studies of the Massachusetts Institute of Technology and Harvard University, 1962), p. 28.

36. Task Force on Land Use and Urban Growth, *Use of Land*, p. 184.

37. Bernard Siegan, *Land Use Without Zoning* (Lexington, Mass.: Lexington Books, 1972), p. 157.

Chapter 7

1. John Delafons, *Land-Use Controls in the United States* (Cambridge, Mass.: Joint Center for Urban Studies of the Massachusetts Institute of Technology and Harvard University, 1962), p. 5.

2. Task Force on Land Use and Urban Growth, *The Use of Land: A Citizen's Policy Guide to Urban Growth*, ed. William Reilly, (New York: Thomas Y. Crowell, 1973), p. 33.

3. Barton-Aschman Association, Inc., *The Barrington, Illinois Area: A Cost-Revenue Analysis of Land Use Alternatives*, prepared for the Barrington Area Development Council, February 1970, p. 48.

4. Thomas Muller and Grace Dawson, *The Fiscal Impact of Residential and Commercial Development: A Case Study* (Washington, D.C.: Urban Institute, 1972), p. 86.

5. Livingston and Blayney, *Open Space vs. Development*, Final Report to the City of Palo Alto, 1971, p. 139.

6. Robert Cahn, "Mr. Developer, Someone Is Watching You," in *Where Do We Grow From Here?* (Boston: Christian Science Publishing Co., 1973), pp. 4–5, reprinted from *Christian Science Monitor.*

7. Gladwin Hill, "Nation's Cities Fighting to Stem Growth," *New York Times,* July 28, 1974, pp. 1, 30.

8. See U.S. Commission on Population Growth and the American Future, *Population Distribution and Policy,* ed. Sara Mills Mazie, Commission Research Reports, 5 (Washington, D.C., 1972).

9. For a comprehensive selection of articles on growth controls, see Randall Scott, ed., *Management and Control of Growth,* 1, 2, 3 (Washington, D.C.: Urban Land Institute, 1975).

10. Steel Hill Development, Inc. v. Town of Sanbornton, 469 F.2d 956 (1st Cir., 1972).

11. David Berry and Robert Coughlin, *Economic Implications of Preserving Ecologically Valuable Land in Medford, New Jersey,* A Report to Medford Township, New Jersey, by the Regional Science Research Institute (Philadelphia, 1973).

12. Molino v. Borough of Glassboro, 116 N.J. 195, 281 A.2d 401 (1971).

13. See Hill, "Nation's Cities Fighting," p. 30.

14. Boulder Area Growth Study Commission, *Exploring Options for the Future: A Study of Growth in Boulder County,* vol. 1, *Commission Final Report* (November 1973), p. 80.

15. Michael Sumichrast, "Area's Existing Home Sales Now Most Expensive in U.S.," *Washington Post,* November 22, 1975, Real Estate Section, p. 1.

16. Congressional Budget Office, *Homeownership: The Changing Relationship of Costs and Incomes, and Possible Federal Roles,* budget issue paper (Washington, D.C., 1977), p. xiv.

17. Federal Home Loan Bank Board, *Economic Briefs,* May 11, 1976, p. 3.

18. See Bernard Frieden and Arthur Solomen, *The Nation's Housing: 1975–1985* (Cambridge, Mass: Joint Center for Urban Studies at the Massachusetts Institute of Technology and Harvard University, 1977), p. 116.

19. Quoted in Hill, "Nation's Cities Fighting," p. 30.

20. Task Force on Land Use and Urban Growth, *The Use of Land,* p. 100.

21. Edwards v. California, 314 U.S. at 173 (1941).

22. National Land and Investment Company v. Kohn, 419 Pa. at 533, 215 A.2d at 612 (1965).

23. Golden v. Planning Board of Ramapo, 30 N.Y.2d at 390, 285 N.E.2d at 309 (1972).

24. Construction Industry Association of Sonoma County v. City of Petaluma, 375 F. Supp. at 586 (N.D. Cal., 1974).

Part III   A Proposal for a New System of Metropolitan Land Tenure

Chapter 8

1. National Commission on Urban Problems, *Building the American City: Report of the National Commission on Urban Problems* (New York: Praeger, 1969), p. 248.

2. See E. F. Schumacher, *Small Is Beautiful: Economics as if People Mattered* (New York: Harper and Row, 1973).

3. David Morris and Karl Hess, *Neighborhood Power: The New Localism* (Boston: Beacon Press, 1975), p. 5.

4. The Real Estate Research Corporation, *The Costs of Sprawl*, prepared for the Council on Environmental Quality, the Department of Housing and Urban Development, and the Environmental Protection Agency (Washington, D.C., 1974); see Executive Summary, p. 14. The figures shown in the text are exclusive of open space and school costs as shown in the government study.

5. *Regional Energy Consumption*, Second Interim Report of a Joint Study by the Regional Plan Association and Resources for the Future (New York, 1974), p. 8.

6. *Income Security for Americans: Recommendations of the Public Welfare Study*, Report of the Subcommittee on Fiscal Policy of the Joint Economic Committee (Washington, D.C., 1974), pp. 1, 11.

7. Ibid., p. 49.

8. Ibid., p. 140.

9. Ibid., p. 28.

10. See *Federal-State-Local Finances: Significant Features of Fiscal Federalism*, A Report of the Advisory Commission on Intergovernmental Relations (Washington, D.C., February 1974), p. 5.

11. Southern Burlington County N.A.A.C.P. v. Township of Mt. Laurel, 67 N.J. at 151, 336 A.2d at 713 (1975).

12. Ibid. at 179 and 727.

13. Quoted in John Delafons, *Land-Use Controls in the United States* (Cambridge, Mass.: Joint Center for Urban Studies of the Massachusetts Institute of Technology and Harvard University, 1962), p. 21.

14. Lester G. Chase, *A Tabulation of City Planning Commissions in the United States*, Bureau of Standards, Department of Commerce (Washington, D.C., 1931), p. 4. Available at Avery Library, Columbia University.

15. Quoted in Seymour Toll, *Zoned American* (New York: Grossman Publishers, 1969), p. 253.

Chapter 9

1. For a study of homes associations, see *The Homes Association Handbook, Revised Edition*, Technical Bulletin 50 (Washington, D.C.: Urban Land Institute, 1970).

2. For a study of condominium ownership, see David Clurman and Edna Hubbard, *Condominiums and Cooperatives* (New York: John Wiley, 1970).

3. For figures on condominium ownership, see the *HUD Condominium Cooperative Study* (Washington, D.C.: U.S. Department of Housing and Urban Development, July 1975).

4. Deed of Dedication, Reston First Home Owners Association, as amended on March 31, 1966.

5. Robert Ellickson, "Alternatives to Zoning: Covenants, Nuisance Rules, and Fines as Land Use Controls," *University of Chicago Law Review* (Summer 1973):761.

6. Ibid., pp. 767–68.

7. John J. Costonis and Robert S. DeVoy, *The Puerto Rico Plan: Environmental Protection Through Development Rights Transfer* (Washington, D.C.: Urban Land Institute, 1975), p. iii.

8. See John J. Costonis, "The Chicago Plan: Incentive Zoning and the Preservation of Urban Landmarks," *Harvard Law Review* 85 (1972):574–631.

9. Costonis and DeVoy, *The Puerto Rico Plan*, p. 10.

10. See Fred Bosselman, David Callies, and John Banta, *The Taking Issue: An Analysis of the Constitutional Limits of Land Use Control*, prepared for the Council on Environmental Quality (Washington, D.C., 1973).

11. Ibid., p. 276.

12. See Task Force on Land Use and Urban Growth, *The Use of Land: A Citizen's Policy Guide to Urban Growth*, ed. William Reilly, (New York: Thomas Y. Crowell, 1973), p. 175.

13. Costonis and DeVoy, *The Puerto Rico Plan*, p. iii.

Chapter 10

1. Another way of saying this, in formal economic terms, is that environmental controls provide protection against "pecuniary" as opposed to "technological" externalities. Many important environmental amenities—such as peace and quiet in a secluded setting—are now distributed outside the market and the price system. But if they were included, the effect of bringing newcomers into an area would be to drive up the price of achieving a given level of amenity. Environmental controls protect the existing residents of areas from such "pecuniary" externalities by keeping out new entrants. In this sense, environmental controls are analogous to efforts by firms to keep out new entrants into their industry. New entrants would drive down prices, thereby creating a "pecuniary" externality. For a discussion of pecuniary and technological externalities, see Otto Davis and Morton Kamien, "Externalities, Information, and Alternative Collective Action," in *Economics of the Environment*, ed. Robert Dorfman and Nancy Dorfman (New York: Norton, 1972), p. 74.

Index